5/10

2

ILLINOIS CENTRAL COLLEGE

W9-BWR-726

Withdrawn

I.C.C. LIBRARY

DEMCO

WRITE THESE LAWS ON YOUR CHILDREN

WRITE THESE LAWS ON YOUR CHILDREN

Inside the World of Conservative
Christian Homeschooling

ROBERT KUNZMAN

I.C.C. LIBRARY

BEACON PRESS
BOSTON

LC
40
.K86
2009

Beacon Press
25 Beacon Street
Boston, Massachusetts 02108-2892
www.beacon.org

Beacon Press books
are published under the auspices of
the Unitarian Universalist Association of Congregations.

© 2009 by Robert Kunzman
All rights reserved
Printed in the United States of America

12   11   10   09   8   7   6   5   4   3   2   1

This book is printed on acid-free paper that meets the uncoated
paper ANSI/NISO specifications for permanence as revised in 1992.

Composition by Wilsted & Taylor Publishing Services

Library of Congress Cataloging-in-Publication Data
Kunzman, Robert.
  Write these laws on your children : inside the world of conservative
Christian homeschooling / Robert Kunzman.
       p. cm.
  Includes bibliographical references and index.
  ISBN-13: 978-0-8070-3291-6 (hardcover: alk. paper)
  ISBN-10: 0-8070-3291-3 (hardcover: alk. paper)   1. Home schooling—
United States.   2. Christian education—United States.   I. Title.

  LC40.K86 2009
  371.04'20973—dc22   2008046811

1/10 B&T 27.95

DEDICATED TO GENE & LUCY ANN KUNZMAN

home educators in the finest sense

And these words, which I command thee this day, shall be in thine heart:
And thou shalt teach them diligently unto thy children,
and shalt talk of them when thou sittest in thine house,
and when thou walkest by the way,
and when thou liest down, and when thou risest up.
And thou shalt bind them for a sign upon thine hand,
and they shall be as frontlets between thine eyes.
And thou shalt write them upon the posts of thy house, and on thy gates.

—DEUTERONOMY 6:6–9 (KING JAMES VERSION)

The unexamined life is not worth living.

—SOCRATES

Then saith {Jesus} unto them,
Render therefore unto Caesar the things which are Caesar's;
and unto God the things that are God's.

—MATTHEW 22:21B (KING JAMES VERSION)

CONTENTS

I

SHAPING A GODLY WORLD

It's a warm March evening in downtown Los Angeles, and the thunderous applause from inside the Kodak Theatre can be heard even out on the deserted red carpet on Hollywood Boulevard. The Academy Award for Best Picture has just been announced, and the jubilant director arrives at the podium. As he begins his obligatory thank-you speech, his cell phone rings. He sheepishly retrieves it from his pocket and glances at the number—and then to the astonishment of everyone, he quickly answers. "Hello, Mr. President," he says with a broad smile. "Thank you very much. Yes, we did it."

This is the dream of a man named Michael Farris, cofounder of the Home School Legal Defense Association (HSLDA) and chancellor of Patrick Henry College (PHC), the nation's first college for homeschoolers—and what matters most about his vision is that the victorious movie director and the president of the United States are former homeschoolers and roommates at Patrick Henry College. Their conservative Christian upbringing and education have shaped much of their lives, and now they help shape the broader social and political culture in extraordinarily powerful ways.

Farris talks about this dream of his frequently as he strives to generate support and enthusiasm for homeschooling and PHC. While we have yet to see such a scene play out at the Oscars, the surge in homeschooling and the growing influence of its conservative Christian organizational apparatus is hard to miss. The most recent data from the National Center for Education Statistics attest to homeschooling's continued rapid growth, measuring a 74 percent increase over eight years—*twelve times* the increase of public school students over the same period. There are probably around two million homeschooled children in the United States today, but the simple fact is that no one knows for sure. Nearly a fourth of states don't even require parents to notify anyone if they homeschool their children, much less offer any sort of verification that they are doing so. Nationwide surveys almost certainly underreport the total numbers, as many home-schoolers are strongly opposed to any kind of governmental oversight of their efforts, and therefore refuse to participate in any data-gathering attempts.

This book explores the world of conservative Christian homeschool-ing, both in the day-to-day lives of families and in its broader aspira-tions to influence American culture and politics. What do homeschoolers do all day, and why do they do it? What makes these parents decide to homeschool in the first place? What do their children have to say about it? Do these kids learn to think for themselves, or are they herded into mirroring the beliefs and commitments of their parents? What do they learn about democratic citizenship and engaging with people who believe differently about important social and political issues? And are parents really focused on the goal of creating culture-shaping political leaders and movie directors?

While estimates vary widely, most observers acknowledge that con-servative Christians constitute the largest subset of homeschoolers in the United States (the 2006 documentary film *Jesus Camp* uses a 75 percent figure, but this seems likely an exaggeration prompted by the dominant profile of groups such as HSLDA). I use the term *conservative Christian* for several reasons: while it includes most of those who would be labeled "fundamentalists," it also extends to many evangelicals more broadly. The term *conservative*, however, alludes to a political as well as a theological perspective. While evangelicals hold political views across the spectrum, the families I spoke with, read about, and visited in their homes were far to the right politically—in some cases, they criticized Republican politi-cians and policies for not being conservative *enough*.

Nevertheless, it's important to point out that conservative Christians are hardly the only ones to choose this educational path for their children. Support and advocacy organizations serve almost every demographic im-aginable. A quick check online, for instance, lists groups for disabled, Jewish, Latino, Catholic, Seventh-day Adventist, Mormon, single-parent, vegan, Native American, African American, and Muslim homeschoolers (the latter two, among others, both claim to be the fastest growing segment of homeschoolers).

So if homeschoolers are actually quite a diverse bunch, why focus on conservative Christians? Admittedly, some of the "big questions" I explore in these pages relate to homeschooling more generally, such as what role (if any) the state should have in the education of children. But other vital issues—such as the value of ethical diversity, what it means to think for oneself, and the preparation of democratic citizens—gain an extra layer of complexity when deeply held religious convictions are involved.

In addition, whether conservative Christians comprise two-thirds, one-half, or even less of total homeschoolers, what seems beyond dispute is their disproportionate influence on public perception and rhetoric, and the ways in which HSLDA and state-level affiliates hold sway over much of the policy environment surrounding homeschooling. For better or worse (and some homeschoolers would clearly say the latter), the perpetual interplay of religious convictions and public life creates a complicated and combustible context wherein we continue to work out the shape and purpose of American education—and the meaning of democracy amidst diversity.

How did this educational phenomenon of homeschooling—what a former research analyst for the U.S. Department of Education called "one of the most significant trends of the past half century"—gain such momentum over the past thirty years? Most observers trace the origins of the modern homeschooling movement to a liberal critique of institutional schooling in the 1960s by writers such as A. S. Neill, founder of the alternative student-directed school Summerhill, and Ivan Illich, a cultural critic who advocated the dissolution of institutional schooling. Within the next decade, former schoolteacher John Holt had begun publishing *Growing without Schooling*, a magazine advocating a form of homeschooling commonly known as "unschooling." Unschooling eschews most traditional structures of formal schooling, instead letting children decide what to learn, when to learn it, and how. At its core, unschooling rests on a philosophical belief that children learn best when the focus and course of study emerge in response to natural interests and needs. While John Holt died in 1985, the organization that bears his name estimates that unschoolers comprise about 10 percent of the total homeschool population.

Holt was not the only educator challenging institutional schooling during that time. In a 1972 *Harper's* article titled "The Dangers of Early Schooling," educational researcher Raymond Moore questioned the "race to the schoolhouse" and, over the next decade, made a case for abandoning schools altogether in favor of homeschooling. Like Holt, Moore also criticized institutional schooling for its standardization and impersonality, but whereas Holt's philosophy of unschooling let the child and her interests determine the pace and direction of her learning, Moore emphasized the importance and authority of parents in the educational process. Regardless of which philosophy they favored, parents who chose to homeschool during the 1970s did so surreptitiously, since most states' laws were unclear regarding its legality. A series of court challenges during the 1980s met this uncertainty head on, with the result that by 1993, all states had recognized parents' rights to homeschool their children.

Coinciding with these legal battles and the rise of the Moral Majority, the early 1980s marked the beginning of significant growth for homeschooling, particularly among conservative Christians. Many of them first heard about homeschooling when Raymond Moore was interviewed by James Dobson on his *Focus on the Family* radio program. In fact, both Michael Farris and J. Michael Smith, who cofounded HSLDA in 1983, credit Moore for introducing them to the concept of homeschooling, and Moore provided a fledgling HSLDA with his important endorsement. (Fifteen years later, however, Moore published a scathing criticism of Farris and HSLDA—part of a wider disenchantment with the organization's disproportionate influence, described further in chapter 5.) The latter half of the decade saw perhaps a sixfold increase of the homeschooling population, to an estimated three hundred thousand. Rapid growth continued in the 1990s, likely topping one million by the end of the decade. Public attitudes in the United States toward homeschooling appear to have improved as more Americans have chosen the option. In 1985 only 16 percent of those surveyed by *Phi Delta Kappa* felt homeschooling was good for the nation; by 2001 this positive appraisal had risen to 41 percent.

Despite the growing popularity of homeschooling, research data about its demographics and effectiveness are fundamentally incomplete. Any statistics claiming to provide a definitive picture of some aspect of homeschooling across the United States are, simply put, wrong. The truth is, we just don't know for sure who is homeschooling or what they are learning. Homeschool regulations, as is typical with much educational policy, vary widely from state to state; some require extensive documentation, while others don't even know (or ask) how many families are homeschooling within their borders. We have numerous anecdotes of spelling and geography bee champions, and the occasional horror story of physically abused children whose parents claimed to be homeschooling them. We have impressive standardized test results volunteered by some homeschool families; plenty of others don't report them or don't administer them in the first place. Many homeschoolers will not respond to surveys, particularly government-sponsored ones. Most education regulations aimed at gathering performance data, such as the No Child Left Behind Act, apply only to public schools. Even in states where registration and/or testing is required, substantial numbers of homeschoolers (including several families I visited) simply ignore the regulations.

While this book focuses on the conservative Christian subset of homeschoolers, I've spent significant time exploring the broader movement as well. When I'm asked to describe the typical homeschool family, I generally respond by saying that you might as well describe the typical public school family—the range of demographics, philosophies, and practices make such a generalization practically impossible. Nevertheless, several common characteristics are worth noting.

Homeschool parents believe they can provide a better educational experience for their child, and are willing to sacrifice their time, money, and/or careers to make it happen. They are frequently (although not always) dissatisfied with more conventional educational options, including a typical distrust of the public school system. Eighty-eight percent of homeschool parents in the 2007 National Center for Education Statistics (NCES) survey mentioned earlier identified "concern about environment" in conventional schools as a significant factor in their decision to homeschool.

Perhaps the most crucial insight into the homeschooler mentality is that they generally view education as more than just formal schooling; as one Virginia parent explained, "It's not just schooling; it becomes your whole way of life." The rhetoric of "raising academic standards" and "restoring economic competitiveness" by policymakers and politicians at least partly misses the point as far as homeschoolers are concerned. For them, the educational process is first and foremost about their child's individual learning needs, and extends well beyond traditional school standards, structures, and schedules.

Describing the "typical homeschooler" remains an imprecise affair even when the focus narrows to conservative Christians. As my travels reveal, a wide range of philosophies, practices, and outcomes exist here as well. Nevertheless, certain aspects seem fairly typical. Whereas homeschool practices among the general population fill the spectrum between open-ended unschooling and highly structured replications of institutional schooling, conservative Christian families tend toward the latter—reflecting their belief that human nature is inherently sinful and in need of regular guidance and correction, particularly during childhood.

But even more central in the mindset of conservative Christian homeschoolers is the fundamental conviction that educating their children is a God-given right and responsibility, and one they can delegate only at great moral and spiritual peril. Like many in the broader homeschool population, conservative Christians see homeschooling as a twenty-four-hour-a-day, all-encompassing endeavor. For them perhaps more explicitly than for other homeschoolers, homeschooling is a shaping not only of intellect but—even more crucially—of character. This means more than just moral choices of right and wrong; character is developed through the inculcation of an overarching Christian worldview that guides those moral choices. These parents share a fierce determination to instill this type of Christian character in their children, a process that entails protecting them from the corrupting influences of broader society. To accomplish this, the family becomes the defensive bulwark and sanctuary wherein children are prepared for eventual engagement with the world.

In *Kingdom of Children*, an excellent sociological study of the homeschooling movement, Mitchell Stevens highlights a fundamental organizational difference between conservative Christians and other homeschoolers. The latter, he explains, lack a singular identity or ideology beyond their status as homeschoolers, making it difficult to advance a detailed policy agenda. By contrast, conservative Christian homeschoolers are successful politically because they work well within hierarchical structures and have cultivated a cohesive ideology that moves their agenda forward. Their

organizational prowess and media savvy sometimes create the false impression that they are pretty much the only ones homeschooling, or at
least the only ones worth our attention. Not surprisingly, this dynamic
fosters an underlying resentment from many in the broader homeschool
population. Even among those harboring such resentment, however, few
will deny the disproportionate influence of HSLDA in setting the tone
and agenda for homeschooling in the United States.

But these machinations of policy and politics, while certainly influential on homeschooling as a movement, tell us relatively little about
the day-to-day world of conservative Christian homeschool families: what
they're doing, why they're doing it, and what it means for their children
and perhaps our broader society. So while I spent plenty of time interviewing homeschool leaders, attending conventions, and exploring curricular
programs and resources, I also wanted to get an "inside look" by visiting families in their homes, observing and hearing from them firsthand.
Over the course of two years, I made more than twenty trips around the
country, including repeated visits with six homeschool families, spending
time in their homes and churches, interviewing parents and children, and
observing their homeschool practices and related activities.

Many homeschoolers are hesitant (to put it mildly) to welcome outsiders into their homeschool settings, much less an educational researcher. I
relied on mutual acquaintances for initial introductions, then explained
that I was dissatisfied with the uninformed assumptions (often for the
worse) that many outsiders—particularly education professionals—make
about homeschooling. I said I was hoping to spend some time observing their homeschooling process and talking to them about what they're
doing and why they're doing it. I tried to assure families that I was not
out to do a hatchet job, but at the same time made sure not to promise a
glowing appraisal either.

Some turned me down, but six families agreed to participate. Their
geographical diversity was an added bonus, not only because the regulatory context of states varies so widely, but also because it seemed likely
that conservative Christianity and the homeschooling inspired by it in
rural Tennessee, for instance, might look quite different than in Los Angeles. To preserve privacy, I have changed the names and identifying characteristics of all but the most public figures. Quotations are taken directly

from recorded material, however, and my notes and transcripts were analyzed by research assistants in an effort to bring other perspectives to bear on the data I gathered.

So what qualifies me to undertake this project, to explore the philosophies and practices of conservative Christian homeschoolers? While I have never formally homeschooled my children (or been homeschooled myself), I empathize with parents as they describe the apprehension they felt about sending their children to institutional schools. Even though I ultimately feel good about the public schools my kids attend, dropping them off each morning and watching their small frames walk into the crowds and through the front doors nevertheless demands a certain blind trust in other adults whom I hardly know and a system that sometimes thwarts everyone's best intentions.

In fact, I know that system quite well, having spent a decade as a public high school teacher, coach, and administrator, in both urban and rural settings. I have faith in the power and potential of public schooling, and I think my students were largely well served by their time in my care. I've also spent eight years as a teacher educator and observed hundreds of classroom lessons as a student-teacher supervisor. I understand the limitations of "dropping in" to a learning context (as I did with these homeschool families), and I know how difficult teaching can be—and that a relatively brief glimpse by an observer will never tell the full story. At the same time, I've developed both a technical understanding and intuitive feel for good teaching and student learning.

I also have a sympathetic appreciation for the depth and complexity of the Christian commitment and culture of the families I observed. While generally a bit "left of center" in my political and theological leanings, I have spent much of my life around conservative Christians, and count some of them as close friends. I see great value in the promise of religious community, and a society in which such communities are allowed to flourish. With this value in mind, then, I am also deeply committed to a democratic public square in which all citizens are afforded respect and the opportunity to deliberate about the shape of our lives together.

The primary goal of this book is to provide a window into the homeschooling worlds of a few conservative Christian families, amidst a descriptive backdrop of homeschooling more generally. Even as I began this project, I suspected that more diversity of thought and practice exists among conservative Christian homeschoolers than appears from the outside, and I wondered what that might look like in the day-to-day lives of families. During the course of my travels, a variety of related topics arose: academic achievement, special education, child abuse, public school connections, cyberschooling, college transitions, and more.

I began this journey with four central questions, which serve as thematic threads running through each family's chapter:

Teaching and learning. What kind of teaching and learning goes on at the kitchen table, and beyond? I wanted to see how homeschoolers spend their time, and what their educational priorities are. What curricula do they choose, and what do they do with it? How do they address the different needs of their different children, and provide the appropriate balance of support and challenge? How do they assess their kids' learning?

This focus on teaching and learning emerges from my own experiences, both as a teacher and someone who prepares future teachers for the classroom. I have come to believe that there is no single model of good teaching—much depends on the context, and a particular style or strategy effective in one setting, with a certain student, may be ill advised in another. A good teacher can "read" the context and make the most of it, while anticipating and minimizing its inherent challenges or limitations. With this in mind, then, I sought to understand what particular opportunities and obstacles exist in the homeschooling context, especially in comparison with conventional schooling, and how parents navigate that context.

Thinking for themselves. If conservative Christian homeschool parents are determined to shape their children's character to reflect their own cherished beliefs and values, what room does this leave for children to learn to think for themselves? We are all born into a culture that instills certain values, particular ways of understanding and evaluating the world around us. If we are to make those beliefs and commitments our own, rather than merely echoing what we are taught, we need to be able to reflect critically on our inherited way of life—not necessarily negatively, nor all at once. Philosophers since at least as far back as the Enlightenment have argued about what exactly it means to think independently in this way, but it generally includes awareness of other values, other ways of life, that might be pursued instead.

With this in mind, I wanted to find out what opportunities these homeschoolers have to interact with the world outside of their families, to engage in critical thinking about a range of ideas and perspectives. Is it more than just learning about how mistaken other ways of life are? Does their homeschooling experience provide room for questioning, dissent, or even rebellion?

Parents have an obvious interest in passing on certain values and commitments to their children. While this may or may not involve specific religious beliefs, it almost certainly includes lessons about what's important in life, how to treat others, and the like. When kids go off to school and encounter teachers and peers with an array of experiences and beliefs, they are often pushed to consider this received wisdom from home in light of other perspectives. Do homeschool kids get the same opportunity to encounter ethical diversity firsthand—and to what extent is this a desirable goal in the first place?

Christian citizenship. Learning to think for oneself is also an essential ingredient in democratic citizenship, since a thriving democracy needs informed citizens who can thoughtfully consider a variety of perspectives. Religion plays an especially powerful role in many citizens' vision of the good life and the good society, and as a result, America continues to wrestle with the question of what role religious convictions should play in shaping our laws, policies, and public square. How do these homeschool parents understand the rights and responsibilities of religiously informed citizenship? And how do they communicate these convictions to their children?

One way that HSLDA seeks to instill its vision of Christian citizenship in homeschool youth is through a civic education curriculum called Generation Joshua. I've spent the last six years following the activities of GenJ and its goal to "take back America for God." Generation Joshua raises challenging questions about what it means to be an engaged citizen, what it means to be a good citizen, and whether the former necessarily leads to the latter. Midway through these homeschool family portraits, I will pause to describe the Generation Joshua experience, as well as examine its parent organization, HSLDA, and its role and influence on the broader homeschooling world.

Homeschool regulation. The ways that homeschool parents answer these questions—about educational priorities and practices, whether their kids learn to think for themselves, and how they understand the relationship between faith and citizenship—have significant implications for whom their children become as adults. It seems clear that both parents and children have profound interests at stake in the shape of a homeschooling education. But the outcome matters to broader society as well, both in terms of having economically self-sufficient members and citizens committed to a healthy democracy.

This triad of interests in homeschooling—parents, children, and society—brings me to my final question: should the state regulate homeschooling, and if so, to what extent? The government obviously regulates public schools, and some private schools. But stepping into the educational details of a couple million separate schools that take no government monies is a vastly more complex proposition, for a host of reasons I will explore with the families I visit.

Besides offering insight into the day-to-day world of homeschooling, these four central questions will help illuminate some of its underlying tensions. I call them *tensions* not to imply some fundamental flaw in homeschooling, but rather that legitimate priorities often pull against one another. The freedom that homeschooling provides parents to shape teaching and learning, for example, holds both positive and negative possibilities ranging from enrichment to neglect. The desire to impart cherished values to one's children can be in tension with helping them learn to think for themselves. Striving for a society in harmony with one's religious values can clash with a democracy filled with diversity of thought and belief. And regulations aimed at protecting the interests of parents, children, and society can threaten the flexibility that makes homeschooling an effective learning experience for many children. Each of these tensions involves competing visions about the proper aims of education as well as the relationship between faith, freedom, and citizenship.

In addition to exploring these central questions, my journey through the world of conservative Christian homeschooling also raises important issues that extend far beyond that world itself. Homeschooling pushes us—as parents, policymakers, and community members—to reconsider what it means to be educated, how it should happen, and what role the state should play in that process.

Homeschool advocates are fond of pointing out that public schools are a relatively recent invention, and that the earliest Americans were actually homeschooled. This latter claim is a bit misleading: the variety of educational approaches—private tutoring, town academies, neighborhood cooperatives, even placing children into other homes to live and be educated—extended well beyond what is generally meant by homeschooling today. Nevertheless, it's true that public schooling as we know it arose in the mid-nineteenth century. Prompted in part by massive waves of immigration, reformers saw in "common schools" the promise of creating an educated citizenry with a common American identity, and by 1880, school attendance was mandatory in all states.

This common school vision, of course, has never been fully realized. While some schools provide opportunities for genuine interaction with social diversity, others suffer from segregation of many kinds. But it would be hard to imagine a public school in which no ethical diversity, no disagreements about the best ways to live, existed. As I noted above, this is where some critics of homeschooling raise concerns—especially when parents hold strong religious commitments—about the opportunities that children have to think for themselves and engage with beliefs and perspectives different from their own. To the extent such concerns are valid, this sort of homeschooling complicates our ideas about preparation for democratic citizenship.

At their extreme, stereotypes of religious homeschooling involve parents creating brainwashed automatons, unable to think for themselves and either sequestered from society or determined to impose their worldview on others. But consider what it means to homeschool (whether religiously motivated or not) in a society where at least 95 percent of the population does otherwise. By virtue of their freedom to shape their child's education in almost any way they choose, homeschoolers are pushed to grapple with several vital and profound questions: What are the central purposes of education? What kind of person do I want my child to become? How can I make her learning experience the best it can be? One might argue that the rest of us, and the schools we support and send our children to, neglect such fundamental questions far too much.

These broader issues certainly deserve our sustained attention. But at the heart of this book are the stories of the families themselves: the opportunities I had to visit them in their homes and churches, to observe their homeschooling "in action" and hear their thoughts on education, faith, and their vision for America's social and political future. My goal in offering glimpses of these six families is not to provide a comprehensive statement about conservative Christian homeschooling, to say nothing of homeschooling more generally. But I am hopeful these portraits will help illuminate some of the central philosophical issues and practical considerations at stake in homeschooling, while helping those outside this world to understand more clearly what it's all about.

Michael Farris and HSLDA want homeschoolers to play central roles in shaping our world, "to accomplish great things for God and for the good of our nation." But there's another kind of world shaping at work among conservative Christian homeschoolers. More than one parent pointed to the biblical passage of Deuteronomy 6:6–9 when explaining to me their motivation to homeschool. *The Message*, a popular Bible paraphrase, puts it this way: "Write these commandments that I've given you today on your hearts. Get them inside of you and then get them inside your children. Talk about them wherever you are, sitting at home or walking in the street; talk about them from the time you get up in the morning to when you fall into bed at night." For these parents, homeschooling is above all an opportunity to shape the hearts and minds of their children from morning until night. In what follows, I explore what this might mean for those children—and the shape of our world together.

2

THE PALMER FAMILY
In the World, Not of the World

My journey begins with what outsiders might consider a stereotypical homeschool family. Debbie and Michael Palmer are parents to nine children, seven girls and two boys, whose ages range from twenty years to eight months. The two eldest girls, Amy and Elizabeth, attend a nearby Christian college in Los Angeles. Unlike all her siblings, sixteen-year-old Carly has chosen to spend her junior year at the local public high school. Joanna (age fourteen), Olivia (age eight), Jason (age seven), and Julie (age five) are homeschooled by their mother. Two-year-old Sam and baby Mindy add to the comfortable chaos of everyday life and the challenges of the homeschooling endeavor.

The Palmers live in one of the many urban municipalities of Los Angeles, in an area marked by tremendous ethnic and linguistic diversity. Their home sits on a relatively quiet side street off a busy thoroughfare, a modest two-story house with yellow stucco and dark blue siding. The second floor was added as the family grew, but even now the home is no more than 2,500 square feet—large for the neighborhood, but certainly not for eleven people. A large, white Econoline van sits in the driveway; beyond a metal gate, various toys lay scattered about in front of the "California garage" (a storage room for everything *but* cars).

My first visit takes place on one of those nearly perfect autumn mornings in Los Angeles: sunny and in the low 70s, with a clear sky and gentle breeze. When I arrive at eight o'clock, breakfast has been cleared and schoolwork is already under way. The ground level's open floor plan—with the kitchen, dining room, and family room all conjoined—serves as homeschool headquarters, with some kids sprawled on the sofa reading books, others sitting with Debbie at the kitchen table, and the rest working independently at the dining room table.

The walls of the house are adorned with plaques and artwork. In the hallway a wooden sign proclaims a verse from the biblical book of Joshua: "Choose ye this day whom you will serve. As for me and my house, we will serve the Lord." Another plaque provides a reminder from the Psalms amidst the perpetual motion of this household: "Be still and know that I am God."

This morning, two-year-old Sam is playing with blocks in the living room, and nine-month-old Mindy explores the kitchen, trying to pry open cabinet doors, pulling herself onto chairs, and occasionally demanding attention from her mom or siblings with an indignant shriek. I'm struck by how smoothly the older children seem to take their turn with their baby sister, stopping to make silly faces at her when they walk by, or offering her a new toy to occupy her attention. Her occasional high-pitched squeals of delight or frustration don't seem to bother anyone—this family is clearly used to working amidst a variety of background noise.

Debbie sits with Julie at the kitchen table, using tiny plastic babies to help her daughter work on adding three small numbers. Debbie engages Julie with questions that push her to use the thumb-sized babies as concrete manipulatives in order to figure out the answers. The five-year-old goes along willingly, although she is also quite adept at using her little sister as a welcome distraction from time to time. Jason and Olivia occasionally venture over from the dining room table to ask Debbie questions or have her check their work. When Jason takes his turn at the kitchen table with his mom, they use weekly offering figures from the church bulletin to explore numerical comparisons—a small but typical example of how their religious identity and commitments are woven throughout their learning.

The "big kids" aren't home. The eldest two daughters, Amy and Elizabeth, live on their college campus about ten miles across the city. During the school year, they come home only on Sundays, often bringing friends—as Debbie good-naturedly points out, the difference between nine and eleven kids for Sunday dinner is hardly noticeable.

Joanna and Carly, the two teenagers still living at home, are only two years apart in age, but move in strikingly different worlds these days. Joanna, the fourteen-year-old, is quiet and shy. "She's my homebody," Debbie says with affection. By the time I arrive, she's already out on her regular Monday morning babysitting job. Joanna would like to work with children in some capacity after high school, Debbie tells me, and perhaps attend community college.

Carly, on the other hand, is *not* a homebody. The family rebel in thought and action, she recently began her first year of public school, entering as a high school junior. For the past couple years, she had been asking her parents if she could stop homeschooling, and they finally agreed. Her classes don't start until mid-morning today, so she's still around the house when I arrive. She's dressed not unlike many high school girls in my classrooms over the years, fashionably but not immodestly, with jeans and multiple layers of patterned shirts. Carly tells me she's enjoying public high school so far, and is particularly interested in interior design or fashion design. "She's discovered she's an artist," Debbie interjects.

A few minutes later, Carly gathers up her lunch and books to leave. "Let me pray for you before you go," Debbie says to her. This appears to be a regular practice, and even with a stranger in the house, Carly agrees easily. Debbie prays: "Father, I thank you for today, and the chance for Carly to go to school, to be a blessing to you and a blessing to others. In Jesus's name, amen."

Debbie looks up at Carly as she shoulders her bag. "Love you," she says to her daughter.

Carly smiles as she heads for the door. "Love you too."

Debbie devotes the bulk of her homeschooling attention to the five younger kids. They have a general sense of routine: in the morning, working semi-independently on language arts and math, with periodic check-ins with Debbie for help and direction. In the afternoons, when baby Mindy is napping, they focus on social studies, science, and art, often in a group format. Beyond that general pattern, however, Debbie leaves plenty of room for flexibility. Whereas some homeschool families have a structured setting and firm schedule that mimics a traditional classroom, Debbie realized early on that this wasn't going to work for her crew.

She uses a mix-and-match approach with her curricular materials, pulling from a wide range of Christian homeschool publishers. "I choose curricula based partly on what works for the kids and partly on what works for me, teaching multiple levels," she explains. "I've never done a whole reading program, because I'd rather have them read full books. I do this sort of thing"—she gestures to a reading workbook—"so they can learn the kinds of reading comprehension they will see on tests. I've decided to help them be a little more comfortable when it comes to standardized testing."

Most outsiders are surprised to learn that the homeschool curriculum market does nearly a billion dollars a year in sales in the United States alone. Anyone venturing into the cavernous display halls at state homeschooling conventions, however, quickly sees just how much is available for parents to choose from. Debbie tells me she only spends $300–$400 a year on materials altogether, far less than the estimated average of $350 per homeschool student. They get away with this, she says, because she never lets the kids write in the books, so each successive child can use the same ones.

Publishers offer a wide range of instructional approaches and philosophies, many with explicit Christian themes and references, but others that an outsider would be unable to distinguish from a public school resource. This variety is evident in the Palmers' various texts as well, but I notice that their science books have biblical quotations woven throughout, with the clear message that Scripture should guide and inform scientific interpretation, from evolution to genetic engineering. In *Eagle's Wings: Considering God's Creation (A Creative Biblical Approach to Natural Science)*, for instance, one recurring feature is "Evolution Stumpers," which question evidence such as the fossil record and examples of random mutation. This critical approach to evolution is, not surprisingly, quite common in conservative Christian homeschooling, and one I encounter in many of the families I visit.

While the physical setting and some of the curricular materials set homeschooling apart, much of Debbie's pedagogy resembles that of a skilled classroom teacher. She devises creative activities for the kids that extend well beyond conventional pencil and paper assignments: wood blocks for Sam to sort by shape and color, "math hopscotch" in the driveway for Jason and Olivia, or even just shaving cream on the kitchen table for the kids to write in and "erase" while practicing spelling (and simultaneously keeping the youngest ones occupied drawing pictures in it). And like any good teacher, Debbie looks for specific ways to praise and affirm her kids in their learning.

Even after just a few hours with the Palmers, it's clear that Debbie is a master multitasker, responding to a steady stream of family needs while paying close attention to the child with whom she's working. Last year was the toughest year for them, Debbie tells me, when she was teaching five kids (Carly was still being homeschooled, and Elizabeth was in twelfth grade). But the biggest management challenge for Debbie—and, it turns out, for many of the families I visit—is caring for the children who are too young to homeschool formally. "Right now," Debbie says, "it's mostly keeping the young ones busy. Honestly, that's always been the biggest challenge." It's a constant balancing act, Debbie admits, trying to plan activities that will appeal to the widest range of ages, and she worries that sometimes the younger ones end up getting shortchanged. On the other hand, she reasons, they've got a bunch of older siblings who give them plenty of attention and undoubtedly spur their learning and development.

The unique context of homeschooling provides a mix of opportunities and challenges here. The curricular options and resources, for example, are immense. As I witness with other families, this can be overwhelming and disorienting. Debbie's experience as a longtime homeschooler, however, enables her to mix and match in ways that engage her children and meet a variety of learning needs. Their family homeschool environment is rich with interaction and assistance among siblings; at the same time, it risks overlooking specific learning needs when joint activities are necessary.

While home is clearly educational headquarters for the Palmers, they get out of the house to combine fun and learning as well, taking advantage of Southern California's many resources: the Museum of Science and Industry, the zoo, and even the L.A. County Fair (yes, there still is such a thing). Many places, both here and throughout the country, offer discounted "homeschool days"; the Palmers regularly take advantage of those at Sea World and the San Diego Wild Animal Park.

Today we're going to the Bridgeway Homeschool Fair. Bridgeway is the Palmers' independent study program (ISP). One of the regulatory options for California homeschoolers is to enroll in an ISP, which serves as an umbrella organization that maintains paperwork, monitors academic progress, and communicates with state and local officials (California homeschool regulations are moderate compared to other states). ISPs come in a variety of shapes and sizes; unlike some, Bridgeway doesn't have its own facility for meetings or activities. Instead, it uses churches throughout the Los Angeles area as satellite campuses for these occasional events.

We're headed to one such satellite campus today. The eight of us clamber into the fifteen-passenger van in the driveway—"we refer to it as the ark," Debbie says with a smile. On our way there, she tells me more about Bridgeway and ISPs. California homeschoolers have the option of filing their own affidavit to homeschool, but Debbie prefers the additional resources and recordkeeping that Bridgeway provides. It costs them $65 per month for four kids. They also belong to HSLDA (a family membership runs $115 per year), although they've never had any legal issues or known anyone personally who has. "We're part of it because we believe in it," Debbie says. "We think it's a good thing what they're doing."

Many homeschoolers throughout the country participate in cooperatives, or "co-ops," that allow them to merge interests and resources with other families and offer their children everything from science labs to drama teams to gym class. While many of these co-ops are informal groups started by motivated parents, Bridgeway Academy offers regular, structured Academy Days that serve a similar purpose. The offerings range from art and music to self-defense and cooking, and parents volunteer to teach classes in their areas of expertise.

Bridgeway requires its members to record daily attendance, as well as semester and year-end grades. In September, parents also have to submit a curriculum outline plan for the upcoming year; during the high school years, this plan must also include course descriptions so it can be used as part of a transcript. But the chore Debbie finds most onerous is keeping track of daily content coverage, which essentially amounts to writing down all the page numbers that the kids worked through during the day. Bridgeway's administrators verify that everything is filled out and spot-check a few of the entries. "I guess I understand why they do it, for accountability," Debbie says, "but it's tedious to me."

No testing is required, either by Bridgeway or the state, but each year Debbie has her kids take one of the standardized tests that California public schools administer. She explains to her kids that this is more *her* report card than theirs, and she finds that the results generally confirm her own sense of their skills, which are primarily at or above grade level. "I look for improvement from one year to the next," she tells me.

Debbie understands the rationale for some homeschool regulation. "I know there are always the irresponsible families out there that are doing nothing," she acknowledges, "but most of the regulations don't have to be there for me." At the same time, Debbie resists the idea of additional governmental oversight. She points out that there seem to be plenty of kids in the public school system who lack basic skills, suggesting that "the government isn't doing that great a job at what they're already doing. And I guess at the risk of those few children who might fall through the cracks and not get a good homeschool education, I'm not really willing to give that over to the government." This perspective on regulation arises repeatedly in my conversations with homeschool parents—as much as they are saddened by the prospect of some kids being educationally neglected, they don't believe it justifies increased intrusion into the homeschooling endeavors of everyone else.

We've reached the church now and pull into a side parking lot. In the front of the building, a dozen or so tables are set up, with parents and children milling about them. Each table has a sign indicating what it has to offer: information about nursing careers, a chiropractor providing scoliosis checks, a karate academy advertising lessons, a dental hygienist demonstrating proper brushing techniques, someone selling beauty products for healthy skin, earthquake safety information, and even a service that will track your child in case of abduction.

We make our way into the church gymnasium, where a buzz of activity greets us. Several lines snake through the cavernous room; some people are waiting to register for photos, others to have pictures taken. As Debbie and the kids figure out where to go, I wander off down the church hallway to see what else is going on. This could almost be a typical school fair, albeit with most kids dressed more conservatively than some of their public school counterparts, and better behaved. As if to remind me of the difference, though, a group of early adolescents sit in the hallway, one strumming a guitar and singing a heartfelt chorus, "God has a plan for you, God has a plan for you."

When I return to the gymnasium to rejoin the Palmers, I see kids lined up on bleachers for the classic school picture, a mix of stiff smiles and genuinely beaming faces, the felt board at their feet proclaiming in plastic white letters, BRIDGEWAY ACADEMY GRADE 4. Other mothers are hastily combing kids' hair, adding a little spitshine to their faces as necessary. An exchange between a preadolescent boy and his mom again makes clear that despite some of the trappings of traditional schooling, there's something different going on here. "Mom, am I in fifth or sixth grade right now?" Wait a minute, I think—he doesn't know what grade he's in? Well, if your instruction is tailored to your own pace of growth, why bother starting a new grade just because it's September, or ending one just because it's June? "You're sixth," she tells him, and he sprints off for that group's photo.

Nearly three hours later, we head for home. On the drive back, Debbie tells me more about Carly's transition to public school. Carly had been pleading for the last two years, but Debbie and Mike didn't feel she was responsible enough. Even when they relented for this eleventh grade year, Debbie had misgivings. But it has turned out to be a great opportunity for Carly to take art classes, and she's had little trouble transitioning to public school academics. Part of this success, Debbie believes, is because homeschooling required Carly to work independently and figure things out for herself. The other reason, however, is less gratifying—what Debbie sees as a lack of rigor in the public school curriculum. "In English," she says, shaking her head, "everybody has a copy of the book, and while they're in class, they listen to it on tape and follow along. Nobody takes the book home. In social studies, the teacher is the football coach, and every week they watch a movie about the period of history they're studying."

On the logistical side, California's homeschool regulations actually ended up making it easier for Carly to enroll in a public school and be granted academic credit for her homeschooling work. California categorizes independent study programs such as Bridgeway Academy as private schools, so Carly's transcript appeared no different than any other student transferring from a private school—they didn't even know she was homeschooled prior to her arrival (although they would recognize that Carly attended a religious school, since Bible classes were listed on the transcript—and were processed as "elective credits" by the public school). Elsewhere, policies for granting credits to homeschool students who enter public schools vary from state to state and often from district to district, particularly when regulations categorize homeschools as distinct from private schools. Some evaluate transcripts, others require tests, and in a few states, high schools put a ceiling on transfer credits or even accept none at all.

Having returned home, we sit down for lunch. Debbie casually quizzes the kids about what friends they ran into at the homeschool fair and what parts of the event they liked the most. When Joanna says she overheard some girls criticizing others for "looking like homeschoolers," Debbie bursts out laughing.

"*You* know," Joanna persists, "some people have this look about them."

"Well, not all the kids are as lucky as you are," Debbie responds wryly, "with a fashion-conscious mother who picks out all their clothes for them!"

For the remainder of lunch, the younger kids gleefully explain an intricate burping game to me, which doesn't seem to faze Debbie in the slightest (although she does smilingly suggest to the kids that the best response to a burp isn't "pickle" or other prescribed code words, but rather "excuse me"). As they finish up their meal, Debbie tells them they can change out of their nice clothes and go play for a bit, and then we're all going to do an art project together.

As we clear dishes, I ask Debbie what prompted her to start homeschooling in the first place. After graduating from college with a child psychology degree, she had been teaching kindergarten in a Christian day school. Amy, her eldest, was born in 1984, and Debbie started contemplating the prospect of homeschooling. "I didn't know anyone who did it and I really think it was something that God put on my heart," Debbie says, "because I really knew very little of it at the time. Even when I started, people were still saying, 'Is that legal?' Nobody knew anything." Eighteen years later, she's still at it, and plans to keep going until baby Mindy finishes high school.

"What would you say are the most important academic skills that you want your kids to learn by the time they're done homeschooling?" I ask.

"Well, beyond the basics of being able to read and write, and math skills," Debbie says, "I want my kids to have the ability to find something out if they want to learn it in the future. With a lot of textbooks, you can read it and you can regurgitate the information, but you really haven't learned a lot other than to get through the test. I want them to be able to know what the resources are and even have that desire, when they want to learn more about something, to go and look at it and be excited about it." She contrasts this with her own experiences as a student in public school, which she remembers as dull and uninspiring.

After lunch is cleaned up, Debbie gathers all the kids together at the dining room table for an art project to conclude the homeschool day. She reviews some color concepts with them (primary and secondary, warm and cool), then sends them out to the front yard to each find one big leaf, which they use to create stencils and ultimately a collage of fall colors on their papers.

Shortly before three o'clock, Carly returns home from school. She's still a bit flustered by the organizational challenges of keeping track of six distinct classes, teachers, and assignments, but remains in good spirits about the whole experience. "Hey Mom," she asks, "if you get a chance can you help me with my geometry?" Carly's arrival has driven the younger kids into a state of rambunctious excitement, so Debbie sends them outside to play for a few minutes, and she sits down to look over Carly's geometry textbook with her. Formal homeschooling for Carly may be over, but Debbie is still teaching.

On one of my subsequent visits, I arrive in time for the Bible study that begins each morning. Except for Carly, who has just left for school, all the kids sit in the living room with Debbie, their Bibles in hand. But their heads are definitely not in it this morning. "We read in Proverbs that we have a choice," Debbie summarizes, scanning the room in search of eye contact. "Which kind of life do we choose to live?" She waits for a response, but gets nothing. "You'd choose the life of God's wisdom, wouldn't you? But you know, every day, sometimes every hour, we make a choice about the kind of life we want, which kind of wisdom. Snack time rolls around and sometimes you choose selfish ambition: 'No fair, he got the last one!' And all of a sudden we have disorder, don't we?"

Debbie continues to prod them throughout the session, but gets only the pat answer or one-word responses that discussion leaders dread. Apparently sensing she had gotten everything out of them that she could, Debbie asks the kids if they have any prayer requests, and then leads them in a closing prayer.

When she finishes, Debbie begins issuing directions to each of her children about where to begin their schoolwork for the day. Within a few minutes, academic study has commenced. Joanna has retreated to her room to work independently, and Jason sits at the dining room table doing handwriting exercises from a workbook. The rest of the kids are in the kitchen with Debbie. She's given Sam and Mindy crayons and paper to keep them busy while Olivia reads aloud to her a textbook passage about planetary positions. Meanwhile, Julie works on a set of simple addition and subtraction problems from her workbook, which Debbie periodically checks over. Debbie divides her time among each child throughout the morning, which is split midway with a snack break and some trampoline jumping to clear the head.

After lunch, Debbie helps eight-year-old Olivia with a project—designing and building a model of a house described in an *American Girl* book she's reading in her Academy Days class. Debbie offers a few suggestions for how Olivia might go about it, but Olivia gets a bit frustrated with her mom's input. The familiarity of the parent-child relationship seems to cut both ways in this regard; Debbie knows her daughter extremely well and Olivia may feel more comfortable asking for help, but I doubt very much that Olivia would ever roll her eyes or give a whiny retort to a classroom teacher.

While Olivia is finishing up her project, Debbie calls to Joanna, who has been ensconced in her room most of the day, to see if she's finished with her work. When I have the chance to speak with Joanna alone, she tells me that she finds most of her independent work pretty boring, mostly just grinding through textbooks, reading chapters and taking quizzes focused on information recall, with few requirements to analyze and synthesize the material. Even Spanish, I was disappointed to discover, consists mostly of just learning vocabulary and grammar, with very few opportunities to practice speaking.

Earlier that day, Debbie had gently chastised Joanna for her lack of progress in her history textbook, and a faint glimmer of "adolescent attitude" emerged—nothing major, but maybe a little disenchantment with her work and her mom's expectation that she had to keep at it.

Perhaps as a former secondary school teacher, I'm more sensitive to the quality of learning experiences for adolescents, but it strikes me that as homeschoolers get older and do more and more independent work—a typical pattern—the risk of an isolated and uninspired learning experience grows. This need not be the case, of course; plenty of teens flourish when given more latitude to direct their own learning, but it's harder to imagine that happening when textbooks and chapter quizzes play a central role.

In Joanna's case, the relative seclusion of her homeschooling experience presents an additional dilemma. On the one hand, Joanna told me she wouldn't want to follow in Carly's footsteps and switch to public school—"I'm just kind of shy and so I wouldn't fit in a lot of things"— but on the other, she regrets not having more friends, and sometimes feels lonely. Perhaps attending a conventional school would be so intimidating that it would hinder her learning, or perhaps it would push her to develop greater social confidence. Hard to know.

What opportunities do the other Palmer children have to engage with diverse people and viewpoints? When I ask them privately, they seem quite content with a social world that certainly extends beyond the walls of their home. Carly interacts all day long with a range of peers and perspectives in her urban Los Angeles public high school. Seven-year-old Jason, while not as immersed in the outside world as Carly, tells me he has several friends who attend public school and are not Christians. (I overhear one conversation with his mom where Jason relates some of the "bad language" his friends use; Debbie suggests that perhaps he can help his friends find some better words to use, but her low-key reaction tells me that she sees such exposure as part of growing up.) Olivia is very active in her church youth group, but also tells me about several non-Christian friends from the neighborhood she plays with regularly. All of the older kids participate in community sports leagues as well, and pop culture makes its way into the Palmer house via computer and television (*High School Musical* and *Xiaolin Showdown* are cited as a couple of favorites).

Even Joanna, while obviously wanting more friends in general, has developed relationships with non-Christians. In fact, her best friend Meredith actively questions Joanna's Christian beliefs. Debbie admits to me she initially had some concerns about this "Of all my children, is she going to be strong in this relationship or is she going to get pulled into something?" But hearing them talk and looking over Joanna's shoulder as she instant messages Meredith on the computer has changed Debbie's mind; Joanna has not only held firm in her own religious convictions but also tried to engage her friend in ongoing discussions about faith. "She has blown me away," Debbie says with admiration.

Another way that the Palmers engage with the broader world is through missions work. The previous summer, eighteen-year-old Elizabeth spent a month in the Ukraine working with children in an orphanage. This trip transformed her own sense of purpose, to the point where she is now organizing a more extensive return trip and contemplating a long-term move there. As Elizabeth told her mom, "I knew it would change my life, but I didn't know it would *become* my life." It has also begun to broaden her appreciation for diverse social contexts, she says, helping her to become less judgmental as she understands different cultural practices. The rest of her family has joined with her to help raise funds, collect supplies, and host Elizabeth's fellow missionaries who will be traveling back with her.

The Palmers' church also provides ample opportunity and encouragement for members to engage with the broader world and see themselves as part of a larger community. During my trips out to Los Angeles, I have several chances to visit. Grace Reformed Church (GRC) is a multiethnic, multigenerational church with nearly two thousand in attendance over five services each Sunday. Attire is "California casual," and worship is an energetic affair with a gospel choir and band complete with keyboard, drums, and electric guitars.

While GRC is theologically conservative, politics are rarely mentioned, according to the Palmers. When they are, the pastor emphasizes that neither Democrats nor Republicans have the answer; instead, it is up to GRC as a faith community to make a difference. "I believe God has placed us strategically to be a thriving ministry center," he reminds the congregation regularly, and encourages them to devote their energies to the many GRC programs aimed at high-poverty areas surrounding them. One morning the pastor calls up a young woman who works as a physician in a county health clinic. She speaks movingly of the tremendous need in their community, including one patient who has been waiting four months for a desperately needed biopsy: *"This is not justice,"* she says, her voice breaking. People around me wipe their eyes, and a couple offer soft calls of encouragement to her as she seeks to compose herself. She concludes by presenting a vision for a church-run, free clinic and invites congregants to help. The Palmers embrace this social ministry vision of their church. "It's exciting to me," Debbie says. "I like the fact that we are looking outside ourselves."

Missions work, whether in communities across the freeway or across the world, has long been a central commitment of many conservative Christians and their churches. Such efforts have an uneven history, of course, marred by cultural ignorance and imposition. But this approach to missions has been changing in recent decades, with a growing emphasis by many missions groups on cross-cultural understanding, humility, and learning from the people among whom they go to live. To the extent that conservative Christian homeschoolers participate in the latter kind of missions, they have the opportunity to learn beyond a surface level how different people understand and experience the world, and hopefully enlarge their own understanding of the world and themselves in the process.

Since Michael Palmer works long hours during the week, I arrange to stop by their home one Sunday afternoon so I can talk with him. When I arrive, Elizabeth is home from college for a visit, and she readily agrees to sit down for a chat. Shorter than Carly but with the same dark hair, she has a friendly, self-confident air about her. Not surprisingly, Elizabeth's transition to college life involved an adjustment period, but her choice of a Christian college seems to have made the shift less dramatic. Besides the typical social changes of living with peers away from home, she was unused to taking formal written exams and writing extended analytical papers—two forms of assessment not typically used by many homeschooling families. As she's done more and more of these in college, however, she feels she's been able to adjust to their format and expectations.

On an earlier visit, I had asked Debbie about writing requirements in their homeschool curricula. They don't do much extended analytical writing—taking a position, formulating an argument, responding to other perspectives—primarily due to the time demands on Debbie of reading and evaluating long papers. "When Amy went away to college the first year," Debbie told me, "that was my biggest fear: oh, we haven't done enough writing! And she ended up being the one that edited everybody's paper!" This was, Debbie suspects, because Amy had done so much reading during her homeschool years.

One facet of college life that Elizabeth says she continues to struggle with, however, is classroom discussion, particularly when disagreement is involved. Initially she avoided verbal conflict, but says she's gotten better at asserting her opinion, as well as offering spontaneous analysis during class. While some of these difficulties she attributes to her personality, she acknowledges that she had little opportunity to engage in large-group discussion during homeschooling. This lacuna turns out to be a common refrain in the homeschooling families I speak with—even if a homeschool family had a dozen or more kids at home, it's not the same as speaking up in a room of mere acquaintances. In addition, I find few homeschool co-ops where group discussion is a major focus. For conservative Christian homeschoolers, it seems Sunday school classes, or youth groups, are perhaps the likeliest venues to develop those skills.

On the other hand, one aspect of college academics that many freshmen struggle with but that Elizabeth felt well prepared for was the expectation that students plan and pace their own studies without a teacher looking over their shoulders. "I think I was good at working on my own," she says, "because that's just what I did all through high school."

Elizabeth's experiences echo much of the broader story of homeschoolers transitioning to college. While formal studies have been limited in scope, they suggest—along with hundreds of anecdotal accounts I have reviewed over the past few years—that homeschoolers generally fare quite well in college. Both university officials and homeschoolers-turned-collegians themselves point to social adjustments as the biggest challenge, as well as learning to adhere to a fixed schedule of classes and assignment deadlines. As with Elizabeth, however, homeschoolers' ability to direct their own learning and pace themselves is identified as a real strength, particularly if accompanied by a zest for exploration and discovery that self-directed learning can foster. Not surprisingly, then, admissions departments around the country are increasingly amenable to homeschooler applications, some actually assigning an official liaison specifically for this population. Others have even begun actively recruiting homeschoolers through state conventions, targeted information sessions, and homeschooler publications.

Despite Elizabeth's overall appreciation for the college experience, her recent involvement in missions work in the Ukraine has made such a dramatic impact on her sense of purpose that she's not sure whether she will complete her degree. This prospect doesn't concern Mike or Debbie; as with many homeschool families I've spoken with, college is viewed as just one post-homeschooling option among many. For conservative Christian homeschoolers, the metric for a successful education is almost always described in terms of "being the person God wants them to be" rather than an Ivy League diploma, high-powered job, or six-figure income.

After my conversation with Elizabeth, Mike Palmer graciously gives me nearly two hours of his precious time at home. By his own account, Mike is relatively uninvolved in the day-to-day homeschooling process. One year he taught science to the older girls, but found it hard to be consistent given his work schedule. On many mornings he reads the Bible to the younger kids during breakfast, and tries to stay involved in the kids' education in other ways: coaching soccer, reading with them in the evenings, helping with their hands-on projects. But especially in recent years, he says, "my role is really just to bankroll the thing," admittedly no small feat for a family of eleven living in Los Angeles.

It seems beyond dispute that women do the vast bulk of the homeschooling work. Some observers, noting Debbie's college degree and professional teaching career prior to the birth of her children, might argue that she has sold herself short. A common saying among conservative Christian homeschool dads is, "My wife's the teacher; I'm the principal." By this they usually mean that they are there to support their spouses and "back them up" in terms of expectations and discipline with the children. Some fathers, however, also use that statement as an assertion of their ultimate authority and influence in the family structure.

But let's stick with that metaphor just a bit longer. As most veteran classroom teachers will tell you, the power of the principal holds far less significance once they close their door and start to teach. And while some conventional principals may attempt to micromanage, I've yet to encounter a homeschool dad who reviews lesson plans or even plays a central role in choosing curricula packages. And just like all the great classroom teachers I've known over the years, the influence that really matters to homeschool moms—if we're willing to take their words at face value—is the influence over their children's learning and the shape those lives will take in the future.

This certainly seems to be the case with Debbie. She readily admits to feeling exhausted on a regular basis, but affirms with no hint of resentment that "I'm doing what I feel I need to be doing and *want* to be doing right now." Debbie knows this time of life won't last forever, and she sees homeschooling as a gift to her children and an investment in their lives moving forward. And while Debbie might not be so bold to claim it herself, homeschool mothers—much more than fathers—are the ones who lead their families on an educational journey that questions and often rejects societal norms and expectations.

While Mike is not nearly as involved on a day-to-day basis, he is firmly convinced of the value of homeschooling. "I always tell people, even if Debbie wasn't the great teacher she is, a mediocre tutor is better than an excellent teacher that's trying to give you one-twentieth of her attention." It's the time commitment that matters so much, Mike insists: "Unfortunately in our culture today, we dabble in parenthood. I think that we view kids as more like pets and there's not the attention that's needed. There's a lot of freedom and lot of things that the kids are allowed to do because no one's supervising them, no one's training them, no one's taking the time to spend with them. The old adage about 'quality time,' you know—it's got to be *quantity*. The quality's *in* the quantity."

This reminds me of Debbie's observation that one of the big benefits of homeschooling is that her kids "get a lot of *life*, real life that goes on, that they don't understand when they are separated for several hours a day." One compelling example she offers in this regard was the time that her children spent with her last year during the serious illness and eventual deaths of grandparents—her kids saw what it meant to care for them beyond a quick visit to the hospital in the evenings. "If they had been in school all day, I think they would have been isolated from that in a lot of ways." It's important not to overlook the significance of this point. In a culture where children seem increasingly programmed with outside activities from dawn to dusk, and family time is fragmented by an array of work and social demands, it can become difficult to learn what it means to travel through life together *as* a family.

Neither Mike nor Debbie claims that homeschooling is the only legitimate choice, however. "Homeschooling isn't for everybody," Mike says, "and it's not the cure-all for everything." They believe public schools serve an important purpose, and don't resent paying taxes for them even though their children don't attend. As for other families, Debbie remarks, "I would never say that they're doing it wrong if they don't have their kids at home. It's what *we* feel that *we* have been called to do, and that's why we're doing it."

What about the Palmers' political views, and their vision of what it means to be a Christian citizen? Although it became clear in the course of my informal conversations with each of the six families I visited that they were strongly conservative in their social, political, and religious views, I also wanted a slightly more systematic way to affirm those impressions. I asked each set of parents to respond to a list of questions drawn from the General Social Survey, a nationwide poll administered to adults across the country every couple years. This allowed me to compare their answers to the general U.S. population and verify that, yes, indeed, these families were strongly conservative on almost every social, political, and religious issue addressed.

Mike and Debbie willingly completed the survey, but when I asked them follow-up questions, it became clear that they don't spend a lot of their time and energy trying to get the rest of America to agree with their conservative viewpoints. Mike does lament the nation's moral and spiritual condition, contending that "as a Christian country," we've moved away from our original aim to please God. This notion of America founded as a Christian nation but increasingly adrift from those roots—and thus risking the wrath of God—is prevalent among many conservative Christians, including the homeschool families I visited. Mike and Debbie used to be more politically active, particularly around the issue of abortion (making phone calls and writing letters, primarily), but the time demands of homeschooling a large family have curtailed those efforts.

Political awareness and engagement don't appear to be strong educational priorities, either. Debbie says they might occasionally discuss a major news event with the older kids, but that's about it. And as I mentioned earlier, political issues are rarely raised—at least overtly—in their church. When I asked the Palmer teenagers a few of the survey questions, every one of them prefaced their responses with some version of "I don't pay much attention to politics." While this was a discouraging refrain to my high-school-teacher ears, it's one I've heard all too often from public school students as well.

Although politics and civic engagement aren't priorities for Mike and Debbie as they raise and educate their kids, they are increasingly confronted with the challenge of how to help their children learn to navigate the world on their own, while still encouraging them to hold fast to their Christian beliefs and commitments. A central tenet—and tension—of the Christian life, drawn from Jesus's words in the gospel of John, is to be "in the world, but not of the world." Christians are not to withdraw from the world, but at the same time must not be conformed to the ways of the world, many of which run counter to the values and commitments Christians are called to live out. In *Thy Kingdom Come*, historian of religion and self-professed evangelical Christian Randall Balmer criticizes conservative Christian homeschoolers for erring on the side of withdrawal, and argues that educating one's children in a religiously segregated context ignores Jesus's command to be "the light of the world."

When I ask Debbie and Mike what they think of Balmer's perspective, they dispute his implication that children are necessarily ready for that type of engagement. "To expect a five-year-old to take on that task, I don't think that's what God's Word teaches us," Debbie says. She paraphrases God's commands from the book of Deuteronomy to illustrate her point: "I think we are to train up our children; I think we are to teach them as we walk along the road and as we sit down and as we eat at a table and everything else and *equip them to be that light and salt*—but not in those formative years."

Mike offers a similar take on the issue. "You don't thrust your children out into a world where you haven't trained them and prepared them for a world that is decidedly at war with God," he asserts, then adds a biblical image: "You know, they're either going to learn real quick and become like David and slay the giant or they're going to tremble before Goliath—and the natural response is going to be to tremble, unless they have faith that God is the author of everything, that he is the source of truth, and all truth finds its origins in God."

With this in mind, Mike and Debbie strive to instill in their children a particular understanding of the world, one that evaluates everything in light of fundamental Christian convictions. In the Palmer household, this process begins with unquestioning obedience to one's parents—not as an end unto itself, but as part of the training and preparation necessary for engagement with a world often hostile to their values and commitments.

But Mike and Debbie also understand that, ultimately, their children will have to decide for themselves what they believe and how they want to live. They want their children to develop into critical thinkers, but see the purpose of critical thinking to be at least as much about interrogating the messages and values of the world as it is reflecting on one's own faith commitments. "I want them to not just accept what they read or what they hear," Debbie says. "I want them to think it through and be able to examine it and weigh it in light of what they *do* know to be true. I want it ultimately to come back to their relationship with God and who he is and who they are—understanding that, apart from him, they really don't have anything." Because the Palmers live *in* the world, surrounded by a culture that sends worldly messages about money, success, pleasure, and power, they focus their efforts on preventing their children from becoming *of* the world.

Mike and Debbie's willingness for their children to ultimately choose their own way is currently being tested with Carly, now in her senior year at the public high school. "Carly in particular is struggling with whether she's going to make the faith her own," Mike tells me. Nevertheless, he supports her decision to attend public high school. "She needed"—he pauses for a moment— 'she needed to be doing something different."

"What makes you say that?" I ask.

"Well, she's been pressing for independence harder than any of the other kids, which is not a bad thing necessarily, but it's brought us into conflict," Mike admits. "Because she wants to do things her way, and you know, her ways and our ways don't necessarily agree all the time."

Here's the complicated calculus of helping your children learn to think for themselves, particularly when you also desire to pass on certain values and beliefs. "How do you respond," I ask, "when she pushes against the things that you think are really important for her to learn or believe or be—when she's saying, 'I'm not sure that's for me'?"

"How do I respond?" He grimaces. "Not well, sometimes. I can honestly say that God's been refining me. I don't lose my temper easily, but she knows what buttons to push. I guess I'm realizing that, ultimately, they're not our kids. They're God's children. And I'm learning to just open my hand and not cling to my ways as much." As if to demonstrate, he turns his palms upward. "All I can do is teach them; I can try to lead by example, I can pray for them—and all I can do is trust God for the end results. There's a limitation to what I can do and at that point then they have to assume responsibility for their life."

Debbie shares her husband's perspective. "It has been a *big* learning experience for us," she acknowledges. "Because, you know, we thought we were parenting pretty well!" She laughs freely and admits that they are still trying to figure out how to navigate things. "But boy, we meet it with a lot of prayer now. A *lot* of prayer."

The next day, I get a chance to talk privately with Carly and hear what the seventeen-year-old has to say for herself about these issues. I ask her if she's found it challenging to decide what she believes as she's gotten older and her world has increasingly expanded beyond family life and homeschooling.

Carly nods. "Yeah, 'cause there's so many different views out there. And I'm realizing, too, that being homeschooled—especially in this Christian family—you just grow up with all those beliefs, and you don't really see anything else. And going to school, there is such diversity and different views on politics or religion, just *everything* about life. And so I've kind of questioned that, and wanted to look into some different things more. But I think it has just really helped me in my faith personally. I *have* thought for myself more."

"Are there ways in which you feel like your views have changed so they're now different from your folks?" I ask.

"Maybe slightly," she says, "but not really anything major. I still have the same faith that my parents have; I've just adopted that as *my* faith more than theirs. I think it's just different opinions on the grayer areas."

"What types of things come up?"

"Just like a lot of things in the church, what people think is right and wrong." She pauses to figure out how to explain herself. "There's just little things my parents and I have gotten into arguments over, from things that don't matter to things that do. It's just kind of like now I'm thinking for myself more and I *can* disagree with my parents. One of us is not necessarily wrong but we just have different opinions."

While Carly managed to transition fairly well to the academic side of public high school life, she acknowledges that there have been social adjustments as well. "It's just like there's so much drama," she tells me. "Peer pressure is a lot stronger at school. There were some things I did compromise and I wish I hadn't." But even though Carly has come to regret some of her choices, she remains firm in her desire to step beyond the social circles of her past. "My parents, when I was homeschooled, they had a really hard time with me hanging out with non-Christians. And a *lot* of Christians have problems with that," she says, with a slight edge to her voice. "But going to school, you *have* to branch out, meet people. Not everybody is going to be a Christian, not everyone's going to have the same faith as you, but they can still be good people and you can still love on them, you know? And I think that my parents are more hesitant about that, whereas I'm just like, 'Come on.'"

We talk some more about the range of perspectives and beliefs she encounters in her school, and how one of the challenges of living in a diverse society is figuring out what to do when we disagree with others about important issues. "So how important is it for *you* to understand where other people are coming from, if you disagree with them?" I ask.

"Oh, that's *so* important to me," Carly responds. "I'm the type of person that you tell me something and I'm not necessarily going to believe it. I want proof, I want facts, I want to look into it."

Carly's determination to get all the facts before making up her mind is of course admirable. But it also seems to me that one of the greatest challenges we face as a democracy is the existence of irresolvable moral disagreements, where neither side can show beyond a doubt that it is solely in the right. Can we recognize the reasonableness of other perspectives, I ask Carly, even when we disagree with them? Or is this just a failure to either get all the facts or think through it carefully enough?

It's a complicated question, but Carly picks up on it quickly. "It kind of depends on what it is, you know?" she says. "Like the whole situation with gay marriage: there are two totally different opinions on that and I think a lot of it *is* religiously based, and so I think that people who aren't as religious, they're just like, 'Oh yeah, whatever makes them happy.'"

"Do you think that it's a legitimate argument for a Christian to make, to give religious reasons for saying same-sex marriages shouldn't be allowed?" I ask.

"Probably not, because it doesn't apply to everybody," Carly says. "It is legitimate for people in the Christian faith, because they understand it. Like I think it would be *so* wrong if Christians were supporting gay marriage, but for people who don't even believe in God or hate God or whatever, how can you make that argument with them?"

Carly makes an interesting—and, to my mind, important—distinction here between reasons that carry weight among Christians versus reasons that the rest of society recognizes as valid. It raises a broader question that political theorists continue to grapple with: are religious citizens justified in appealing to reasons that others don't recognize as valid (for example, drawn from holy scriptures) when they're advocating policies that affect everyone? While Carly hasn't thought through all the details of these complicated questions, I'm encouraged to see that even though she holds some strong conservative opinions (for example, abortion and homosexuality are wrong), she is nonetheless willing to consider other perspectives and the need to make room for them in our pluralistic society.

As I depart the Palmers' home for the final time, I am largely impressed with what I've seen. Some observers will no doubt disapprove of certain aspects of their homeschooling, but it would be tough to argue that their children are receiving a demonstrably inferior education than what is provided in many public schools. Even with so many children to teach, Debbie takes good advantage of homeschooling's opportunity to individualize instruction, particularly among her younger kids. She offers a variety of activities that appeal to a range of learning styles, and provides a supportive mixture of affirmation and criticism informed by an intimate knowledge of her children's personalities and needs.

While politics and civics aren't an overt focus for the Palmers, their children do have a variety of opportunities to engage with the outside world. My individual conversations with the kids suggest an openness to considering the viewpoints of others, even though they don't see this as related to good citizenship or express much interest in the political realm. Either way, it hardly echoes Michael Farris's vision of a homeschooled president.

The Palmers' biggest challenge, it seems, is navigating the tension between instilling a foundation of Christian commitment in their children while also providing them the freedom they need to make those commitments their own. Carly's story, of course, is the most wrenching manifestation of this challenge for Debbie and Mike. When I check in with them via e-mail the next summer, Debbie tells me that Carly graduated from high school with honors, but doesn't have immediate plans for college, since she's unsure what studies she wants to pursue. Currently, she's working two jobs and trying to afford an apartment, Debbie reports, and "is struggling to find her own way right now, and wanting little advice or counsel."

As becomes clear throughout my homeschooling travels, being "in the world but not of the world" poses a challenge of balance. Even when homeschoolers overemphasize the latter half of the admonition, the world often has a way of intruding nonetheless. I recall hearing about one homeschool family whose young girls mentioned to their mom as they drove past a local strip club that "that's the place where ladies show their bottoms." After nearly driving off the road in shock, this mother discovered that they had been informed of this little tidbit from a slightly older homeschool boy, who had in turn learned about it from the neighbor kid next door.

In the case of the Palmers, some homeschool proponents will undoubtedly point to Mike and Debbie's decision to let Carly switch to public school as the source of her problems. Other readers will likely say, "What problems? Good for her!" Regardless, it seems clear that Carly had already begun to question much of the received wisdom around her well before she made the switch. I appreciate Mike and Debbie's commitment to homeschooling their children, but I also admire their willingness to let a sixteen-year-old have a real say in her education—and their desire to walk with her in that process as much as she will allow them.

CALIFORNIA HOMESCHOOL CONVENTION

The Christian Home Educators Association of California stakes its claim as the largest state-level homeschool organization in the country. Their annual convention draws nearly five thousand participants over three days, and during one of my trips to Los Angeles I count myself among them. As I enter the convention complex, it's clear this is a well-staffed, highly organized event. In the massive main hall, a contemporary Christian band leads early arrivers in worship. The room gradually fills with casually dressed attendees. There's more racial diversity here than I see in homeschool gatherings around the country, but it's still a predominantly white crowd.

After the band finishes, a conference official welcomes the audience and leads them in prayer. Next up on the dais is Roy Hanson, representing a California organization called Family Protection Ministries. He tells us that 80 percent of homeschooling legal issues are decided at the state level, and explains that FPM's job is to keep track of what's going on and advocate for homeschoolers as necessary. "We are very busy at the state capital," he assures us.

Michael Smith, president of the Home School Legal Defense Association, rises to speak next. He offers a fiery endorsement of FPM and urges attendees to donate generously to their cause as the offering plates begin to circulate through the conference hall. Smith mentions the specific threat of universal preschool, which he says is just the precursor to mandatory preschool and an effort to keep lowering the compulsory attendance age. FPM deserves our thanks, Smith urges, for protecting homeschoolers against this type of legislation, as well as against intrusive social workers who view homeschoolers as guilty until proven innocent. The next great battle in home education, Smith warns, will be over regulatory issues. If we lose the battle of regulation, he contends, we will lose the genius of home-schooling, which is individualized instruction.

I agree with Smith that one of the greatest potential benefits of home-schooling is the opportunity to provide learning experiences that closely match a child's needs and interests, but Smith's implication here—that fixed standards destroy this flexibility—ignores the distinction between means and ends. Regulations could require basic literacy and numeracy, for instance, while leaving the teaching methods (and the rest of the content) entirely up to the parent.

The convention schedule includes over one hundred speakers to choose from, not including the promotional workshops offered by curriculum vendors eager to showcase their programs in detail. Speakers' topics range from inspirational ("Trials, Tears, and Triumphs of Homeschooling") to administrative ("Home Ed Basics: Recordkeeping") to practical curriculum ideas ("Hands-on Science Guaranteed to Knock Your Socks Off, Not Your Hands").

One speaker I'm especially interested in hearing is Ned Ryun, founding director of Generation Joshua, the youth civics program from HSLDA "dedicated to helping teens to become effective citizens and future leaders." Ryun's first of six talks is entitled "Christians and Politics," and draws more than four hundred people, many of them teenagers. While dressed more conservatively than the high schoolers I've taught, they still have the "adolescent look"—lots of baseball caps turned backwards, T-shirts and jeans, even one long-haired guy who wouldn't have stood out from the public school surfers or stoners. I see a T-shirt—"Body Piercing Saved My Life"—with a picture of Jesus crucified on it. Ryun gives a fifty-minute lecture and, with the exception of some whispering among a few teens leaning against the back wall, these kids sit quietly and attentively, offering raised hands when Ryun quizzes them on American history.

Ryun's version of this history emphasizes the Christian devotion of the "Founding Fathers" and their Judeo-Christian intent in the design of our government. Ryun equates America with ancient Israel, urging us to remember that when the Israelites followed God, they flourished, and when they didn't, they perished. Christians need to be involved in politics, he argues, reciting numerous unattributed statistics to argue that conservative Christian views are actually the majority ones on social issues, but

Christians must do more to make their voices heard. If we elect Christian men and women who rule in accordance with natural law and God's Word, Ryun claims, the nation will be blessed, and if we don't, the nation will be cursed—"it's cause and effect."

This call to engagement is echoed by the convention keynote address of Jeff Myers, a professor of communication arts at Bryan College in Tennessee and a frequent speaker on the conservative Christian lecture circuit. "The race of life is a relay," he urges. "We only win when we pass the baton of faith to our children." To do this, he says, we must recognize that our children will either be shapers of culture or shaped by the culture. What Myers suggests (and what the activist message of Michael Farris, Ned Ryun, and HSLDA echoes) is that staying on the sidelines in hopes of being left alone isn't an option. Unless Christian homeschoolers learn how to engage their culture—whether through politics, business, science, or the arts—they will be swept away in a riptide of values antithetical to the Christian life.

After a morning of speakers, I wander into the cavernous exhibit hall. A must-see for most attendees, it's filled with aisle after aisle of vendor booths, more than two hundred in all. By mid-afternoon I'm ready to leave, worn out by crowds and carrying a four-inch stack of promotional material: demo CDs and DVDs, science lab supplies, "reading systems," record-keeping software, online virtual academies, special education consulting, tutorial services, Christian college guidebooks, and catalogs listing hundreds of curricular options for every school subject imaginable, from genetics and biotechnology to music theory and Latin. I can certainly see how homeschool parents would find these conventions a valuable source of information and encouragement and—for better or worse—inspire a vision for how to engage with the broader culture.

3

THE RIVERA FAMILY

"I Can See That I'm Doing the Right Thing"

Lydia and John Rivera live with their three young children—and one or more troubled teens they take in—only a few freeway exits away from the Palmers, but in a decidedly rougher neighborhood. The small houses, many with peeling stucco, push up almost to the sidewalk of their sparsely landscaped street, the tiny patches of front yard grass surrounded by chain-link fences. The Riveras rent here; when they began homeschooling five years ago, Lydia quit her job and they had to sell their house. "We decided we were raising a family and not a house," she explains. "We'll get by somehow, because this is more important."

I arrive at nine in the morning to find Lydia and her two girls sitting on the living room floor, making decorative construction-paper chains. Their eldest, Anna, is ten years old; her sister Veronica is seven. Both have long, dark hair and beautiful smiles, and both treat me with warmth and respect throughout all my visits. Their five-year-old brother, Daniel, is still sleeping. The decorations, I discover, are for the weekly dinner, games, and socializing they host for fifteen or so local teens they've befriended. "A lot of these kids, ninety percent of them, are broken kids," Lydia says, "so our family is being a light to them."

Lydia and John describe their home as a "ministry house," and their doors are open for the handful of adolescents who stop by almost every evening, sometimes staying until one in the morning or later, hanging out and talking about life and its challenges. Two eighteen-year-old girls from abusive homes are currently living with them, crammed into one of the house's tiny bedrooms.

The homeschooling day for Anna and Veronica generally runs from around ten in the morning until they break for a late lunch, usually one or two in the afternoon. The girls' typical morning routine, Lydia tells me, is to begin the day with their devotions (Bible reading and prayer), then work their way through history, science, English, math, health, and fine arts. But as I learn, there are many exceptions to this schedule. On Mondays, they generally stop early, so they can shop and prepare for the teen dinner that evening. They also have annual passes to Knott's Berry Farm and make frequent "educational" visits there or to other area amusement parks during the week.

While the girls continue working on the party decorations, Lydia tells me about why they started homeschooling in the first place. "It was laid on my husband's heart," Lydia says. "He was listening to Dr. Dobson about how the best thing you can do is quit your job and find a way to stay home with kids. So John was like, 'Lydia, you need to do this. This is something we need to do for our family. You need to quit your job.'"

Lydia says she agreed, but with some reluctance. "I was worried about the money, I was worried about the house, I was worried about messing up my kids for the rest of their lives, because they're gonna be sick of being with me and I'm overbearing," she says. "Is this gonna work for our family? Are my kids going to adapt?"

"So do you think you'll continue to homeschool all the way through?" I ask.

"We need to see who they are as kids, as young adults, because if they have the values that they're not gonna be swayed, if they're not going to be taken under by the world, then maybe we'll consider them going to junior high," Lydia says. "I'll be willing to stay here as long as I need to for them, because in my opinion, raising kids is not just providing an education. They are getting a certain kind of love, a certain kind of heart training. They're getting a positive way of behaving instead of having everybody influence them, because they *are* on their own when they're at school and surrounded by all these kids that don't have the right values—even at the private Christian schools. Homeschooling is more about values."

With the paper chains finished and hung around the living room, the girls turn to their schoolwork, with Anna studying in the kitchen and Veronica staying put with her math book. Throughout the morning, Daniel occupies himself with toys, drawing, and a variety of children's television shows such as *Sesame Street* and *Calliou*.

A short while into their bookwork, Veronica asks her mom for help in explaining a problem in her math text. At first, Lydia is stumped as well. "I don't know what they want because I don't buy the teacher's books," she explains to me. "That's just an extra twenty-five dollars that I try to manage without. It's a first-grade math book—I'm sure I can figure it out." She scans the instructions again, and they eventually reach the correct answer. "We don't usually do tests," Lydia explains to me. "We usually just talk it out and talk it out, because they've got to convince me they know it."

While her girls continue to work independently, I ask Lydia what she thinks is the best thing about homeschooling.

"It's probably that I get to spend time with my kids," Lydia says. "I can see that I'm doing the right thing. I'm trying to raise good kids, and I don't know how I'm supposed to raise good kids if they're in school and I'm not raising them."

"What would you say is the toughest thing about homeschooling?" I ask.

"Attitudes," Lydia responds without hesitation. "Attitudes and disrespect. I don't want any friction; I don't want my kids hating each other and fighting each other and snapping at each other. We've got to be with each other all day long, so we need to behave with each other all day long."

Another big challenge, Lydia explains, is her younger daughter's ongoing health issues with her ears, including several surgeries. Veronica's hearing problems mean that "she didn't process a lot of stuff that I was saying. It was such a struggle to have her listen to how to pronounce this word and how the sound goes, because these are the building blocks. And then you hear people say, 'Well, my son didn't start reading until he was about eight.' Well, why? Was it the school or was it the kid? Was it him being taught or was it his desire? Or was it difficult and he was ashamed and embarrassed?"

Lydia wants to provide a learning environment where Veronica can catch up on her literacy skills without fear of embarrassment, but I discover that Lydia herself has difficulty maintaining a positive attitude when Veronica struggles. Later that morning, when Veronica is reading aloud to her mom, I witness an example of Lydia's frustration.

She stops her daughter in midsentence. "What's this?" Lydia asks, pointing to the word *word* on the page.

"*World*," Veronica answers.

"Is it *world*? Because you're making a sound that's not there."

Veronica tries again. "*World*."

Lydia sighs in exasperation. "Okay, you're saying *world*. *World*. This is not *worllllld*," she says, stretching it out to emphasize the extra letter Veronica is mistakenly inserting.

This time Veronica pretty much eliminates the *l* sound from her pronunciation: "*Word*."

"It's *word*? But you've been saying *world*. It's not *world*." For some reason, Lydia is not content with the correction—she needs to drive home the error.

"*Word!*" Veronica says loudly, getting frustrated with the interrogation.

"Pronounce this again!" Lydia meets her emotion with a rising tone of her own.

Now Veronica is losing focus, and reverts to her original mispronunciation: "*World!*"

"You're not listening to me," Lydia retorts. "You're putting an *l* in there. Okay, let's try it with the sounds that are right there."

"*Wo-ord*," Veronica says, stretching out the *o* to help her avoid the *l* sound.

"Say it again."

"*Wo-ord*." Tears start to roll silently down Veronica's face.

"Okay—is that round?" The sarcastic edge to her mother's voice grows sharper. "The *word* is round? No, the *world*—okay, you're crying, whining, and complaining, but you're not listening. I know your ears don't work, but they do. Listen to me and stop getting frustrated with me! You know these sounds! Say the sounds!"

Veronica's spirit is broken, but she does her best to respond. "*Wo-ord*."

Lydia won't let up. "*Word*," she repeats. "If Momma says 'the *word* is round' does that mean that we live in the *word*? Okay, what *is* that?"

"*Word*." This one is Veronica's best pronunciation yet.

"Okay," Lydia relents. But now she's angry about Veronica's attitude. "Why are you whining? Why are you doing that? What's wrong?"

At this, Veronica doesn't yell back again. Instead, she just shakes her head and says quietly, with great sadness in her voice, "Because I can't say it right."

This dynamic of Veronica struggling, Lydia pestering, Veronica getting frustrated, and Lydia getting frustrated and angry and sarcastic, which cycles into more emotion and even a mocking of Veronica's speech patterns, repeats itself on several occasions during my visits. Lydia interprets Veronica's wrong answers as either carelessness or willful resistance.

Part of me understands these frustrations, as I consider my behavior when helping my own children with their homework. When the answer or concept is blatantly obvious to me, and my daughter just keeps missing it, I can transform from an experienced teacher of nearly twenty years into an impatient, sarcastic parent who thinks his kid is being obstinate or lazy. (But I think it's significant to note—not in my defense, but as an observation about the parent-as-teacher dynamic—that I've never treated one of my students that way. The familiarity of the parent-child relationship has many benefits, but it can also "push our buttons" and cause us to act in ways we wouldn't in public settings with others.) The difference, however, is that my daughters only have to endure my shortcomings on occasion. In the case of the Riveras, Lydia conducts the vast majority of formal instruction.

Pedagogically, Lydia seems to think that if Veronica has trouble with reading, her daughter should simply be made to read the same story over and over again until she gets it right. Not surprisingly, this only adds to Veronica's frustration and disenchantment with reading in general. It also produces an unintentionally humorous moment (at least from my perspective). After Veronica complains to her mother that she has read the first story of her *Eclectic Reader* so many times that she has it memorized, Lydia—apparently interpreting this as a challenge to her authority—demands that Veronica immediately recite the story back to her. Lydia is certain that Veronica can't do it—after all, she can't read correctly, so how could she have it memorized? Veronica proceeds to recite the story, almost word for word, from memory. This demonstration seems to annoy Lydia even further, and she tells her daughter that she now has to practice by reading the words in the story in reverse order (so she can't just recite the words from memory). The problem is, this procedure also eliminates contextual clues that are so helpful in learning to read.

Veronica's *Eclectic Reader* is one of the nineteenth-century McGuffey Readers that are popular with many conservative Christian homeschoolers for their moralistic stories and phonics approach to literacy (this loyal following contributes to their ongoing status as the third best-selling texts in American history after the Bible and Webster dictionaries).

"So what made you choose that reader for them?" I ask.

"It was my husband," Lydia says. "It's a Christian book. He bought it one year for Christmas for them. He knew that it was something that *Little House on the Prairie* used, and that it's an old book and it talks about God and Christian stuff." As a corollary to their indictment of America's ongoing moral decline, many conservative Christians embrace the texts and tools of an earlier era. The pro-homeschooling retailer Vision Forum, for example, describes its mission as "dedicated to the restoration of family culture" and "building a culture of virtuous boyhood and girlhood." It sells books and paraphernalia nostalgic for a supposedly purer past: prairie bonnets and quilting kits from the Beautiful Girlhood Collection, cowboy vests and plastic Crusader swords and shields from the All-American Boys Adventure Catalog. In the same way, McGuffey Readers, New England Primers, and Blue Back Spellers hearken for a mythical era that combined rote learning (no modern learning theories or fads, thank you very much) with an unambiguous moral code.

Shortly thereafter, Lydia tells the girls to watch a Pee-wee Herman video as their health lesson for the day. Pee-wee is afraid to go to the dentist even though his tooth hurts, but eventually he relents and finds out that the dentist can help him feel better. Beyond that message, there's little health content, but no matter—the girls don't really pay attention anyway, since they've already seen it several times. Seven-year-old Veronica remarks that she's never been to the dentist before.

Their current health curriculum, Lydia explains to me, generally consists of videos she checks out from the library, as well as Veronica's many medical appointments to treat her ears. "I forgot to buy them a new health book," Lydia says. "So that's why we've been using videos from the library and stuff, until I can get around to figuring if I want to buy a new book."

Their fine arts curriculum includes more videos, listening to classical music CDs, and home crafts such as today's paper chain decorations. Anna walks over to the stereo and inserts their "fine arts" CD for the day. The opening stanzas of Beethoven's Fifth Symphony begin to fill the room.

"What do you like about classical music?" I ask her.

"It's pretty," she says. I probe a bit more about whether she and her sister can tell the difference between different instrument sounds, or different composers, but it turns out they don't do much beyond play the CDs as background music during their other activities. The music shifts to Gershwin's *Rhapsody in Blue*, and then on to other selections as we sit and talk in the living room. During this time, Veronica cuddles up with her mother on the couch; despite the tense encounter earlier in the morning over her reading assignment, there is clearly still great affection between them.

The Riveras belong to the same independent study program (ISP) as the Palmers—Bridgeway Academy. "I have to give them, every nine weeks, a daily log of what we do," Lydia explains. "I have to write down what they do in Bible, in English, in math, in social science, science, health, fine arts, and physical education." For recordkeeping, she has the kids use Post-it Notes on their books to keep track of their progress, and then she goes back later and writes things up more formally. "This is all pretty much for us to keep ourselves covered and I understand that. I'd rather be safe than sorry."

Lydia is also cautious about letting the kids play outside during school hours. "When the other kids come home from school at one or two, then these kids see the light of day. We don't go grocery shopping at nine in the morning. Because if you start doing foolish things, you start getting truancy officers. But when they come to the door, you don't have to invite anybody in. We know all this stuff, because we've been practicing. They don't have any right to come in; you are enrolled in a private school."

It's now early afternoon, and academic work has given way to preparations for Monday ministry night with the local teens. They spend the rest of the day cleaning and grocery shopping, which Lydia counts as doing health and math (budgeting). A range of activities can receive school credit in Lydia's recordkeeping: "When they're playing," she explains, "they'll have classical music going on, which counts for music credit, and they'll watch an educational video or something on PBS that might be half-related to science. The learning keeps going on its own. But sometimes we'll figure, did you do Heritage Studies? Well, maybe we should watch *Little House on the Prairie*. We have *Good Eats*, which is a Food Network show that we have on DVD, and it's just so cool, so educational—we watch that a lot, just because it's fun, but then *they don't know they're learning*, too."

When I arrive at nine thirty the next morning, the atmosphere is subdued, and the only light in the kitchen is what seeps around the drawn window shades. The girls sit at the tiny breakfast table in their pajamas, quietly eating cereal. Lydia seems tired, and as the morning unfolds, her patience wears thin and she snaps frequently at the kids.

They tell me the St. Patrick's Day party went well last night, and the fifteen or so teens departed before midnight, a bit earlier than usual. During the festivities, Anna and Veronica stayed in their bedroom and watched one of their favorite movies, *What a Girl Wants*.

After finishing their breakfast, the girls and their mom settle down in the living room for their morning Bible reading.

"Where are we at?" Lydia asks, opening her Bible.

"Job," both girls reply simultaneously.

"Job?" Lydia repeats. "What chapter are we in?"

"Chapter three," Anna answers. At her mother's direction, ten-year-old Anna begins to read, and continues for about three minutes, fluidly and with little difficulty with syntax or vocabulary.

After she finishes, Lydia asks, "Was Job complaining?"

"Yeah, kind of, I guess," Anna says. She looks at the next section heading. "Tomorrow will be the first speech of Eliphaz," she informs her mother.

Lydia nods, and directs them to their next activity with no further discussion of the reading. "Okay, time for science now."

"No Heritage Studies today?" I ask, remembering their history study usually follows Bible reading.

"That's going to be on TV," Lydia answers, as she jots down "Job, Chapter 3" in their school activity logbook.

Lydia picks up their new science textbook—*Science for Christian Schools*, published by Bob Jones University Press—and begins to read the introduction to chapter 1, about geology. She starts skipping ahead in the passage, reading pieces aloud as she tries to make sense of it. "This is like fancy, fancy stuff," Lydia says, looking up at her daughters. "And I'm bored with volcanoes, so let's find something better to start with."

"Let's read about minerals and stuff," Anna suggests. "Are there rocks in that chapter?"

"No," says Lydia, flipping through the textbook. "Let's do some—let's do this right here. Okay, these are the five senses." She begins reading: "Our five senses help us be aware of the world around us. Without these senses we would not be able to understand or appreciate God's creation." The passage goes on to describe different parts and functions of the ear. When Lydia finishes reading, she decides that for a follow-up activity, the girls should color in diagrams of the ear that she has in her supplies. While she looks for them, she tells the girls to move on to Heritage Studies.

Today's Heritage Studies lesson, it turns out, is in honor of St. Patrick's Day—in the form of a fifteen-minute video segment from VeggieTales (a popular Christian series featuring animated vegetables). The story offers a brief summary of St. Patrick's travels and influence, and as it finishes, Lydia tells her girls, "You can write about it tomorrow. Tell me a story about it tomorrow, in a paragraph."

A short while later, we all assemble in the living room, where Lydia plans to read to the girls from *The Horse and His Boy*, a book from The Chronicles of Narnia series. While waiting for everyone to get settled, I flip through Anna's Heritage Studies textbook. "Do they have teacher's editions for these?" I ask Lydia.

She nods. "They have teachers' editions for *everything*. They're about $185 a book." Lydia, however, spends only about $200 a year total on curriculum materials, plus $45 per month for Bridgeway membership, $115 for HSLDA membership (which Bridgeway requires for legal protection), and $35 for CHEA (Christian Home Educators Association of California) membership. She saves money on materials by having Veronica use some of Anna's old books; Anna has already written in them, but her mother gets around this by having Veronica start at the point in the book where Anna left off. Veronica gets clean pages to work with, but it's hard to imagine that this doesn't make for a pretty haphazard learning experience for her.

Lydia's practice of not purchasing teacher's editions of textbooks seems to be a fairly common one among homeschoolers. And while I've certainly seen—and ignored—my share of unhelpful teacher's guides over the years, it does make me wonder if important things might be missed, particularly if the parent doesn't have much expertise in a given subject. I ask Lydia how often she finds herself wondering what textbook writers mean by something, or what answer they're looking for.

"Sometimes I look at the teacher's edition and think, do I really need this to explain something to them?" Lydia says. "I want to teach them our values and what we feel is right. So I don't even bother with the teacher's edition, unless it gets to a point where it's getting to fifth and sixth grade and it's like, 'Wow, I need help and support, because these things are getting complicated.'"

"Have you come across that yet?" I ask. Lydia has an associate's degree in creative writing, but I'm not sure about the breadth of her academic background.

"I know that with science it's going to be like that," Lydia acknowledges. "My strong points are English and math, so when it gets to science, I know that I'm probably going to need to get some kind of support. I'm worried about having science be too difficult for them to understand, because it's difficult for *me* to grasp it. I'm waiting for the point where one of these kids is actually like, 'Wow, science is just the coolest thing!' Then that kid is just going to jump into it and help explain it to us." She pauses, then adds, "That's one thing about homeschooling: you don't *have* to have the answers—you can learn it together in the book. But I'm also afraid of confusing them when we learn it."

"Are there co-ops or other resources through Bridgeway where you can access more expert knowledge in areas that you're not as comfortable in?" I ask.

"They're probably out there," Lydia says. She mentions a co-op they used to be involved with when Anna was in kindergarten and first grade, which based its activities on a curriculum called KONOS, an interdisciplinary approach that incorporates an impressive range of hands-on experiences and projects to supplement the learning process. The KONOS materials were expensive, however, and the time commitment involved in planning and coordinating with other families turned out to be more than Lydia wanted to take on.

Lydia has also found the various co-op opportunities to be less than satisfying on a personal level. She's not sure whether her lack of success in developing friendships with other homeschool mothers is due to differences of ethnicity (the Riveras are a Latino family, and most of the homeschoolers she knows are white), in socioeconomic status (she mentions feeling uncomfortable with a couple of wealthier families), or her relative newness to this ISP (people already have well-established relationships and don't seem motivated to enlarge their circle). Whatever the reason, it makes her reluctant to risk trying to forge friendships and become more involved in group opportunities for support and guidance.

Lydia picks up *The Horse and His Boy* and begins reading aloud to the girls. Every now and then she pauses to explain some of the vocabulary, especially dated or unfamiliar words, such as medieval military items. "What does loquacious mean?" she asks at one point. Getting no response, she suggests, "It's like your mouth—your talking—it has to do with your talking." There's clearly a lot of vocabulary in here that the girls don't understand, making it harder for them to stay interested. And since Lydia hasn't been reading along with the girls throughout the entire book, she doesn't know the story line very well herself. After about twenty minutes of reading, Lydia closes the book. "You know what? We're going to stop. I thought it was going to be a short section. We've got like another two pages and I'm getting cold sitting here." Without any summary or check for overall comprehension of the reading, she instructs Veronica to review her spelling words and Anna to go do her English and practice her handwriting.

I ask Lydia if she's ever thought about participating in Academy Days, the parent-led enrichment classes offered by their independent study program.

She nods. "Yes, but two things would say no to me: it's getting me and my three kids up and ready and thirty minutes away by nine o'clock in the morning, and then I'd still have to take care of Daniel. So I was thinking, well, that might be better when he gets a little bit older, so they could all three be in it. And just us and our lifestyle," she adds, pointing out that teens are at their house many nights until midnight or later. "It's draining in some respects, but I know that we're still doing a good thing here. And I'd have to pay for Academy Days; they're not free. And I just never know what our days are going to be from day to day."

Veronica brings some handwriting work over to her mom to inspect.

Lydia glances through it and says, "This is really sloppy. You know that, don't you?" She picks up a pencil and shows Veronica how she needs to write more slowly and carefully. "I want you to do your work and make it look right." She hands back the workbook and asks her daughter, "So what do I want you to do?"

Veronica mumbles unhappily. "Do it again."

I wander into the kitchen, where Anna sits at a tiny desk in the corner, working on her grammar workbook. Lydia follows me and tells her older daughter that she needs to check what she's done. "Okay," Lydia says, reading the directions aloud, "underline the plural possessive noun in each sentence." She pauses, then repeats the directions to herself, trying to figure out just how much should be underlined. Without the teacher's edition as a reference, she is left to make her best guess. For these exercises, it probably doesn't matter much what exactly gets underlined, as long as the correct rules are learned for possessives.

But they run into a problem here as well, when the sample sentences involve words that are automatically plural, such as *oxen* or *children*. As far as I can tell, Lydia isn't familiar with this grammar rule. "*Oxens*—this is driving me crazy right here," she admits. "The plural of *oxen* is *oxen*—and then *yokes*. Hmm. The *oxens*—that's nuts. Doesn't make sense to me."

She looks at the next sentence, where Anna has hedged her bets with two apostrophes: *geese's'*. "Which one is right?" her mom asks her.

"I don't know," Anna admits.

"Well, you need to know," Lydia says. "Because maybe if you explain it to me, that will explain my thinking." She scans farther down the page. "*The boys' hats.* Is the hats apostrophied? Is it possessive? Is it many hats or is it somebody's hats? It says a plural name—a plural noun names more than one person. And so here's *children*, okay? Should the *childrens's noises*—now that's lots of noises, but is it the noises are owning something? Because if it's owning something, then you have your apostrophe. Do the noises own something?"

At this point, I'm pretty lost by Lydia's explanation, and it's hard to imagine that Anna is tracking it either. They continue working on it for another five minutes, discussing different examples, but I don't get the sense that either of them reach any sort of clarity before Lydia decides it's time to move on to the next subject.

Anna's math, her final task for the day, focuses on rounding numbers in order to estimate large multiplication products. Lydia spends about five minutes walking Anna through the sample problems, until it seems clear her daughter gets the concept, and then she leaves Anna to work through the assignment on her own.

Homeschooling offers enormous flexibility in scheduling, curriculum, and teaching methods. This allows parents to treat learning as a much broader, more holistic endeavor than public schools, which are typically constrained by fixed standards, mandated texts, and unyielding demands of "curriculum coverage." This latitude, however, can also result in a haphazard array of activities and materials. This seems to be the case with the Riveras, who also contend with financial limitations (can't afford enough books) and competing priorities (late ministry nights, for example, make morning co-ops unappealing).

The second year of my visits finds homeschooling at the Rivera household relatively unchanged. Lydia is very enthusiastic about a bowling class that she and Anna have started taking together through Bridgeway Academy. Lydia now works part time in a nearby university clerical position, so the kids spend Fridays at their grandmother's house. They generally don't do formal schoolwork there; their grandmother is physically ailing, so Lydia is just happy that they have that regular time to spend with her. The two teenage girls no longer live there with them; in their place is an eighteen-year-old boy who is currently estranged from his own family.

Veronica's ear problems seem somewhat improved, but she's still working in the same math and English books as last year because of her ongoing difficulties with reading. I ask Lydia about accessing specialist services through the local school district, having Veronica evaluated to see if any interventions or therapy might be helpful, but she's not interested.

"I know Veronica so well that I know it's just going to take an extra long time for her to get it," Lydia says. "And sometimes that's just the way a kid is. Here I'm struggling and frustrated with my eight-year-old who just started reading last year, when there are still some boys who can't read. Every homeschool mom thinks she's a failure because her kid hasn't reached those building blocks, but all I know is she just needs to be told a hundred times, over and over, and sometimes that's how a lot of us learn."

Lydia pauses and shrugs. "But as far as getting tested and stuff, it never really crossed my mind. People have told me that she'll outgrow her speech impediment. Some of it might be attributed to her lack of hearing, but she'll outgrow it. And if I got her tested, what's going to be the result: Somebody teaching her at a slower pace? Teaching her some special things that I'm trying? All I can think of is, they're just gonna go slower with her and give her stuff at her rate—and that's kind of what I'm doing."

Although no comprehensive research exists, homeschool advocates contend that the customized, individual attention made possible in a homeschooling context can be of particular benefit to students with special needs. In the 2007 NCES survey, 11 percent of homeschool parents pointed to their child's "physical or mental health problem" as a reason they chose to homeschool, and 21 percent of parents said their child had other kinds of "special needs" that schools didn't address to their satisfaction.

Parents don't necessarily need to choose between special education services and homeschooling their children, however. The Individuals with Disabilities Education Act (IDEA) requires school districts to locate and evaluate both public and private school children in the district who may have special education needs. Whether homeschoolers are considered private school students—and thus eligible for special education services—varies from state to state. California views Veronica Rivera as a private school student in Bridgeway Academy, so Lydia and John could request an evaluation and likely receive services.

In recent years the Home School Legal Defense Association has sought to clarify IDEA regulations involving homeschoolers, especially the right to refuse such evaluations. They argue that any decisions regarding testing children for disabilities, or what services they need, should rest entirely with the parents. Thanks in large part to HSLDA lobbying, the revised regulations issued in 2006 specify that school districts may not evaluate homeschool students for disabilities if the parent refuses consent.

Lydia tells me that her husband does attempt to help out with homeschool instruction on occasion, primarily reading aloud to the kids. "He read all three of The Lord of the Rings books to Anna, and Veronica and Daniel would hear a lot, and they would just sit down and color while

Daddy was reading." Problems arise, however, when John—who works in construction—is home for long stretches because of bad weather and spends his time watching TV and playing video games, disrupting the homeschool routine.

When I sit down with John Rivera on a Sunday afternoon to hear his perspective, he readily acknowledges his minimal involvement in the day-to-day process. I ask him what role he thinks the father should play in homeschooling.

"The biggest thing is backing up Mom," he answers. "I'm not here when she's doing all the academics or whatever. And if there are problems that come up during the day, the biggest help I can give is just making sure the kids know that Lydia and I are a team."

"Are there ever times when you think you might have done things differently than Lydia?"

"You know, I can give my input," John says, "but I'm not here so I can't see it. So I've got to trust her judgment, because she has that working relationship with the kids and I don't."

"Do you have any sort of hopes and dreams for your kids, in terms of what you want their lives to look like after school?"

John responds confidently: "If you ask them, they might even tell you: 'Whatever God wants me to be,' because that's what I'm really trying to put into them. You kind of have to go where you feel led. So I have no idea what the future holds for them—I just want them to follow Christ. And sometimes that doesn't look like somebody else following Christ; it's usually pretty different."

John says he'd consider letting his kids attend public school when they get older, but only if they all felt God was leading them in that direction, perhaps "to minister to kids and be a light in the public school."

"Do your children have much opportunity now to interact with kids other than at church and the teens who hang out here at your home?" I ask.

"Pretty much it's church," John acknowledges. "We really do depend on church quite a bit. Our oldest girls are in dance there and they do the weekly church activities. And that's pretty much where their friends are. Their best friends are homeschoolers and they have the same interests; they're kind of at the same place. They're playing with dolls. They're still very innocent."

"And that's the best of all worlds, from your perspective—for them to be with kids who are at that same place?"

John nods. "Yeah."

"Would you want them to have more interactions with non-Christian friends?" I ask. "Or do you prefer that they only interact with Christian friends?"

"I prefer they only interact with them at this age," John says. "I mean, that's not the way *my* life is and it would be impossible for it to be that way. But for them, I don't think they are prepared."

"When do you think that will change?" I ask.

"Somewhere in high school," he says. "I don't think my kids are prepared to deal with non-Christians and have their beliefs put on them right now. I don't think they are ready to handle that. It's hard for *me* to handle that, you know? I'm the only believer at work and it's hard for me to walk the right path when the guys are talking about things I shouldn't be listening to or doing things that I shouldn't do. So I wouldn't want that for my kids—how are they going to handle it?"

I pose a hypothetical. "If you could imagine one of your kids coming to you when they're a teenager and saying, 'Dad, I've been thinking about this creation/evolution thing and I'm not so sure anymore. Not only that, I'm not so sure about my Christian faith.' What would be your instinct in how to deal with that?"

"Sometimes you've got to just step back and let them figure things out," John says. As an example, he points to the teenage boy who's living with them now, who says he doesn't believe in God. John appreciates his honesty and encourages him to keep asking questions, keep trying to figure things out. "We never push him, we never press, we just kind of let him do his thing and try to figure things out. I think it would be harder if it were one of my own kids," John admits, "but it's something you'd still have to do. You've got to step back and let them figure things out."

In light of Lydia and John's obvious desire to protect their kids from the world's negative influences, their "ministry house" environment, with troubled teens visiting at all hours and some even living with them, seems at least a bit incongruous. But as John explains it—and Lydia echoes almost word for word when I ask her later—the difference is that "we're there supervising it and we wouldn't be able to do that if we just sent them off to public school. And the time our kids have with the teenagers is limited. What I hope happens with my kids is they will see these older ones who aren't believers, see that their lives are messed up and won't get any better if they don't start walking on the right path. And if my kids see that, I don't mind—that's life."

Similar to the Palmers, politics aren't much of a presence in the Rivera household, other than voting. But John's conception of citizenship reflects a fairly common perspective among conservative Christians, one that mostly rejects a distinction between the believer's personal convictions about the good life and the proper shape of our democratic life together.

"Do you think that it's the role of the Christian citizen," I ask him, "to try and get the United States to look as much like biblical life as possible?"

John nods. "I think we do have an obligation to steer things in that direction, because that's the right direction. And if you're a Christian, you believe that's the right direction and that's the direction you want it to go," he asserts. "I don't think we should ever force it on anybody, but we do live in a country where we can vote, and we have the right to speak up and say what we need to say. Because if it goes the other way, it's going to be forced on *us*. Just like abortion is legal. I mean, we can't do anything about it, so in a sense that is being forced on us, too." He pauses before adding with a chuckle, "Tolerance goes both ways."

"That's democracy in action?" I ask.

"That's just the way it works."

I pose another hypothetical to John: if he got to choose all our legislators and judges, would he select just those who reflected his own beliefs, or would he want people who would represent the diversity of perspectives in this country—and thus might be more likely to strive for compromise and accommodation in our public policies?

"I don't think I'd want people who looked for middle ground," he answers. "To me, that's like a 'yes man'—you know, somebody who is there to please everyone. I just don't think you're gonna get anywhere with that, because you can never please everyone. You need someone in there who's got strong convictions one way or the other. God said, 'I'd rather you were hot or cold; if you're warm, I'm gonna spit you out.' Pick a side, you know?"

John is referring to a passage from the book of Revelation where God condemns believers for lukewarm faith, but it seems a stretch to claim it applies to centrist politics. I try to suggest a distinction between personal religious convictions and the desire for our government to endorse that way of life at the expense of all others: "So God clearly gives Christians that message in their private lives," I say, "but do you think that God would want that in their public lives as well—'go all out and try and win as many battles in the public square as you can,' and reject compromise?"

"I think your private life is going to *reflect* your public life," John answers.

"So there really shouldn't be a distinction?"

"Right."

John tells me he doesn't believe Christians should force their beliefs on anybody, but in the next breath implies exactly that—he sees democratic politics, and the citizen's role in them, as essentially adversarial in nature. Whichever side prevails in the political arena can legitimately make the rules, and for Christians, those rules should reflect their convictions about the right ways to live.

My final homeschool visit with the Riveras unfolds much like the others. Early on, Lydia spends about twenty minutes reading together with Veronica from the biblical book of 1 Samuel. I note that same edge of impatience from Lydia when her daughter mispronounces, especially when she does it repeatedly on certain words.

Partway through, Anna comes in from the kitchen and checks in with her mother about her progress and what's next for the morning. When she leaves, I ask Lydia how much her eldest daughter is expected to do each day in their workbooks. Basically, it's up to Anna—usually just one section heading, "about a page and a half."

Self-sufficiency is expected of the girls in other ways as well, such as when Lydia stays up late talking with a visiting teenager. "My kids know that if I'm still in bed at ten, they'll get up and read their devotions and have their breakfast," Lydia explains. "They'll turn on a quiet-time movie until Mom gets up and organizes school, just because that's the way our house operates."

Lydia shows me an official-looking certificate with Anna's name on it. It's from the homeschooler honors society that Bridgeway sponsors and entails regular volunteer work in the community as well as monthly organizational meetings. "My kids are getting their socialization," Lydia asserts. She lists church, Sacred Dance, choir, and youth group as primary activities. "They do spend a lot of time with their friends, but the best thing is that they're *our* friends right now. We're trying to instill them with *our* values instead of their friends' values. And if they were at school, how can their teacher instill them with values?" Teachers are too busy just keeping control, Lydia says, and peer pressure prevents kids from asking for extra help when they need it.

When I talk with the girls privately, they also express their preference for homeschooling. "If your mom and dad told you that you could go to school instead, what would you think?"

"I wouldn't want to go," Veronica answers.

"How come?" I ask.

"I like to stay home," she says, "because when we finish with school we get to spend time with Mom and Dad, instead of coming home and doing your homework and going to bed, and not being able to see them all day."

Her older sister agrees. "I feel very comfortable doing school here," Anna tells me. She is an avid reader, and spends much of her free time immersed in books—The Boxcar Children, The Chronicles of Narnia, and Little House on the Prairie series are among her favorites.

They assure me they have plenty of friends, most of them through church. The Riveras attend Grace Reformed Church, same as the Palmers. As with GRC as a whole, the large youth programs include a wide range of ethnic and socioeconomic diversity. The girls aren't completely sheltered from popular culture, either—*Hannah Montana* and *The Suite Life of Zack and Cody* are top TV choices, and *The Princess Diaries*, *Spiderman*, and The Lord of the Rings trilogy are favorite movies.

When I talk with Veronica alone, she says the year is going well. Her ears still hurt, though, and math remains a struggle. She has finally finished her math book from last year, but doesn't have a new one yet, so her mom gives her worksheets pulled from the Internet.

"What's your favorite thing about homeschooling?" I ask.

"Sometimes we get to skip school and go out to the mall early in the morning and go to Disneyland and stuff." Veronica smiles. "And we never do our school that much. Like around Christmas time, we didn't do our school."

I'm not sure if she means a typical two-week holiday break. "Oh yeah? How long?" I ask.

"All of December. And then like at the last day of December we started doing our school," she says, chuckling. "Mom said, 'You need to do extra school because you haven't been doing it for a while!'"

I wonder if Veronica might be exaggerating a bit here, or unsure of the actual length of their holiday break, so when I talk later with Anna, I ask if there are times during the year when they take extended breaks.

"Well, usually around Christmas time," Anna says.

"How long of a break do you take usually?" I ask.

"Kind of before Thanksgiving until after Christmas," she says.

Anna tells me she's enjoying this year of homeschooling, following a similar schedule of subjects as before. She's studying fractions in math—her favorite subject—and plant classifications in science.

"And what are you doing for Heritage Studies?" I ask.

"Well, it's a book I read last year, about Egyptian history, but I like it."

"You've read it before?" I ask. "How come you're doing it again then?"

"Well, we really don't have a lot of books sometimes," Anna says, "and I like it, too."

"Do you do any writing?" I ask.

"Sometimes we watch a movie like *Oliver Twist* or *Swiss Family Robinson*, and then the next day we write a report about that," she says.

This "watch a movie, write a report" assignment appears to be a common routine; on this particular day, Anna is working on an essay about the movie version of *Bridge to Terabithia* (she hasn't read the book) and another one comparing the two *Cheaper by the Dozen* movies.

"Are there any things that you don't like so much or that are frustrating about homeschooling?" I ask Anna.

"Well, there are some things in math that I don't understand," she says. "Sometimes in my English book, too."

"And what do you do when you don't understand things?"

"Well, usually I go ask Mom, unless she's asleep," she says, "and then I just skip that and wait until she wakes up."

"So do you usually get going by yourself in the morning?"

Anna nods. "Yeah."

"And how long do you work by yourself until your mom gets going with you?"

"Well, she usually sleeps until eleven or sometimes later than that," Anna says.

If this is the usual routine—and Anna doesn't strike me as prone to exaggeration—then it appears that Lydia scheduling my arrivals at nine in the morning has necessitated a significant adjustment for their home-school day. Perhaps this has contributed to Lydia's short fuse with her kids as well.

Later in the morning, Anna and Veronica bring their essays—Anna a summary of *Bridge to Terabithia* and Veronica a description of her trip to her grandma's the day before—and Lydia reviews them line by line for grammatical errors, and also pushes them to add details and explanations where they are lacking. These teaching interactions strike me as the most comfortable and effective for Lydia, probably because it draws on her own strengths and college coursework background.

I ask Lydia if I could see examples of the records that Bridgeway requires her to keep, and she pulls out her attendance chart, with a small square for each day of the week, Monday through Friday. Each box needs to be filled for each subject, she tells me. She could classify a day here or there as a holiday, but she has to reach 180 school days each year. "And that's one thing about homeschooling," she adds. "When you're traveling, you can still be doing your school. If we're spending the week at Disneyland, we can still say 'Well, we went and saw this, which was fine arts.' And we could be sitting there doing spelling games in the lines, which is spelling. And we could bring a book and read during lunchtime. As for math, you could do budgeting—give them two dollars and say, 'Okay, go buy three things.' If you think about it, there is just a lot of education. And they know when we go to Disneyland, we don't go to have fun and buy treats and go on rides, because we're always busy. We go to walk around, experience it, and just hang out. We've been doing that for years."

While we're on the subject of recordkeeping and regulation, I ask Lydia whether she thinks parents should have sole responsibility for their children's education, or whether the state should be able to intervene if concerns arise about the quality of a homeschooling situation.

"It would be funny if they had the nerve to care about what a home-school family is doing," Lydia says. "I mean, they can't even take care of their own government schools. It just seems hypocritical for them to really nail down *us* when you see that the kids who have credentialed teachers are getting Ds and Cs. Is it the teaching? Or is it the student? And for my kid, is it my teaching or is it her ability to learn?" This is the objection I hear regularly from homeschooling families—in essence, let the public schools get their own house in order before they come knocking on our doors.

But Lydia's other point here is also worth considering. It's quite possible that some homeschool students who have learning difficulties would be having at least as much trouble in an institutional setting. To assume outright that a parent-teacher is a failure because her child doesn't meet a fixed standard at a particular age or grade level may be just as unfair as expecting a classroom teacher to have all students excelling in June, regardless of where they started in September. This doesn't mean that interventions are never justified or helpful—just that they shouldn't automatically begin with the assumption that poor teaching is the cause of slow academic progress.

John is less resistant to current homeschooling regulations. "The government should at least hold us accountable," he says, "that kids are getting an education."

I point out that in California's present system, though, it would be possible for parents to report academic activities but not really do them, since no formal testing is required.

"They could, but what parent is gonna go through all this time to keep all these records and do all these things and their kids aren't getting an education?" John says. "I mean, what really is the point of that?"

I ask him if he thinks some sort of basic skills test would be a fair expectation for homeschoolers.

"Yeah, that's really tough," he says, "because you look at public schools and most of the kids who are graduating don't know a lot of these things. Most of the kids who are graduating public schools can barely read. So I don't know."

"It's a double standard in your mind?"

"Yeah."

Educational researchers would dispute John's assertion about the illiteracy of public high school graduates. But as I've explained before, debates over regulation focus on more than just students' basic literacy skills. Homeschool critics also worry that parents could teach their children values that are antithetical to democratic citizenship. I ask John if he thinks homeschool parents should be able to teach their kids any beliefs about the world that they want, whether it be racial supremacy or other worldviews that most people would find abhorrent.

"They're the parents and they're gonna teach them that anyway," he says. "I mean, who's really gonna stop them?"

"Well, some people would argue that at least if they go to school, they hear other messages," I suggest. "If they're just at home with their parents, they're in this world that their parents mostly control and there is a greater chance for their parents to essentially brainwash them into this ideology. If they have to go to school, at least they'll have other influences."

"Well, you kind of have to take it," John says. "I mean, they're the parents and they have the right to teach their kids whatever they're going to teach their kids. Because you can just turn that totally around—what if people say, 'No, you can't teach them Christianity, that's a whacked belief; that's wrong'? It's got to go both ways."

"So it's sort of the luck of the draw if a kid gets born into a family where they're teaching all sorts of awful things?" I ask.

"Yeah, I get your point—if they were at school they'd be taught other things," John acknowledges. "But who's your biggest influence? It's gonna be your parents anyway." As we continue to talk, it becomes clear that for John—like most homeschoolers I speak with—the cost of regulating the ideological content of homeschooling is not worth the uncertain possibility of preventing a few children from growing up with belief systems entirely at odds with what a democracy requires to sustain itself.

Lydia's follow-up e-mail at the end of the school year provides an update on Veronica's ear problems: "We had to cancel an appointment to see the doctor and haven't been back but need to because they just aren't well!

That is on our list for the coming week." She admits to continuing frustration with Veronica, and mentions that she spoke with a mom from church who suggested Veronica may have attention-deficit/hyperactivity disorder (this mother's own two children are taking medication for ADHD).

"I then had to wonder if my child was needing such a diagnosis while at the same time defending that I KNOW that Veronica's problem is NOT ADHD," Lydia writes. "We had a LONG family talk and analysis of ADHD and realize that it's not a disorder, it's an early lack of discipline (many times, we feel) on the parents' part to have the kids just 'check out' and not pay attention to anything except toys and TV. No kids should be on medication at that age and it doesn't make their brain work better or make them smarter. It just makes it easier for them to SIT in class for a long period of time!"

It's true that significant disagreement and controversy exists about the treatment of ADHD among schoolchildren. Many health professionals express concern about overprescription of ADHD medications, but most also agree that a combination of chemical and cognitive-behavioral treatments can be very effective in helping diagnosed students focus and excel in academics and everyday life. It may very well be that an ADHD diagnosis is completely off the mark for Veronica, but my sense is that the Riveras' suspicion of "professional expertise"—a not uncommon attitude among homeschoolers—may ultimately be hindering their daughter's educational growth.

In her e-mail, Lydia also admits that they fell far behind in their academics this year: "We will be catching up on school work I HOPE! I really hope! Every summer I want to do that but every summer WE DON'T! It's really important to me that we do." But then Lydia goes on to mention that they are consumed with planning for Veronica's birthday party: "It has been a very exciting project to plan with the kids and we've been planning it for weeks already and we KNOW it's a month away! I spend all day looking for crafts and fun projects to make for the occasion. We love doing stuff like that, planning parties, games, just organizing hospitality times!"

Lydia Rivera does not claim to be a perfect homeschool teacher; in fact, she alternates between asserting that "I know I'm doing the right thing" and worrying that she's not up to the task. While it may be unfair to characterize homeschooling in the Rivera household as an afterthought, Lydia's comment that "I just never know what our days are going to be from day to day" speaks not only to scheduling, but also to the structure and method of their homeschooling overall.

Are the Rivera children learning to think for themselves? Lydia describes homeschooling as primarily "heart training," but I see little to suggest that Anna and Veronica are being forced into an intellectual or ideological mold of their parents' choosing—the entire homeschooling experience seems much too haphazard for that. Lydia and John shelter their kids from a public school environment beyond their control, but expose them to the broken lives of local teens. As the kids get older, perhaps John's vision of democratic citizenship—trying to shape society in accordance with his religious convictions—will influence their own conception of civic engagement, but it seems just as likely these issues will remain unexplored in their formal curriculum.

For all the paperwork that California requires of the Riveras through their ISP, there seems little opportunity to ascertain what their kids are really learning. Does Bridgeway Academy believe it can vouch for the quality of homeschooling provided by its member families? What interests do they perceive as being at stake in the realm of homeschool regulation, and how do they understand their role in that? In the interlude that follows, I get a chance to explore these questions with the leaders of Bridgeway.

Bridgeway Academy

I make one more visit to Los Angeles, this time to talk with the leaders of Bridgeway Academy, the homeschool umbrella organization for both the Palmers and the Riveras. I meet with Alan and Priscilla Bartlett at their administrative headquarters, located in an aging office building amidst the city sprawl. Alan is a middle-aged man with abundant gray hair and gray beard. His voice is soft but with an underlying firmness, even certainty, about what he says and believes. Priscilla has long dark hair, well below her shoulders; she smiles frequently, trying to keep the conversation good-natured whenever Alan and I start arguing philosophy.

Bridgeway Academy currently has about 100 families enrolled, around 170 kids total. The Bartletts are longtime homeschool parents themselves, having begun back in 1982 with their eldest daughter. "Since there weren't private schools running homeschool programs," Alan explains, "people began looking at how to satisfy the compulsory attendance requirement, which was either public school, private school, or tutorial exemption. So somebody decided to get a bunch of people together and file one affidavit, which is what you have to do if you're operating a private school. It's not a license or a permit; it's just simply a notification to the state: 'Here we are.'"

As I noted earlier, Bridgeway Academy requires member families to belong to HSLDA as well. The Bartletts knew its president, Michael Smith, before HSLDA began back in the 1983, when Smith was a personal injury attorney practicing in Southern California. As the Bartletts explain it, he started volunteering his time defending local homeschoolers from harassment by public education officials. "If there hadn't been a Michael Smith donating his time," Priscilla asserts, "everything in California would be different, because the fact that homeschoolers could say 'call my attorney' made all the difference in the world at those very beginning stages."

In the eyes of California regulations, Bridgeway Academy is simply a private school. But one of the unique things about running a homeschool independent study program, Alan adds, is that Bridgeway is not only enrolling a student; it is also engaging parents to be the teachers. This means the Bartletts have to ascertain whether parents are capable of supervising their child's education. "We have some single moms," he explains, "and they've had to work out arrangements either to live with their parents or to have a grandmother in the home or something like that, so there is somebody supervising. And the paperwork, of course, is the parents' responsibility—if they're unable to do that, then we have to terminate their enrollment."

Since Bridgeway ultimately relies on parents' self-reporting of their progress, I ask if there's anything—apart from parents' own sense of moral obligation—that would prevent them from claiming they had finished schoolwork that they really hadn't.

"Our paperwork is pretty minimal," Priscilla concedes. "I'm sure somebody could be dishonest about it some way. There is always a way around the system. But we have daily lesson logs that are reviewed once a quarter in all the subjects and then we have final grades. So short of them putting false stuff every single day on the lesson logs—"

"What type of detail is required on those logs?" I'm curious to see if their expectations match what Lydia Rivera described to me.

"They're tracking their course of study," Alan explains. "So if the course of study says 'U.S. History, 8th grade, Bob Jones,' then on the daily lesson plans they put 'chapter 1, pages 21–22.'"

This strikes me as a pretty weak oversight system. Even if parents are honest about what material they are "covering," there's no evidence that students have actually learned anything in the process. Perhaps sensing my skepticism, Priscilla wants me to understand the type of parents she works with in Bridgeway: "The people we're dealing with aren't going to fill out their paperwork incorrectly," she says. "They are so overly involved and overly concerned. They're really not as worried about what we think, as what *God* thinks."

"Homeschooling is not easy," Alan adds, "and people generally don't undertake it lightly with the idea, 'Oh, this is a way to keep my kid home.' Why would you do that? If you don't want to be engaged, send them to the public school or something. We very rarely have a situation—usually it's that they are not able to do it after they start it. And those families pretty much will recognize that and will leave the school after a year or something."

In light of my experience with the Riveras, I find the Bartletts' confidence in Bridgeway's accountability system to be misplaced. But I discover I'm even more skeptical of their underlying educational philosophy, which holds that parents alone should control their children's education—there is no triad of interests involving children themselves or broader society.

"I don't believe that the child has a right to an education," Alan asserts. "Rights aren't things that the government is responsible for providing. The government's responsibility is to ensure that somebody else doesn't infringe on my God-given rights to life, liberty, and property." In his view, the state should play no role in the education of children, because God has assigned that responsibility exclusively to parents.

"So would you then say that parents have the right to instill any philosophy or worldview in their child that they so choose?" I ask.

"Not in relationship to their responsibility to God as parents," Alan says. "It's very much the contrary."

"But if parents fail in that responsibility," I ask, "the state has no business in intervening?"

"Well, how would we decide what that would be?" Alan responds. "*I* certainly think that the teaching of another religion, or no religion, is destructive to children because I believe that Christianity is true. So some parent who is teaching their children Islam or Mormonism or atheism is, to me, harming their child. But do I want to organize the power of government to stop them from doing that? No, I don't."

It's certainly true that people are going to have differing views about what constitutes an ideal or even minimally sufficient education. Reasonable disagreement clearly exists, for instance, about the value of religiously based schooling, and so the state generally stays out of it by giving parents choice in this regard. But state deference to parental authority over their children is not limitless—physical abuse is perhaps the clearest example of where the state properly steps in and takes control, as the child has an obvious interest in not being abused by her parents.

But it seems clear to me that the child also has a strong interest in becoming a self-sufficient adult, including developing basic skills of literacy and numeracy, and I say as much to Alan.

"But that's an assessment that you want to make for someone else," Alan counters.

He's right—I *do* want to make that claim for all children. "In our modern American culture," I persist, "if you cannot read and write, you are going to be severely limited in your ability to be self-sufficient."

"That's not self-evidently true," Alan insists.

I have trouble keeping an incredulous tone out of my voice. "You don't think so?"

"That's not self-evidently true," he repeats. 'There are millionaires right now who are functionally illiterate because they are able to perform. They make more money than you or I will ever imagine making. Do you think all of the guys in the NFL are functionally literate? So saying that a child has an interest in learning to read and write is an arbitrary statement. Does a child have an interest in learning? Well, yes, of course he does. But who's going to be the arbiter of that? Is it going to be the civil government, which has to choose among a virtually infinite number of value systems, to say this is the one that the child should be directed toward? Or is it the parent? And failing the parent, is it then the child, when he becomes capable of directing his life?"

Alan's implicit claim here is that any attempt by the state to stipulate a basic educational minimum will inevitably reflect a value system, and it's not the state's role to push particular values on citizens. I can see how this would be a legitimate concern if regulations mandated certain literature, for instance—but there's a huge distance between saying "all kids should learn to read" and saying "these are the books they should read."

"So is the child just out of luck," I ask, "if she happens to be born to parents who neglect their responsibility to educate her, and she's functionally illiterate at age eighteen?"

"The child is not out of luck, because, see, there are larger issues here," Alan says. "There is the providence of God. Children don't just arrive in families by happenstance. And as hard as it is for us to be willing to understand, every family, every individual, is under the providential direction of God. But the other issue is, the family doesn't exist in isolation. You don't just jump from the family to the state government. There's extended family, there's community, there's church. And all those things used to have a tremendous force, and to the extent that government has this larger and larger role, those forces have broken down. And the state can't raise children."

Alan Bartlett relies on the providence of God and concentric circles of community to care for children and their needs. For him, the price of state oversight and intervention, in terms of God-given parental authority, is too high—even if some children are deprived of an education as a result. "That's the cost of freedom," he says, "the risk that some people will not behave in ways that we want them to."

It's true, we're all willing to accept a certain degree of risk that people will abuse their freedoms in order that the rest of us may enjoy them. But isn't there a middle ground here where education regulation is concerned? Can't we agree on some basic expectations and still avoid an intrusive government that tells parents how to teach or what to believe? The sad fact is there are going to be parents who neglect their responsibilities toward their children, and in some of those cases, the concentric circles of extended family, church, and community are not going to be influential enough to step in. Nowhere in my homeschool exploration is this clearer than in my visits with the Branson family in Tennessee.

4

THE BRANSON FAMILY
"A Godless Conspiracy"

The Bransons' small, weathered house sits back from a winding Tennessee country road, a few miles from the Mississippi border. In the driveway, a white pickup and a red Econoline van are adorned with bumper stickers: BUSH/CHENEY, FRIST FOR U.S. SENATE, and ABORTION STOPS A BEATING HEART. A white, wooden cross, a good seven feet tall, leans against a tree out near the road. Two yard signs, supported by metal stakes, flank the front door. One lists the Ten Commandments and the other proclaims, A WISE MAN FEARETH AND DEPARTETH FROM EVIL.

I sit in the tiny kitchen, having just arrived, surrounded by the Branson family: Gary, Lauren, and seven of their ten children. The table is still sticky from breakfast, and the littlest children squirm in their seats. The Bransons are about to begin their morning Bible study, but first Gary asks me more about my book project. I explain that I'm especially interested in the role of religion in education, so Christian homeschooling seemed an important angle on that.

Gary nods, his broad face framed by large, square-rimmed eyeglasses. "Well, I think that's the main attack against us as American citizens and Christians," he says in the mild southern drawl shared by his family. "The educational system wants to do away with the actual foundation of all learning, all existence. And you want to put your children up under that type of philosophy?"

Sharon, his sixteen-year-old daughter, has been listening closely and jumps in. "They're trying to take the Bible out of public schools—"

"*Did,*" interjects Gary.

"—and they're going to let the Muslims pray during school, but we can't read our Bible during school," she concludes.

"It's specifically attacks against Christians," Gary says. "And Jews. They don't want Judaism talk. But any godforsaken religion is welcomed. My whole purpose for not wanting to send my children to school is because I felt like if we did that it would be tantamount to turning our children over to the devil. That's the depth of my philosophy." He lays his palms upward on the table and says in a quiet, matter-of-fact voice, "I'm not a wise man in the world's things. I'm not even academically able to teach a lot of subjects and neither is my wife. We resolved in ourselves years and years ago that if we were able to teach our children character, teach them how to read so that they could read the Bible, we would have done all that is necessary for them to survive this world. And we're not going to put ourselves up under other people's ideas of what an educated person is. So we've taught each one of them that we would be just as proud to see them hanging off a garbage truck, knowing that they don't lie, steal, cheat, and despise God."

Their family Bible study lasts a full forty-five minutes and consists of a discussion of the eleventh chapter of the New Testament book of Hebrews, interrupted by various tangents ranging from whether horses will be in heaven to what they'd be willing to do for a hundred dollars. Except for Sharon, the kids have a hard time staying focused. Twelve-year-old Aaron has his head propped in his hands, a glum look on his face. Christine, who is two years younger than Sharon, alternates between paying attention and whispering comments back and forth with Aaron. Nine-year-old Stephanie looks decidedly bored, but still tracks the conversation, occasionally adding an insightful comment or question. For the most part, five-year-old David sits quietly. Remaining calm and attentive seems a lost cause for Jacob, however, whose four-year-old energy repeatedly tries Gary's patience. Little Jessica, only two years old, squirms incessantly in Lauren's lap, as her mother tries valiantly to keep her still.

After Gary closes the Bible study with a prayer, the younger kids scatter quickly. Gary turns to me. "A lot of our activities is done on the spur of the moment," he says. "The earlier we get up, the more we can accomplish. A lot of times we don't get up early. Usually I leave the house for work by two o'clock. I like to get in all that I can accomplish before I leave; I teach civics, the Bible, art, and music. Right now I'm trying to work with Sharon mostly, with the civics stuff and our form of government. We're working on the three branches: legislative, executive, judicial."

"Do you have a textbook or anything you use for that?" I ask.

Gary nods. "Yes, we have a videotape that's actually very, very good."

"I do U.S. history in the textbooks," Sharon interjects. "Well, they're not really textbooks, they're like little pamphlets and you finish so many of those for the whole year."

"I like to have them understand why we go vote for our state and local representatives and so forth," Gary explains. "how it is ungodly judges can get up there, try to kick God out of his own throne room, how that sort of thing can happen. I listen to Sean Hannity on the radio quite a bit and one of the things that I find so amazing, he's got some people that go out and just asks people on the street who the president of the United States is or who the vice president is, and they don't know!" He shakes his head in bewilderment. "People have no idea what's going on in the Mideast. A lot of them don't even know who the governor of their state is! Just absolutely oblivious. And then I would ask one of my children something like that and *they* don't know it and then I think"—here he pauses and makes a face of self-recrimination—"I am not teaching my children!" At this, the kids break into laughter. He turns to Sharon. "Do you know who the vice president of the United States is?"

Her brow furrows as she considers her answer, and Gary chuckles. "The Cheney dude," she finally says.

This confuses twelve-year-old Aaron, a broad-shouldered boy with short sandy hair. "Well, who's that black lady with the gap in her teeth?" he asks.

"Secretary of state," Gary answers.

"I keep forgetting who she is," Aaron says. "I keep seeing her on TV."

"Her name is Condoleezza Rice," Gary adds. He then turns to me and says, "But anyway, we usually head down to the other room to do music now. You want some coffee?"

Gary works the afternoon-evening shift as a meat cutter at a nearby supermarket, which enables him to participate in part of the homeschool day. "If he worked that schedule and the kids went to school early in the morning," Lauren explains to me, "they'd be in bed when he gets home and there'd be no family life."

I soon discover that playing music is Gary's love, and it dominates the homeschool day for the Bransons, despite Lauren's attempts to steer things back to other subjects and activities. Oftentimes, Lauren says, they have to wait until Gary goes off to work. A narrow room off the kitchen holds a piano and multiple guitars, and Gary is constantly exhorting his kids to join him there for practice. He doesn't read music fluently, but teaches by ear. His eldest son, Seth—a nineteen-year-old who lives on his own now—is a talented pianist and periodically plays in Sunday morning worship services as well as local music groups.

Christine, a fourteen-year-old with long dark hair, sits down at the piano and Gary grabs a guitar. He gives some pointers to Aaron, who is learning to play the bass, and they begin to play, loudly and spiritedly, stopping occasionally for Gary's corrections and suggestions. After a few minutes of listening to Gary and his kids perform, I head back into the kitchen.

Lauren is standing at the counter, washing some dishes. Her long, dark hair is starting to streak with gray, and she uses the back of her soapy hand to push some wisps from her eyes. The last couple years have been especially trying for her, ever since little David was severely injured in an automobile accident. He is still undergoing reconstructive surgeries and ongoing therapy. Often when I speak with Lauren about homeschooling and family life, she seems hesitant, almost an apologetic air about her. "It can get really loud in here," she says, a smile on her tired face, her voice raised to compete with the music around the corner. With seven kids living in a 1,900-square-foot house, I suspect it's tough to find much in the way of quiet and solitude.

Sharon and Christine share a tiny bedroom just off the kitchen. Sharon, whose hair is shorter and lighter than her sister's, has just emerged from their room carrying some papers. "So what do you like about home-schooling?" I ask her.

"You can do it at your own pace," Sharon says earnestly. "You don't have to have a schedule. You can go to your friend's house in the afternoon and then do your school at night—as long as you finish it." She places on the table the stack of pamphlets she's brought with her. "That's my English. We finish five of those a month. They're really easy. And then for extra credit, I already finished Latin. That was pretty much looking up words in the dictionary and so it counted for learning a different language."

Sharon and Christine are expected to complete three pages in each booklet, for a total of fifteen pages a day. When they've finished a booklet, they take the test at the end, which consists almost entirely of recall questions—no higher-level thinking required. Lauren records their scores and submits two reports each year to Mission Academy, the homeschool umbrella program they use (this option is similar to the independent study program option in California, except that in Tennessee the sponsoring organization must be "church-related"). The Bransons use the least restrictive regulatory option, the Complete Home Education Program, which allows them virtually total control over curricula and pedagogy— no standardized tests or other state assessments are required.

Gary has returned to the kitchen by this point and has been listening to his daughter describe their schoolwork. "We started homeschooling back before it became popular," he recounts. "Our eldest daughters are twenty-five years old now and they never went to a public school for a day." He pulls out a chair from the kitchen table and settles himself in it. "The public schools are being assaulted by Satan," he continues. "In the public schools, we'd be worried about our daughters being raped, assaulted, learning Satan worship, fighting, all the guns, the deaths in the schools, knifings. Teachers molesting children. Homosexuals, you know, demanding their wickedness be crammed into the classroom."

Sharon shakes her head in disapproval. "The only reason that I would want to go to the public school," she says, "would be for the socialization. That's the *only* reason."

"But you have that at church," Gary points out.

Sharon agrees. "We have that anywhere else."

"And you have that going to Wal-Mart," Gary adds. He turns to me and explains his reasoning: "The Bible tells us that *we* as parents are responsible for our children. The Bible says teach *your* children, not have someone else teach your children. And so we feel like that it is our responsibility to teach our children how to be productive, honest citizens in their country, in the town that we live in. And we'll do our best to see to it, that whether they're academically intelligent or not, they're contributors to a responsible community and not a hindrance."

Gary distrusts schools because of the social environment, but his resistance goes beyond that. As becomes evident in my time with the Bransons, Gary seems pretty much leery of all human authority. "If you join up with the public school system," he says, "you are sacrificing a lot of liberty and freedom to be able to just pack up and go somewhere if you want to," he says, "instead of having to answer to them why your children isn't in school, or have some lousy teacher that thinks they know better how to raise your child than you and start meddling in your affairs. If your kid goes in there and tells them, 'My daddy, he was drunk last night and he was hollering and screaming at my momma'—and then they call the department of human services and then the school board and everybody is meddlin' in your life. That's not freedom." Gary shakes his head and adds with conviction, "The more of the system's tentacles that you can break off from you, the healthier you're gonna be."

Gary is not alone in this sentiment. Several groups, such as Exodus Mandate, Considering Homeschooling, and GetTheKidsOut.org, whose mission it is to encourage conservative Christians to pull their kids from public schools, have sprung up around the country. "The very soul of your child is at risk," one warns. What's going on in schools, they claim, isn't Christian kids shining their light to help others as much as "reverse evangelism": misleading Christian youth into adopting "Marxist-socialist" or "secular humanist" worldviews. Public schools seek to create "a population of sheep, suited to work in a global planned economy regulated by a world government." In recent years, a resolution has been sponsored repeatedly at the annual meeting of the Southern Baptist Convention—the largest Protestant denomination in the country—to encourage members to remove their children from "government schools" (the term favored by critics to emphasize control by the government instead of we-the-public). So far, the resolution has been rejected each year.

Public schools are not the only governmental target of many home-schoolers' criticism and suspicion. In their regular e-mail updates and state alerts, HSLDA portrays social workers and child protective agencies as a dangerous combination of bumbling bureaucrats ignorant of home-schoolers' constitutional rights and devious ideologues intent on removing children from their homes. The reality, it appears, is that the vast majority of homeschoolers never come into contact with these agencies.

That said, homeschoolers' apprehension about child protective agencies doesn't seem entirely unfounded. While I'm no fan of HSLDA's ongoing attempts to induce hysteria and to present itself as a legal savior to homeschoolers everywhere, some public school officials and social workers do have a decidedly jaded view of homeschooling. The prospect—however remote—of such a person, prompted by an anonymous tip and backed by the power of the state, knocking on your door and demanding to interview your children is enough to make any homeschooler wary.

Of the families I visit during my research, however, only the Bransons have had dealings with state social workers. "The state pretty much does whatever they feel like, especially that department of human services," Gary remarks. "They just pop up at our door. They've been out here four or five different times."

"They gave us all interviews," Sharon adds. "People call them on us."

"One time we got reported," Gary says. "We don't know what it really was, if it was some person that just wanted to hurt us or some busybody or something like that. Maybe they saw our kids out playing four or five times when they drove by here and they're concerned that we're not living our lives like *they* think we should. So they call them on us."

Lauren chimes in: "I told Gary, just let them come in and observe, or they'll think you're hiding something. We don't want to hide anything."

"We're very friendly to them," Gary says. "We've actually been counseled *not* to let them into our house, but I decided we *don't* have nothing to hide. We don't treat them like an enemy right on the front end." I'm not sure who counseled the Bransons not to let social workers into their house, but this approach is explicitly endorsed by HSLDA, which offers members a tip sheet titled "Social Worker at Your Door: 10 Helpful Hints."

"So you never hear any follow-up from them afterward?" I ask. "They just come, do their thing, leave, and that's the end of it?"

Gary nods. "Right. As a matter of fact, the last visit, the man opened up to me quite a bit about how he raises *his* children. He told me he smacks *his* children!" The Bransons breaks into laughter.

"It's a touchy issue," Lauren concedes.

Gary nods again. "Children are abused; they're beaten. I just don't like the state stepping in, taking over authority. There's been times—many children get whipped pretty good and hard, with bruises left on them— they *need* it, sometimes. But to hurt and break bones, to bruise other parts of the body than the buttocks, is cruelty. It's abuse. Whips is ideal, but not bruising. Even though the Bible says, 'Blows that wound cleanse away evil,' I think it might really be talking about a full-grown man who gets caught stealing; he gets tied to the stocks and gets whipped with a cane to cleanse evil out of his heart. I don't think we have to put bruises on a child like her," Gary says, pointing to two-year-old Jessica. "But a little old switch, put a whip on her—ooh, she hates that. She just stands there and she just"—and here he mimics her flinching—"and that's all it takes, just one little switch and she *knows* she don't ever want that to happen to her again."

"She's cute, too," Sharon adds, smiling at little Jessica, who looks up at us happily, clearly oblivious to the content of our current discussion.

Gary chuckles, smiling at Jessica as well. "Yeah. But this right here"—he reaches across the table for a thin black rod about eight inches long—"is one of the finest little things I ever seen." He hands me the small whip, which appears to be made out of flexible rubber. "If we want their attention—once they realize that this thing will sting, all you've got to do is—" He picks it up and waves it around the table, and the kids simultaneously flinch and laugh.

"We believe in *training*," Gary explains. "The more you train children, the less you have to use these," he says, holding up the rubber switch again. "But I don't believe there isn't a family in the world that doesn't need this in the beginning." Gary pauses, considering how to explain himself most clearly. "The Bible says, 'The child comes forth from the womb speaking lies.' It's just something you don't have to learn, it seems like. It'll cry for no reason, when he's this little"—holding his hands about eighteen inches apart—"because he knows if he cries, you'll come pick him up, you know? But he's lying." Gary chuckles. "He's lying when he acts like he needs attention. He doesn't, he just *wants* it."

Lauren, perhaps worried I'm getting a negative impression of her husband, puts a hand on his arm and smiles. "But you *like* babies."

Gary returns her smile. "Yeah. We know some people with fantastic children, and that's the Pearls. Are you familiar with Michael Pearl?"

"No, I don't think so," I say.

"Michael and Debi are the authors of these books"—he points to a couple of titles on the table, *To Train Up a Child* and *No Greater Joy.* "We was neighbors. He's the one that actually inspired me to homeschool. He was homeschooling his children when I met him, thirty years ago." Gary's tone grows animated. "He has inspired me. I have never read anything more encouraging, more uplifting, more knowledgeable in homeschooling."

When I return home to Indiana, I look up *To Train Up a Child* on Amazon.com and see that nearly *seven hundred* customers have written online reviews of the book. People either love it or hate it—95 percent gave it either the highest or lowest rating possible. *To Train Up a Child* promises "immediately obedient children" if parents will follow certain training and discipline techniques. Comparing children to stubborn animals, the book urges parents to conquer their children's will and produce "complete and joyous subjection" through the use of rulers, belts, and tree branches. The Pearls' methods are very controversial within the homeschooling community as well, with some parents horrified by their approach and others finding it appropriate as long as it is implemented calmly and consistently.

But here lies one of the dangers of corporal punishment. As most parents will attest, it can be hard to step back emotionally when you're angry at a child and need to discipline her—and the likelihood of bringing those emotions into the situation seems greater when spanking or paddling is involved. The line between restrained, measured correction and child abuse can blur in the heat of the moment.

What about the situations that clearly cross the line, where even Gary and Lauren would agree abuse is occurring—is this more likely to happen in homeschooling contexts? Stories of horrific abuse by parents who claimed to be homeschooling appear periodically in the media. But homeschool defenders respond that these are isolated incidents and there's no evidence demonstrating that abuse occurs more frequently in the homeschool setting than anywhere else—a fair point, given the lack of reliable data about both homeschooling and child abuse.

Some critics worry that since some homeschooled children do not come into contact with adults outside the home on a daily basis, the opportunity to detect signs of physical abuse are greatly diminished. But homeschoolers point out that it's children younger than school age who are most likely to experience abuse, and increased scrutiny of homeschooling will do nothing to address this. Furthermore, the U.S. Department of Health and Human Services says only about 16 percent of reports of suspicion of child abuse are filed by teachers, whereas almost half come from parents, relatives, friends, and neighbors.

Also, defenders protest, what about the double standard: if we care so much about the physical and emotional welfare of children, why are our public schools places where bullying is rampant and substance abuse, violence, and even predatory teachers remain ongoing problems? These images of public schools as perilous war zones appear with some regularity in homeschool advocacy materials. In truth, just as child abuse among homeschoolers often receives widespread news coverage, the same holds true for public school violence. Certainly, violence toward children—whether in schools or at home—deserves both our attention and condemnation. At the same time, some perspective seems in order: according to NCES data from 2003, for example, 1 percent of middle and high school students reported being victims of school violence. While it's true that critics are often guilty of unfair stereotyping toward homeschooling, some in the homeschooling community regularly return the favor where public schools are concerned.

The Bransons' homeschool day continues haphazardly through the morning. Amidst caring for the younger children, Lauren moves primarily between twelve-year-old Aaron and nine-year-old Stephanie, answering questions and encouraging them to stay focused. Aaron is a friendly, somewhat self-deprecating boy, unassuming and easygoing. Working at the kitchen table, he's having trouble with workbook exercises focusing on different ways to tell time, such as "2:35" and "twenty-five minutes 'til three." Lauren spends a few minutes helping him, then heads off to check on a shouting match in the living room. Later, she has to break up the whole gang watching television, telling the older kids to get back to their assignments while the younger ones watch their shows.

Toward the end of the morning, Gary and Lauren's adult daughter Beth arrives for a visit, bringing her infant son with her. Now twenty-five years old, Beth is a quiet, articulate woman who seems to have a more confident air than her mom, perhaps fostered by her solo experiences off at college. Located in Mississippi, Wood College has since closed (apparently for financial reasons), but Beth says she enjoyed her program there, studying "equine practitioning."

Gary admits that he wasn't supportive of Beth's desire to attend college, and while he didn't prevent her from going, he didn't help, either. On her own, she researched schools, applied for loans, and made the decision to attend. Gary explains his resistance: "Since I didn't go to college, what I'd seen and heard of it—to me it was just a waste of money. If you really wanted to educate yourself, you'd do it with books your own self or go to technical school and learn a trade. I felt like most colleges were just a playground for young kids to get involved in sex, drugs, and rock 'n' roll and boozin'.

"But at the end of it," Gary concludes, "Beth proved *me* to be wrong. When I was there for her graduation, and seen all that she accomplished and how determined she was, I apologized for not supporting her the way I should have, and told her how proud I was that she made all these achievements against incredible odds. She has just done exceptionally well." For someone as opinionated as Gary, this seems no small concession. Even more noteworthy, however, is that despite a homeschooling environment that discouraged higher education, Beth Branson was able to step beyond that limited horizon and decide for herself what was important and how she wanted to live her life.

Gary heads off to get ready for work, and the older kids continue their schoolwork around the kitchen table while Beth and I talk. Aaron interrupts: "Hey Beth, what's four times six?"

Beth helps him figure out the answer, then adds, "I need to drill you on flash cards. What's two times two?"

"Four," he answers quickly.

"What's three times three?"

"Twelve," Aaron says.

"No."

"Oh, I didn't do that right," he says with an embarrassed smile. "I started to do that fast."

Beth's tone is patient. "Think—what's four times four?"

Aaron counts on his fingers to get the answer. "Sixteen."

Beth nods. "Now I want you to remember those and not have to count up," she says, pointing to his hands. "What's five times five?"

"Five times five is—" His brow furrows and he doesn't answer.

"Twenty-five," Beth says. "What's six times six?"

Aaron ponders for a few moments, and mild despair creeps into his voice: "Oh, I don't know."

Later that afternoon, I ask Aaron if he'd ever want to attend public school. "Not really," he answers. "I like homeschooling because I've already done it half my life. I don't really know what public school would be like anyways. I would probably have a few friends if I went to public school half my life instead of homeschooling. But I like homeschooling, because you can sleep until twelve thirty."

His mother, who has been working with him at the table, scoffs. "You do not!"

"Yes, I do," Aaron says.

"Daddy lets you sleep until twelve thirty?" Lauren asks, a bit embarrassed. "I can't believe that."

"Yeah, he does. When you're gone, Daddy lets us sleep as late as we want. When Daddy doesn't have to go to work, he stays in there until at least twelve thirty. I stay in bed at least—"

Lauren starts to laugh, warning Aaron: "You're sticking your foot in your mouth!" She turns to me and explains that she periodically needs to take David to medical specialists in Atlanta for a few days at a time. When she's gone, the other kids take advantage of Gary's leniency. She redirects Aaron's attention to his workbook: "Do you know what an adjective is, Aaron?"

He shakes his head. "I don't really remember."

"It describes a noun," Lauren says. "An adjective tells about a noun." They spend the next fifteen minutes or so reviewing basic parts of speech. Aaron continues to struggle, but he doggedly persists as Lauren helps him along.

Shortly thereafter, as I gather up my things to leave, I tell the kids that I'll be back tomorrow to hang out again. As I head toward the front door, four-year-old Jacob starts getting silly, laughing uproariously and yelling out, "I'll kill you! I'll kill you if you come back!" He is giggling and running circles around me. Aaron laughs and reprimands him casually. But Jacob is too wound up; he runs up to me and starts to swing his fists against my legs, a mischievous smile on his face. With a look of chagrin, Lauren gently pulls Jacob away, scolding him in her soft voice.

"We'll see you tomorrow," she says as she closes the screen door behind me.

When I approach the Bransons' front door the next morning, Jacob is waiting for me. "I apologize for my behavior yesterday," he says to me, his tone solemn.

I smile at him as I enter the house. "Oh, that's okay," I tell him, "but thanks for apologizing." I walk into the kitchen, where I find Gary sitting at the table with the older kids, and Lauren at the stove. The atmosphere seems strangely subdued.

"They're not going to have good attitudes this morning," Gary informs me.

"How so?" I ask.

"They're not where they're supposed to be in their schooling," he says. "They deceived us; they led us to believe that they were doing their work. They would come in and they'd show you, but then Momma last night sat down and started examining it, and all they had done was pencil-whupped it, you know."

"Instead of asking if they did their school," Lauren muses aloud, "I should have asked them, 'Have you finished your completed *pages* for the day?' That's what I needed to ask."

"And it's my fault for not being as scrutinizing as I should be," Gary adds, "when Momma's gone to Atlanta and then I go to work. Plus I realize the girls were washing clothes, folding clothes, caring for the kids and the house and all that kind of stuff. But I wish they'd just be a little more honest about it, so that when Momma starts examining everything that *I* was supposed to be overseeing—she come to find out that five of the eight days they conned me."

I turn to Lauren. "How do you grade those pages?" I ask. "Do they give you an answer key?"

"No, I have to go back and look through the book and find the answers," Lauren says. "It's not really hard; it's not like a college exam where you have to find the little bitty print under the pictures."

The kids start to discuss some of the questions they got wrong, but within a few moments, the family dog comes bounding into the kitchen,

the phone begins to ring, and arguments break out about completely unrelated topics. Interruptions and distractions such as this fill the days I
spend with the Bransons. My presence probably makes it harder for everyone to stay focused, but a consistent pattern emerges each day—the kids
quickly grow tired of their independent work and distract one another
in turn; their parents tell them to get busy, but there is little follow-up
or enforcement. Other times, the kids ask for help and their parents tell
them to wait for a minute while they finish up something else, but then
everyone gets waylaid by another distraction.

Gary gestures toward Jacob, who is passing through the kitchen on
his way out the back door. "Was you satisfied with his apology?" Gary
asks me.

I reply affirmatively and nod enthusiastically, but suspect that discipline has already been meted out.

"He got his little tail warmed up last night," Gary confirms. "He's
a very strange little fellow, you know. He's dear to us, but he's—I don't
know how to describe him. He does what you tell him *not* to." Gary
shakes his head. "I don't know. Davey has been our most obedient child.
He has *always* obeyed. A year old is about when we start serious training
with them. Like this: 'Jessica, come.'"

Jessica, who has been playing with some toys in the corner, looks up.
"Come over here," Gary repeats in a stern voice. She gives a beautiful
smile and serenely walks across the kitchen and stands next to him. "Sit,"
Gary orders. There's no open chair anywhere nearby, and the two-year-old
remains standing next to him, smiling happily.

"Sit," Gary repeats.

Lauren attempts to intercede: "She's like, 'Where do you want me to
sit, Dad?'"

"Sit down," Gary says. His tone is one of disappointment: "All right,
see, she failed. Maybe it's the strangeness of this area, but that's the point
I make with all of them. Because you're not *in* a training environment, it's
even *more* important for you to *obey my voice.*" Gary looks over at me and
says, "I'm going to try to take advantage of this situation right now." He
turns back to his daughter: "Jessica, remember? When I say sit, you sit
right then. No matter if you have a chair or anything."

"Sit on the floor if you have to," Stephanie advises.

Gary's voice grows stern. "Jessica, go down to the den." Jessica obediently walks back across the room toward the doorway. Before she gets there, Gary blurts out, "Stop!" Jessica stops. "Come!" Jessica turns and heads back to her father. "Sit." She immediately sits on the floor, next to his chair. "All right," Gary says approvingly. "Stand up," he continues. Jessica rises. "Go in there and touch the living room door." She begins to walk in that direction. "Run!" Jessica increases her pace. "Come!" She turns and goes back to her father. "Stop!" She halts in front of him. "Sit!" She sits again on the floor. "Stand up!" She rises again.

Gary turns to me. "Some of these liberal-type thinking people, you know, think that you're creating mind-numbed robots out of your children. But they don't understand the concept of trying to train your children in the way that they should go, training them to obey your voice. When you're at Wal-Mart, and the kids start screaming and grabbing everything and embarrassing you to your wits' end, you know? Or when you're trying to talk to somebody on the phone and kids are screaming and carrying on. Your kids will humiliate you if you don't train them."

"Is there a point at which you see training them to obey your voice should change into them thinking for themselves?" I ask. "Making their own choices in the way that *you* do when you interpret Scripture for yourself and not necessarily toe the line someone else tells you?"

Gary pauses. "Hmm—you mean that they would be independent thinkers?"

I nod. "Yeah, the idea that by the time they're adults and they're away from here, you want them to be able to think for themselves, make their own decisions, judge and evaluate things. Is there a point in their training, in their education under you, that you start to push them or help them to start to do that for themselves?"

Gary is quiet, considering my question. "Yes. But it's—" He pauses. "It's not planned. You just start seeing that the time is there. We start letting them be who they are without—I guess it's called loosening the reins. Like I'm just adamant about makeup; I don't want my girls wearing it. I think they're pretty without it. But their friends all do it and I see that they've gotten to a point of individuality where they're mapping out their own likes and dislikes. So I've kind of loosened up the reins a little bit and allow them to use it, even though I told them I don't like it. And both of them went hog wild. It just broke my heart, you know."

During Gary's explanation, Sharon and Christine keep quiet, look increasingly chagrined.

"But I've got to keep my hand off of it," he continues, "because I've trained them in the way they should go. They need to have enough character to make decisions based upon *their* ability to discern what is good and what is evil, rather than my opinion—as much as it may break my heart or cause destruction in their life. But I'm almost sure that if I tighten the reins on them and started choking them, it would cut off any help that I might be able to give them later on, you know? There's a degree where training has to stop. But I don't know where it is."

Gary recognizes that his children ultimately have to make decisions for themselves, and that his attempts to subvert that process will likely drive them away from him. Many parents can relate to his uncertainty about how and when to "loosen the reins." But Gary seems to have less insight where his "training" methods are concerned; if he and Lauren don't implement them on a near-daily basis, he tells me, the kids become undisciplined. "It's like the homeschooling, you know: if we don't stay right on top of it, they're busy right before your eyes, but then you go away and come back in, they're gone." In the realms of both behavior and academics, it seems, their children do what's expected when the external motivations—supervision and threats of punishment—are near, but the values their parents seek to instill have yet to be internalized.

The afternoon finds Gary and nine-year-old Stephanie getting started on her art lesson, and this hour is easily the most impressive teaching interaction I witness during all my time with the Bransons. With relaxed confidence, Gary helps Stephanie learn to create lighting, shading, and perspective in her drawings. Although he's a bit formulaic in his approach, Gary's instructions are patient and descriptive: "Keep in mind the light comes from over here, okay? Then you just kind of *creep* up the side of his jaw like this, and it kind of curves and gets darker as it goes into his mouth, see?" He watches Stephanie practice what he demonstrated. "There you go," he says encouragingly, "there you go." Even the language Gary uses is evocative: "Remember you've got to *sneak* over to the middle. It doesn't matter how many times you have to go back—the idea is to creep over there so it will be very, very light."

As I observe this lesson, I can't help but think that if Gary and Lauren devoted similar attention to the kids' other academic subjects, their homeschool experience would be far richer. Gary's offhand comment during the lesson suggests why art might be a different story: "Art was the only thing I really excelled at in school," he told me. "I failed everything else or just made a D." Art and music are the subjects within his comfort zone and skill set, and so they receive the most attention and direct instruction. The other subjects seem largely relegated to independent study, with Lauren checking over their work and answering occasional questions.

The consequences of this relative neglect of other subjects aren't difficult to see. During the art lesson, for instance, twelve-year-old Aaron struggles with his math, which involves multiplying two-digit numbers. He continues to use his fingers to multiply, even with problems such as "five times nine"—counting forty-five fingers in all. A girl mesmerized by an art lesson, next to her twelve-year-old brother doing math on his fingers—the potential and peril of the Complete Home Education Program.

"I guess you could say we're church-hoppers," Sharon laughingly tells me during one of my visits. Not only have the Bransons moved from church to church, but family members attend different churches from one another as well. It turns out that Gary's independent streak extends to churchgoing; his unorthodox biblical interpretations—many of which surface during family morning Bible studies—end up causing problems with his fellow congregants. "Once they realize what I teach," Gary observes, "they start trying to straighten me out. They love having their little traditions and their religion, and if you bring something in that doesn't fit, they will try to correct you, try to get you to repent and straighten out. And if you don't, no longer do they like you singing and no longer are they too interested in hearing your contributions to Sunday school class." Anecdotal evidence suggests that more than a few homeschool families end up moving to smaller churches, or even house churches attended by several like-minded families—they seek to avoid not only school and government authorities, but the institutional authority of the church as well.

Greenway Full Gospel Church sits on a country road about a mile off the state highway, next to a cornfield and a few old houses. This is the current church home of Gary, Lauren, and the younger children (the older kids attend a bigger, modern church in town). I arrive early on Sunday morning and spy Gary up front, rehearsing with the worship band. I choose a pew near the back corner, and during the next ten minutes before the service starts, at least a dozen people introduce themselves and shake my hand. It's clear they know who's a regular there and who's not. About one hundred people attend the service, an all-white congregation as far as I can tell. The small sanctuary feels roomy, with its warm wood ceiling peaked high in the middle.

The service begins with the worship leader bounding up the steps in front, his shoulder-length blonde hair bouncing around as he begins slapping his hands together vigorously and jumping up and down to stir up the congregation's enthusiasm. This is old-time, foot-stomping gospel music—every song involves vigorous clapping and hearty singing, with simple repeated choruses about "running to the light" or "being saved by the blood." Eventually, the pastor ascends to the pulpit for his sermon. "We are in spiritual warfare—and not just on Sunday morning," are his opening words. "We are fighting for people's very eternal souls." During the sermon, congregants call out various affirmations and encouragements: "That's right!" or "yes it is!" Early in the sermon, the pastor breaks into song, which the congregation immediately joins: "Oh the blood of Jesus, it washes white as snow." This mixture of song and preaching continues throughout.

With the exception of one parishioner who asked for prayers for the upcoming elections, the worship service contains no explicit references to politics or even controversial social issues. The church bulletin, however, includes an insert encouraging people to vote for the Tennessee Marriage Amendment—"to prevent activist judges from ruling against the majority's wishes." When I ask Gary and Lauren about this later, they indicate that this insert wasn't a usual occurrence, but understandable since the election was just days away. "And you know," Gary adds, "I'd say it's a disgrace that our nation has come to a point where this even has to be discussed or that it's even considered. That's what makes it so damnable, that it actually has arisen to this point."

———

When I return to Tennessee for my second year of visits, Lauren asks me not to show up until eleven in the morning, as the family attends an exercise class beforehand at the local YMCA. Soon after I arrive, the Bransons get things rolling with their usual Bible study. Since last spring, they have progressed to the New Testament book of 1 Peter, and I observe a similar mixture of yawns, squirming by the younger kids, and occasional engagement by the older ones. During the study, Gary rails against hierarchy in churches that designate the pastor as the authority.

Seventy-five minutes later, the Bible study concludes, and Gary is eager to transition to music. First, though, I want to find out what the kids are doing for their other subjects this year. As I start to talk with Sharon and Aaron about their studies, Gary loses interest and heads off to the music room, where he begins to pluck away on the bass and tune the other instruments.

Sharon shows me her materials. "I read almost the whole book for economics and the way the country runs and stuff," she says. "And this is the book I'm reading now, in the Left Behind series." This collection of sixteen books, a mixture of action thriller and end-of-the-world prophecies, is wildly popular among conservative Christians. As I scan her materials, a distinctive textbook cover catches my eye—*Biblical Economics and Comics*—and I pick it up and page through it.

"It's funner to read," Sharon explains to me.

Sharon has bookmarked her place in the text, so I flip back a few pages. "Do you remember anything you learned about unions?" I ask.

"I don't know, I'm just reading it," she says. She then shows me her English workbook, explaining that she does one practice section a day, filling in answers—no extended writing, no cumulative exams. "And these are some of the other things I've done." She pulls out an activity log on which her mother has listed daily activities: "Typing lessons on the computer," "WordSmart," "Home Ec," "Survival Math," and "Music."

I ask Lauren how she decided on the curriculum for her kids this year. "Different sources, different magazines," she says. She reaches into a kitchen drawer and pulls out about fifty direct-mail postcards, the kind that come wrapped in plastic and advertise everything from curricular materials to correspondence programs to home health remedies. "I got a stack of cards and there are boocoodles of different companies." She holds up one promoting a math program they recently purchased. "Now you can just put a disc in the computer and have each lesson taught; if you don't want to teach algebra, you can just put the lesson in and it shows them step-by-step what to do." She hands me the stack of cards to peruse.

"I have a hodgepodge of different things," Lauren continues, "because I've used A Beka and I have so many different reading programs. I have Hooked on Phonics, I have the *Blue Back Speller*, I have the Montessori reading program on the computer, I have this *Reading and Writing* workbook."

"Have you found anything to work particularly well?" I ask.

"Well, I just need to stick with one thing for the year," she says. "You know, if I go a month or two and it doesn't seem like it's teaching them anything, then maybe I'll change to something different." This seems like a fad-diet approach, hoping for the product to "teach them" and jumping to a new one when it doesn't happen. Public schools can fall victim to this approach as well, as any teacher who's sat through an in-service presentation of the latest and greatest curricular program can tell you.

Gary leaves curriculum purchases up to Lauren. "He just lets me get whatever I need to get," she says. "And I try to pray about it, you know, so I can get the right thing and God can point things out to me. Or somebody else might tell me what's worked for them." The moms' homeschool support meetings have been a good source of information and moral support, Lauren adds—in fact, when she talks about this moms' group, her tone is more animated, her expression happier, than any other time I've seen her. Homeschooling five kids and caring for seven (including one with serious health problems) is hard enough—trying to do so without the support and encouragement of other homeschool mothers would probably be more than she could bear.

Gary has returned to the kitchen, so I ask him what he's doing for social studies with the kids this year. Other than the occasional History Channel videotape, he admits, he has "kind of put civics on the back burner. We have made such major advancements in art and music that we're just consumed with it right now." They frequently play a couple hours in the evening, plus the mornings when Gary is home from work.

The Bransons are also starting to experience the sometimes labyrinthine world of special education, as they have decided to seek services for five-year-old David through the local school district. As with Veronica Rivera in California, David is considered a private school student by the state of Tennessee and thus is eligible for special education assistance. He now has a formal IEP (Individualized Education Program) through the local school district and receives services—occupational and physical therapy—at district expense. Lauren admits to being a bit overwhelmed with the special education procedures. "When we first went, I had to sign all these papers, like buying a house." For a family determined to avoid the "system's tentacles" as much as possible, this strikes me as a significant concession, prompted by the daunting challenge of meeting David's many needs.

While the paperwork for government-financed special education services is extensive, the reporting requirements for the Bransons' homeschooling efforts are pretty minimal—just submitting periodic progress reports to Mission Academy, their umbrella program. I ask Lauren if she thinks it would be reasonable to give homeschoolers a test every few years, just to make sure they're learning basic skills.

"Well, yeah," Lauren says, uncertainly.

"Do you think requiring certain types of curriculum would be reasonable?"

Now Lauren's answer is more definitive. "No, because all children learn in different ways," she says. "And a curriculum that might work for one child might not work for the other one as well. In public schools, they put kids in a box and they have to learn like everybody else, and they have to keep up with everybody else." Lauren's voice grows with conviction—this is the most forceful I've seen her "Well, that's not right, because they might just have a different way of learning. You have to find what works best. And each family is an individual family, so I don't know how you legislate right and wrong in that area."

Gary is even more resistant to state regulation of homeschooling, insisting there should be "none whatsoever." He agrees that physical mistreatment qualifies for intervention, but even there he's wary: "The government would like any excuse to get into a family and start running their business for them."

I ask him if he thinks parents have the right to instill in their children any worldview or beliefs they want—even if, say, they were part of a hate group advocating racial violence.

"Boy, that's a tough one," Gary concedes, then unintentionally illustrates my concern. "Because I'm of the mind right now to kick Muslims out of our country. They say openly that they hate our lifestyle and they want to kill us and take our country away from us; I think they ought to be kicked out of our country."

"But wouldn't that be the government intruding?" I ask.

"Yeah, that's exactly the point," Gary says. "Do people have a right to teach their children that type of business without the government intervening? Oh, that ol' devil wants his foot in the door, doesn't he? I say keep the government out. I'd rather err on the side of the family's security, away from the government, and then trust neighbors and the church to intervene with guilty people."

I point out that plenty of people don't necessarily belong to a church or let their neighbors see what they're doing at home. "What if regulation didn't intrude in the home," I suggest, "but it was, say, a simple test every three or four years? You don't have to know Shakespeare, but you need to be able to show that you're learning how to read and write and do simple math. Wouldn't that be a way to show that your kids are learning the basics, so the government should stay out of your way?"

"Yeah, but it also gives them authority over your life," Gary says. "It gives them access to your family." He starts to sound a bit annoyed at my persistence here. "See, you're using an extreme unlikelihood to validate an intrusion—it's saying, 'Well, if you don't let government check and make sure everybody is being educated, you want to protect the wicked parents that are too lazy to teach their children.' And that's not it. I believe that there are people who probably are irresponsible and don't love their children enough to teach them. But to take *all* the responsible families and subject them to government tyranny and government intrusion and government bureaucracy because of somebody's irresponsibility—I just couldn't do that to anybody. I'd say, let's me and a few other brothers go visit that guy and give him a blanket party."

"Give him a what?" I ask.

"A blanket party," Gary repeats. "Put a blanket over him and whoop the fire out of him with rubber hoses and then explain to him, 'You're causing the rest of us to have to be subjected to government scrutiny and we expect you to have your children educated. If you can't do it your own self, you're gonna have some tutors over here and we're gonna help you. But you're gonna get yourself straightened out or we're gonna visit you again.'"

Gary pauses, searching for a way to summarize his perspective. "We have two opposing sides in this life, for sure. The state, and those of us who want to live peacefully and responsibly without their intervention. We need them: we'll pay them taxes to create us some roads and give us a military and help us with our food production. But we don't need them anywhere else; we'll take care of it. The government is just too big, too intrusive."

In the midst of her managing a household of nine, I finally get a chance to sit down alone with Lauren and hear her thoughts on homeschooling and childrearing. "So as you think about what you're trying to accomplish with homeschooling," I ask, "are there particular skills that stand out to you as the most important, that you want them to have by the time they're done?"

"The main thing is that they know God," Lauren says with quiet conviction. "The main thing is that they are grounded and settled in the Word and that they can tell others. That they have the character they need to continue in life and they're happy and productive. You know, good citizens—they vote and make their voice known in the world."

"What does it mean to you to be a good citizen, beyond voting?" I ask. "Are there other things that you would want them to understand, or that you think are important?"

"Well, we visit a nursing home at least once a week if we can, and we bring the patients to the cafeteria. My husband plays the piano for them and we talk to them as best we can and be their friends and just try to help them not be lonely." Lauren points to these visits as important in broadening her children's socialization as well: "They don't feel like the old people are a burden because they're helping them." Teenagers, she says, often only want to be around other teenagers, but homeschooling "gives you more of a balance instead of being in a segregated age, where the only thing you know is what's in that age group, and then you're afraid to get out from that one age group."

"How about political involvement?" I ask. "Do you think that's important for a citizen as a Christian?"

"If they're led that way," Lauren says. "I'm not politically minded; my husband is more than I am."

In a home that emphasizes "training" so strongly, the question about whether there's room for their children to think independently and make choices for themselves seems especially relevant. "Are there times when, as the kids get older, they start to push boundaries, and issues or conflicts or disagreements come up?" I ask.

"Oh, yeah," Lauren says. "We've had battles with Seth, who his roommates were and what he did in his spare time—you know, should he drink or smoke or take drugs. Just things that you have to deal with as parents."

Seth's transition from homeschooling to the adult world was not an entirely smooth one, but it seems to his parents that he's on the right track now. He began working at Walgreens when he was sixteen and is now taking classes to qualify for their management positions. This has confirmed for Gary his view that "work ethic and character seem to me to be the primary success principles. How smart they are while they're in your home doesn't seem to matter much—it's when they actually put their hands on the real world and embrace personal responsibility and handle it their own self."

Seth is gracious enough to stop over one Sunday afternoon so I can talk with him about his homeschooling experiences and transition into adulthood. Twenty years old now, he has dark hair and a slimmer build than his father. His attitude is very respectful, almost deferential toward me. He says his homeschool experience was quite similar to what his younger siblings have, except that his mom had more time to work one-on-one with him.

"If you want your kids to come up in the right way," he tells me, "I recommend homeschooling. If I had gone to public school, I would have been introduced to a lot of things, such as drugs and alcohol abuse. I mean, I've been into some things like that, but the fact that I was homeschooled has kept me away from *a lot* of things." Not encountering those temptations and challenges until he was a young adult, Seth says, meant he was able to navigate them more successfully.

Seth admits that public school students probably had more exposure to writing and grammar than he did, and likely more expert instruction than his parents were able to provide. But if he could change one thing about his homeschool experience, it would be to "study harder—they pushed me, but a student will only go as far as he wants to go." Now he's realizing how useful those academic skills are as he takes management classes.

I ask Seth about some of his views on social and political issues, and it appears that—while still conservative overall—he sees more room for reasonable disagreement about some issues, including gender roles and even abortion to some extent. Nevertheless, he endorses his parents' approach of instilling a firm belief system in their children; once he got out on his own, he feels he was able to make his own decisions and adapt their teachings to his own life.

By Seth's own admission, the homeschooling environment ultimately did not protect him from, or prepare him for, avoiding worldly temptations once he left the home. Gary remains concerned about his son's moral and spiritual condition. Seth doesn't attend church regularly, and they know he's fallen prey to "boozing and fornication." Some observers might even blame his upbringing, where freedom to choose was significantly curtailed, for leaving him ill prepared for such choices once he left home. Others, including Seth himself, would contend that his relatively cloistered childhood prevented his eventual moral stumbles from being much worse.

When I get a chance to talk privately with Sharon, Christine, Aaron, and Stephanie, all of them express contentment with homeschooling. They indicate no desire to attend public schools, which they view with great suspicion and at least a little fear. They have learned this lesson well from their parents. Popular culture still finds its way into their home, however—they are all avid video game players; among their favorites are *Halo* and *Grand Theft Auto*, two particularly violent games.

Not only do they tell me they are glad to be homeschooled, but none of them voices any major complaints about their parents' rules or expectations, either. "My dad used to say that I couldn't do a lot of things by myself," Christine remarks, "but now he's letting me hang out with my friends. And he used to be really big on not dyeing your hair, because it's the way that God made you and everything. But lately, he says it's our hair, so we can do it if we want to."

"And so you dyed it," I say, pointing to her new red color.

She chuckles. "Yeah."

While not as engaged socially outside the home as many of the other homeschoolers I visit, the older Branson kids do stay active in their church youth group, which has nearly two hundred teenage participants and meets every Wednesday for activities such as singing, skits, and socializing. Much like Seth, the three Branson teenagers seem to have somewhat less rigid views on social and political issues than their father. They each express a recognition that plenty of people in society believe differently than they do, and imposing their own beliefs on others would be a bad idea. But beyond this general sentiment of "live and let live," none of them seem particularly interested in—or informed about—the political process or ways they might get involved.

In the months that follow my final visit, I receive several e-mail updates from Gary and Lauren. Seth received a promotion to assistant manager at Walgreens in a nearby town, and Sharon is now employed at the local Walgreens as well. At the end of the school year, Lauren reports that she isn't satisfied with some of the kids' skills in math and spelling. "I just need to find the right curriculum to meet the multilevel teaching and learning that we have," she writes. David continues to receive occupational and physical therapy through a specialist provided by the local public school, and will participate in a district reading program during the summer months. "He was exposed to the system without it hurting him," Lauren notes. "I have benefited from the public school system this last year more than ever, but I will not let them babysit my children. God is the main focus of our school." The big family news is that Sharon is engaged to be married to a young man who was homeschooled in a family of nine children. "Life is a continual learning process," Lauren concludes. "It unfolds a little here, a little there."

ACADEMIC ACHIEVEMENT AND SOCIALIZATION

What do we know about homeschooler academic performance across the board? Not much. Anecdotally, it seems clear that homeschooling works very well for some students; supporters can point to homeschooled winners of national spelling and geography bees, debate competitions, art contests, and so on. Even stalwart critics of homeschooling acknowledge that the "high end" of academic homeschooling performance compares favorably with other forms of schooling, and as I mentioned earlier, elite colleges and universities count homeschoolers among their student bodies.

But where empirical research data are concerned, we have little to go on, despite the frequently misleading claims made by some homeschool advocates. In a typical example of overstatement, one HSLDA spokesperson claims, "The average eighth grade home-schooler scores higher than the average 12th grader nationwide on standardized tests (per Dr. Lawrence M. Rudner, University of Maryland)." The Rudner research cited here is a favorite of homeschool advocates; commissioned by HSLDA, the study reports that homeschoolers scored two to four grade levels and 20 percentage points higher than national averages on popular achievement tests.

But Rudner's study is perhaps the most misrepresented research in the homeschooling universe. As the study's author himself acknowledges, the homeschool participants (unlike the public school students' scores) were an unrepresentative sample, and it was not a controlled experiment. Among a range of inconsistencies, the study drew only from homeschoolers who elected to take these tests through a Bob Jones University standardized testing program (in which parents typically administer the exams to their own children), then compared this narrow slice of homeschoolers to national averages for public and private school students. Even with the caveats Rudner offered in his analysis, the study came under heavy peer critique in the same academic journal in which his findings appeared.

Despite these many shortcomings, the study's "findings" were trumpeted in a 1999 HSLDA press release: "In the race to scholastic excellence, typical home school students sprint to the front in the early grades, and generally finish far ahead of students in public or private schools." Clearly, there's no grounds for claiming the homeschoolers tested were "typical," and several good reasons to suspect they in fact were not. Simply put, no studies exist that can substantiate HSLDA's claim about the academic performance of "typical" homeschoolers.

And what about the concern raised by many homeschool detractors that children will not have the opportunity to develop important social skills with other children their age? Few criticisms of homeschooling seem to annoy parents as much as the "socialization question." Their typical response is to argue that the type of socialization that public schools typically offer is hardly the most desirable or useful sort for later life. Furthermore, they contend, homeschoolers get to interact more with the full range of ages—rather than almost exclusively with their peers—in a greater variety of learning settings throughout the community.

It's true that opportunities abound for all but the most geographically isolated homeschoolers to have significant, face-to-face interactions with those outside their family, including same-age peers. As with questions about academic performance of homeschooling, however, comprehensive empirical evidence about socialization is unavailable. Homeschool advocates routinely cite one particular study—a 2003 report by Brian Ray, commissioned by HSLDA—as evidence that homeschool graduates are engaged citizens, involved in their communities, and leading fulfilling lives. But this study relied on the self-reports of volunteers without accounting for parent income, education, or other variables, so neither definitive statements about homeschoolers nor reliable comparisons with the general U.S. population can be made.

The question of what constitutes healthy and desirable socialization is at least part of the issue here. In an effort to bring greater precision to this question, psychologist Richard Medlin reviewed dozens of studies on homeschooler socialization. He concluded that the evidence, while still preliminary, suggests that homeschooled children in general are engaged in their community, acquire necessary rules of behavior, and demonstrate social maturity and leadership skills. Medlin emphasized, however, that more and better research is needed before definitive conclusions about homeschooler socialization can be drawn.

5

GENERATION JOSHUA AND HSLDA
"A Few Good Soldiers"

"America is in a culture war. A few good soldiers can make a difference. Equip yourself and come join the battle!" So proclaimed the founders of Generation Joshua, a civics program from the Home School Legal Defense Association begun in 2003. "Our goal is to ignite a vision in young people to help America return to her Judeo-Christian foundation," its leaders explained. "We provide students with hands-on opportunities to implement that vision." As I began my homeschooling research six years ago, the birth of Generation Joshua caught my attention. Here was a civics education program aimed at homeschoolers, one that clearly sought to help nurture in students an idea and practice of citizenship informed and energized by their deep religious convictions. Perhaps the homeschooler president of Michael Farris's dream would emerge from such an education.

Designed primarily for high-school-aged students, Generation Joshua combines online components with periodic opportunities for face-to-face interaction and real-world political engagement. The online elements of the program include extensive civics coursework, adult-moderated "chats" about current events, and thousands of bulletin-board forums where students can post entries on topics ranging from immigration reform and international relations to popular movies and rules for courtship.

This civics education program extends far beyond a virtual electronic community, however. Students are encouraged to participate in summer camps, voter registration drives, regional clubs, and an intriguing feature called Student Action Teams (SATs). These adult-supervised teams of students engage directly with the political process through participation in electoral campaigns. In fact, several victorious candidates for state and national offices have credited SATs with playing a pivotal role in their races.

But assisting with current political contests, while certainly appreciated by candidates, is ultimately a means to a much broader end. An ABC *World News Tonight* profile described Generation Joshua as developing "Christian soldiers with a mission to take back America for God," and GenJ leadership clearly agrees. Founding director Ned Ryun designed a strategy of creating a new generation of leaders who will bring their Christian values and commitments with them into the public square of policy, politics, and culture. "Great movements begin from the grass roots, from the bottom up," he told one magazine interviewer. "With the homeschooling movement, we've only seen the tip of the iceberg so far. In another ten or fifteen years, we may see a disproportionate number of homeschoolers in positions of highest leadership." In the first six years of its existence, Generation Joshua has seen steady growth in its membership, with a 2008 roster of more than four thousand students.

Michael Farris sees Generation Joshua as playing a vital role in the long-term goals of HSLDA and conservative politics. "We are not homeschooling our kids just so they can read," he told the *New York Times*. "The most common thing I hear parents telling me is they want their kids to be on the Supreme Court. And if we put enough kids in the farm system, some may get to the major leagues." It was Farris who coined the program's name. He describes current homeschool parents and leaders as the Moses Generation, the ones who led the exodus from public schools (the equivalent of pharaoh's Egypt). But just as it was Moses's protégé Joshua who finally brought his people into the Promised Land, Farris sees the homeschooled youth as the ones who will ultimately "take back the land" for God.

This vision of conservative Christian homeschooling, while still rooted in the primacy of the family and parental freedom to direct the upbringing of their children, reaches beyond to instill a particular philosophy and practice of citizenship. Even on first glance, Generation Joshua— with its battle imagery and strong emphasis on real-world engagement in the political arena—promised to be something quite different from the lowest-common-denominator, controversy-avoiding, inert civics curricula sadly typical of public schools.

So I decided to follow the development of this program, to see how they go about "igniting a vision" of citizenship focused so squarely on bringing their Christian values into the public square. What kind of citizen are they trying to develop? Are students encouraged to think for themselves, or parrot a party line? And how is such a citizen supposed to engage with the diversity of beliefs and perspectives at play in our democracy?

Generation Joshua provides a range of online learning opportunities for students. Their formal curricular offerings include a variety of topics, such as Constitutional Law, Founding Fathers, Campaign School, Revolutionary War-Era Sermons, The Federalist Papers, The Great Awakening, and Democracy in America. For the most part, however, it's pretty dry stuff. I had high hopes for the Democracy in America course, but like most of the other topics, it essentially consists of selected readings followed by quizzes that can be submitted online, with a certificate of completion awarded at the end of the unit.

The GenJ Book Club offers a yearly reading list, with titles ranging from mainstream historical fare such as David McCullough's *1776* to more partisan texts such as Mark Levin's *Men in Black: How the Supreme Court Is Destroying America*. GenJ staff moderators lead online discussions of the selected books throughout the year; these conversations vary in quality from fairly detailed exchanges about central themes in a text to a series of unrelated and unsupported opinions typed haphazardly by contributors.

The most active online participation, however, takes place on the forum bulletin boards, where GenJ members can share their perspectives on a variety of issues. These "threads" are usually started by student participants, although occasionally one of the adult moderators will pose a question or issue and invite comments.

Forum threads exploring the broad and complex relationship between government and religion appear regularly. The vast majority of forum participants agree that the Founding Fathers intended for the United States to operate according to Christian principles, and many cite political speeches by these men that urged a strong link between government, religious devotion, and Christian morality (the GenJ Web site itself provides a page of over forty such quotes). GenJers recognize freedom of religion as a pillar of American democracy, but don't see this conflicting with their desire for laws that reflect Christian convictions on topics such as abortion, same-sex marriage, religious references in public displays and the Pledge of Allegiance, and so on. The United States can (and should)

be governed by principles of Christian morality, they contend, as long as
no one forces people to *be* Christians.

Approximately 90 percent of GenJers are homeschoolers, so it's not
surprising that threads weighing various forms of schooling would be
popular. "Public schools are quite simply humanist churches," one student writes. Another charges that public schools "have become the Enemy's tool of indoctrination and demoralization of today's society." Some
students seek support in their Scriptures, such as one who argued, "The
Word of God says that parents are to raise their children in the 'nurture
and admonition of the Lord.' What does this mean? It means that it is
a sin for Christian parents to submit 20,000 hours of their child's childhood to an influence which teaches them that there is no God." Another
puts it quite simply: "Children are not spiritually strong enough to attend a humanist church five times as much as a Christian church."

While many forum participants sound absolutely convinced that public schools are the worst possible choice and they would never send their
kids there, a few wrote about their public school friends whom they see
as both good Christians and successful, happy students. "Public schools
are a problem right now in this country, but it is a generalization to suggest that they are all failing, miserable examples of schools," one student
asserts. "Remember there are a lot of Christians in the public system as
well."

On the whole, however, cautionary views of public schools and secular
society rule the day, conveying an implicit conception of childhood as a
defensive posture, protected by parents. Only when they reach adulthood
can they step out and contend with the influences of the world. As one
student remarks, "It is the job of the adult, who is already steadfast in
his/her belief, to do the evangelizing, not of the naïve child who is still
being taught about the Bible and Christianity." A few, however, see the
pathway to adulthood as ideally more of a gradual transition. "I believe
going to a local high school while you are still living at home is much
better than being thrown out into the real world during or after college,"
one participant writes. "It provides a nice transition to the real world
because your parents are still there to guide and direct you."

Some forum topics address, at least incidentally, broader philosophical
issues such as tolerance, compromise, and ethical reasoning. Arguments
against moral relativism crop up regularly, and many students seem un-

willing to consider the possibility of moral shades of gray. "Scripture is not neutral," one insists. "Something is either for God or against God." Another writes, "We shouldn't be lukewarm; there shouldn't be a gray area." A related thread entitled "What Is Truth?" makes clear that most GenJ participants interpret the Bible literally, and if scientific knowledge or personal experience doesn't line up with their literal interpretation, the science is flawed or the experience is misunderstood.

While some public school classroom settings approximate the engaging back-and-forth interactivity that these online chat rooms and forum postings provide, Generation Joshua offers participants a much richer layer of experience beyond that. Voter registration drives, Student Action Teams, and GenJ Clubs: here is where the transformative power and lasting impact of Generation Joshua reside, and where public schools have great difficulty keeping up.

One way in which GenJ members are encouraged to become politically active is by conducting voter registration drives in their local areas. One GenJ staff member made the underlying goal quite clear in his advice to students:

> If it is a secular realm (a county fair, for example), place a huge Bush-Cheney sign and Republican yard signs in the area. This will make it very unlikely that people will show up who want to vote Democrat. You are not a partisan organization, but you can indeed register voters in a partisan manner. When ignorant people come up, make sure you explain things in such a way that they would feel largely stupid to register Democrat. In other words, tell the truth. :)

The vision of civic education offered here promotes partisan victory at the expense of encouraging full participation in the process.

Perhaps the most powerful impact, however, occurs when Generation Joshua members participate in Student Action Teams, which provide hands-on experience in a political campaign. "The balance of power is so close in America right now that a small army of young people, placed in the right place at the right time, can make a difference," Ryun wrote in his pitch to get students involved in SATs. "But we can't make a difference sitting at home. We've got to get out of our comfort zones and go for it." GenJ members get the message that they truly *can* make a difference, even before they're eligible to vote: "This Presidential election and the next could dictate the direction America takes for the next generation. There is so much at stake that will influence your life in the years to come, and you can help change the course of a nation by being involved."

The Political Action Committee of HSLDA identifies "pro-family and pro-homeschooling" candidates to support, and students (and their parents, if they volunteer to serve as chaperones) within driving distance of the campaign are encouraged to join an SAT. Travel expenses are reimbursed, and pairs of Patrick Henry College students serve as team leaders, often supervising as many as one hundred teenagers, thirteen minivans, and twenty-two hotel rooms. Not surprisingly, GenJ requires a strict code of conduct, but it's easy to see how this would present itself as a great adventure for homeschoolers (or any student wanting to get involved in the political process, for that matter).

Political analysts observe that volunteers are even more important than money in campaign success, and the efforts of SATs would seem to bear this out. In 2006 alone, 1,300 GenJers made more than 400,000 phone calls and knocked on over 100,000 doors. SAT participation was slightly less in 2008, but volunteers still made direct contact with more than half a million voters. Numerous victors in the House and Senate over the past several years have credited SATs with playing a pivotal role in their campaigns. Oklahoma senator Tom Coburn proclaimed, "I'm a U.S. senator today" because of the grassroots volunteers who were "just energized and believed in what we were talking about." Generation Joshua, he added, "was the most successful thing I've ever seen in politics, and my hope is that it'll continue."

The testimonies of SAT participants speak to the powerful impact the experience has on them as well. Adolescents in particular crave the opportunity to be involved in meaningful endeavors that provide them with a sense of efficacy in their world, and SATs have the potential to feed this passion. "It is amazing to see the impact that just a few people can have when they work together for a common goal," one says. Another observes, "Going door-to-door was not always fun, but it was good to know I was *doing* something rather than just talking about it."

Not surprisingly, the students who get involved with SATs tend to increase their GenJ participation across the board. "Some of them are getting good enough, we'll fly them in" for high-priority races, Ryun said. These are the ones targeted for development as future leaders for Generation Joshua and beyond, the ones who will make it out of the farm system and into the big leagues.

The primary means for raising up future leaders and recruiting new members, however, are the GenJ Clubs. Ryun spent much of his time in 2006 and 2007 out on the lecture circuit, generating enthusiasm for Generation Joshua and recruiting new members. He also began to encourage current members to start forming local GenJ Clubs, which have two main purposes: "Prayer for our nation and involvement in local civic and political activity." By mid-2008, more than seventy clubs had formed. Largely self-governing but expected to submit regular activity reports to Generation Joshua, club members contact regional legislators, attend public meetings, organize demonstrations and protests (Planned Parenthood seems to be a popular target), and campaign for candidates in local elections.

The GenJ Clubs also have the potential to serve another purpose, one arguably neglected in the rest of the program: emphasizing to participants that their responsibilities as citizens extend beyond political activity. "I'm trying to encourage them not only in politics, but civics," Ryun told me. "How can you be a good citizen? That could be serving in a soup kitchen or helping build a hospice, which one of the clubs in Ohio did." A club in Kansas, he added, helped paint the house of a single mother. This broadening of civic purpose strikes me as a welcome development, and one that might provide opportunities for students to engage with diverse people and perspectives without feeling compelled to win a political battle at the same time.

After spending the last six years following the growth and activities of Generation Joshua, I am genuinely torn in my appraisal. In many ways, this is a compelling example of genuine civic engagement. In fact, in my ten years of teaching public high school English and social studies, I have rarely encountered students whose civic knowledge, skills, and participation matched those of Generation Joshua participants. (The most recent National Assessment of Educational Progress civics assessment in 2006 bears this out as well, with only 27 percent of high school seniors scoring at or above "proficient.")

All this is somewhat ironic given the concerns raised by critics of homeschooling—and of educational privatization more generally—about the threats such alternatives pose to civic engagement. A vital sense of community and civic involvement is neglected, they contend, when families opt out of their public schools, and such a shift only contributes to the culture of individualism, fragmentation, and polarization that threatens the civic fabric of our democracy.

At least some research, however, appears to suggest otherwise. Sociologists Christian Smith and David Sikkink use data from the 1996 National Household Education Survey to argue that religious school and homeschool families are consistently *more* involved in civic activities than families with children in public schools. This held true even controlling for differences in education, income, age, race, family structure, region, and the number of hours per week that parents work. Their conclusion: "Private schooling is absolutely *not* privatizing." In fact, they claim, "The associations and practices of private schooling often create denser relational networks of greater solidarity and shared moral culture than those of public schooling."

Smith and Sikkink use homeschooling as a prime example of the rich array of networks, support groups, and political advocacy efforts that privatized schooling can foster. They acknowledge that "of course, some people do not like the purpose of home schoolers' networking and activism" but claim that "the relevant fact here is that social capital generates the civic participation that strengthens public life, whether or not this is the primary intentional goal of the association."

But the purpose of civic activism—and the methods—*do* matter when considering what strengthens public life. And here lies my concern with Generation Joshua: as a training ground for future democratic citizens and leaders, some vital elements are missing. Rather than framing democratic citizenship as a shared endeavor among a diverse citizenry, where compromise and accommodation are not only necessary but often desirable, GenJ fosters a vision of adversarial political engagement informed by narrow ideological boundaries.

One of the things that's so compelling about Generation Joshua for these Christian youth is the cultivation of group identity and purpose. Many conservative Christians see themselves as an embattled minority desperately resisting the growing secular society around them. This sense abounds in Generation Joshua discussion threads as well, and many students see their involvement as a way to find kindred spirits and like-minded encouragement. One participant writes, "I've found a place where people agree with my political views, and they are willing to stand up for them! It's great!"

But there's an inevitable tension between creating this powerful group identity while still preserving room for ideological diversity, or at least the room to question dogma and consider alternative perspectives. This is not to say that Dennis Kucinich should be made to feel at home, or that GenJ leadership shouldn't advocate certain policy positions or political candidates. But if the tenor and content are so one-sided that participants would have a hard time acknowledging that someone could be a good Christian *and* a good Democrat, then there's a problem. On the whole, Generation Joshua seems a good example of what political theorist Cass Sunstein describes as "ideological amplification": like-minded group members push one another toward more extreme versions of their already-held beliefs.

When I sit down with Ned Ryun in 2007 to hear his thoughts on Generation Joshua and political engagement, he acknowledges this tension between developing a certain ideological cohesion while avoiding an unreflective groupthink mentality. Ryun, who was homeschooled for part of his childhood, surprises me with his candor about the dangers of unreflective acceptance of parental values and beliefs in the homeschool setting. "The thing that's a little scary for me sometimes within the homeschool community is that they aren't challenged in some ways to think," he says, and so run the risk of making bad choices when they go out on their own. "I want them to experience other thoughts, other ideas. I don't think you can actually be effective as a person unless you really have to come to that point and say, 'This is what I've been told—but is it real?'"

These laudable sentiments, however, lose some of their luster when compared to the steady diet of dismissive stereotypes, overgeneralizations, and one-sided assertions that pervade the online realm of Generation Joshua—some of which are made by Ryun himself. "I'm telling you, the Democrats are Socialists," he writes in one post. "That's why the stakes are so high in this election and in the ones to come. We don't have two capitalistic parties competing for control here in America. We have a capitalist one fighting it out with a socialist one." Whether such caricatures are fair game in a political ad may be an open question, but it's hard to see how this qualifies as encouraging critical thinking or careful analysis among impressionable students.

Ryun cheapens the rhetoric even further when he writes, "The left cannot engage in a rational, truthful debate simply because it has no rational, intelligent ideas." This assertion, made in an article he also published on another Web site (and thus not the type of tongue-in-cheek throwaway line made during an online chat session), is so profoundly dismissive of his opponents that I make a point to ask him about it when we talk. He chuckles sheepishly, with a rueful smile: "Yeah, probably not the best statement to make." As if to demonstrate his open-mindedness, he mentions a new friend he made during a conference in Europe, one of the founders of Emily's List, a pro-choice organization for Democratic women. "You know, she's not stupid," he says. "She's very intelligent." At the same time, he says, "we realized we were diametrically opposed on a lot of the issues."

Here was a chance to explore what Ryun and GenJ might think about the value of dialogue across difference. "Do you feel obligated, as a responsible citizen, to try to understand what her line of reasoning is?" I ask.

"I do try," he says. "Probably for strategic reasons, because I have to know how they're thinking." But this merely echoes the debating approach of his boss, Michael Farris, who describes the investigation of diverse perspectives as simply "opposition research." The sole purpose is to ferret out weaknesses, rather than respecting others enough to try to understand what's important to them. I try to push beyond this: "I wonder if another part of it is not only understanding what they believe, but *why* they believe it?"

Ryun nods in agreement. "Yeah, I definitely want students to understand the opposing ideas, where they came from. I just don't know how"— he pauses, as if in contemplation—"with a sixteen-, seventeen-year-old, you start doing that. I want them to realize there are opposing ideas out there and you can't just automatically dismiss them or else you're not going to be able to be engaged." He falls silent again, drumming his fingers on his desk. Then he shakes his head. "I don't know. I don't know how we do that."

Perhaps as a result, appreciation for why others believe differently (not necessarily *agreement* with those beliefs) seems largely absent from the Generation Joshua educational experience. Rarely do GenJ students or leaders engage with opposing arguments on their strongest terms, or consider that reasonable disagreement might exist on important issues. Such an approach results in seeing others as simply wrong-headed adversaries to be opposed at every turn.

When this is the attitude, then compromise and accommodation make sense only in pursuit of an incrementalist strategy, serving merely as tools to be employed toward ultimate (and total) conquest. Ryun, who has mentioned during online chats his intention to run for political office in the next few years, explicitly advocates this incrementalist philosophy. He exhorts his GenJ students: "We fight the secular humanism in politics. We fight it in the arts. We fight it in law. We get more and more evangelical Christians involved who will make a difference. In time, if we are incremental and take ground bit by bit, we will win."

Ryun sees compromise as "part of politics," but only in pursuit of eventual victory—"if I have to give a little bit, lose two yards to gain three," he says. But the idea that compromise and accommodation with differing viewpoints might constitute a democratic good in and of itself doesn't seem to have a place in Ryun's or GenJ's ideology.

Generation Joshua seeks to recruit and train "a few good soldiers," and this warfare imagery of adversarial politics runs throughout the program. In one post, Ryun challenges:

> Will Christians be ready to do battle in the public arena, or will we stand by and watch the direction and future of this nation dictated to us by the secular humanists? Do evangelical Christians have the willpower and desire to make a difference? If we have the desire, we can win. The numbers are on our side. But we must rise up. The battle call is being sounded. The time has come to take up arms and take the fight to the enemy. We must win. There is too much at stake for us to lose.

While perhaps effective at stirring the emotions of adolescents eager to belong to a righteous cause, such imagery reinforces the idea of civic and political engagement as warfare and conquest. Fellow citizens who disagree are enemy combatants rather than deliberative partners, and one listens carefully to their perspectives to gather military intelligence rather than to discern common ground and opportunities for respectful compromise.

But to my mind, good democratic citizens don't just adopt an ideology, identify a cause, and do everything they can within the law of the land to bring society closer to that vision. They also recognize a distinction between the private and public realms, between personal convictions about the best ways to live and the more complicated process of figuring out how we live together. Good citizens recognize that even if they believe in absolute Truth (religious or otherwise), this never will translate perfectly into a government run by fellow citizens. So while Christians, for instance, may believe with passionate conviction that "Jesus is the Way, the Truth, and the Life," they must also recognize that our life together in a pluralistic democracy requires that we make room for others.

"Making room" for others doesn't mean simply giving them the legal right to do battle in the political arena, and may the best politicos win. It means making a sincere effort to understand not only *what* others value, but *why*—to engage imaginatively with the way they see the world, and to meet opposing arguments on their strongest terms, not merely pinpoint their weaknesses in pursuit of rhetorical victory. This sort of deliberative generosity certainly doesn't imply that we will ultimately agree with our opponents, but it might help us to better recognize the reasonableness of other perspectives, and make us more willing to strive for compromise and accommodation, even—*especially*—when we hold the upper hand politically. Christians with a good sense of history will recognize the danger that exists when religious and political power are too closely intertwined; Christians with a good sense of theology, I would add, might also recognize that such a pairing is what Jesus himself rejected, despite numerous entreaties and temptations to assume such power himself.

I realize it would be naïve to expect that all politics will model such virtues. But we would do well to remember that civic *education* should be about more than just politician training. If education has any role in providing a vision for strengthening our democracy, then ideals deserve a prominent role in the preparation of our citizens. Just settling for the simpler dynamic of adversarial politics shortchanges our democratic possibilities. Anyone who takes a long look at the tenor and quality of American political discourse, and the deep discontent and profound alienation many citizens feel, might agree that it's important to aim higher.

Adversarial politics are hardly the fault of conservative Christian homeschoolers alone, of course, or political conservatives more generally. Many GenJ supporters point to similar tactics by the political Left. They would also likely argue that public school civics curricula inculcate their own ideology, one hostile to conservatism and especially the role of religion in the public square. While this may be the case in some settings, this is probably giving public school civics courses too much credit; few will be as powerful in the shaping of citizens as GenJ appears to be for its members.

Consider what public school civic education generally consists of: textbooks stripped bare of potentially controversial material in a desire to boost sales to the widest possible swath of districts and communities; teachers and administrators understandably skittish of having their students directly engage in politics; and a curriculum narrowed to the point where names, dates, and events constitute the bulk of civics instruction. Numerous reports and white papers have emerged in recent years decrying the lack of attention paid to fostering civic engagement among public school students.

Researchers advocate several ways to reverse this trend, including encouraging students to cultivate their own political understandings and convictions; providing students with the opportunity to observe role models and connect with peers who share their commitments; and helping students develop a sense of efficacy that they truly can make a difference. This sounds a lot like Generation Joshua—it offers students an identity, a cause, and a hands-on opportunity to impact the world around them. Can public schools spark a similar engagement, or does their required political neutrality short-circuit the type of passion evident in GenJ participants? And can this passion be fostered in a way that also makes room for respectful dialogue and reasonable disagreement? I believe it can, but it will require a different set of priorities—for both Generation Joshua and our public schools.

I figure it's time to pay a visit to the source of Generation Joshua, and what is clearly the most influential homeschool organization in the world, the Home School Legal Defense Association. While its presence has already made itself felt in previous chapters, I want to hear directly from its cofounders and highest profile leaders, Michael Farris and J. Michael Smith.

The Home School Legal Defense Association (and the campus of Patrick Henry College) sits off the local state highway in Purcellville, Virginia, a small town about fifty miles west of Washington, D.C. When I visit in 2007, it consists of five dormitory buildings for PHC student housing and a much larger building called Founders Hall. The latter serves as office headquarters for HSLDA and provides PHC with classrooms, cafeteria, library, and administrative space. A few hundred yards across the lawn, however, heavy construction equipment is busy at work on a large student center. Estimated to cost more than thirty million dollars when completed, it will add classroom, library, and dining space to the campus.

A quarter-century earlier, two lawyers who were homeschooling their own children found themselves starting to defend other homeschool families in court, and in 1983, Mike Farris and Mike Smith formed HSLDA. Now their organization employs more than sixty staff and counts approximately eighty-five thousand homeschool families as members, a quarter of a million children total. HSLDA claims to respond to more than ten thousand inquiries each year from members who have questions or concerns, ranging from simple regulatory requirements to full-blown confrontations with state authorities.

HSLDA provides a variety of resources beyond legal information and support to its members as well, including advice on working with special-needs children, homeschooling at the high school level, preparing transcripts, and applying to colleges. At the core of their philosophy is the conviction that parents are simply the best teachers for their children, and any parent—given the desire and willingness to work hard—can homeschool his or her child.

HSLDA has been particularly effective at monitoring the regulatory climate surrounding homeschooling and advocating for reduced requirements and oversight whenever possible. In some cases, they actively sponsor such legislation at the state and even federal level, and other times they move forcefully to derail proposals calling for greater regulation that arise occasionally in state legislatures. Friend and foe alike recognize their effectiveness in this regard, especially in terms of mobilizing homeschoolers themselves to express their views on pending legislation directly with their elected representatives. Former congressman Bill Goodling, who chaired the House Committee on Education and the Workforce, told the *Wall Street Journal* in 2003 that homeschoolers were the most effective education lobby on Capitol Hill.

With this status in mind, Farris regularly encourages homeschoolers to stay aware and engaged in the political process. "Our kids need to understand voting and they need to know how the political process works," he urges members. "Take your children to see your city council or state government in action. Go listen to a political candidate speak. Read the newspaper aloud and discuss the issues of the day with your children. Citizenship is best learned by doing." HSLDA helps organize yearly homeschool days at state capitols, such as Maryland's "Shine on the State House Day" and Indiana's "Home School Day at the Capitol." Members are urged to make appointments with their representatives and prepare baked goods with a note saying, "Good things are made at home, including education." Parents are encouraged to bring well-behaved children and to help their kids prepare a response in case they're asked what they like about being homeschooled. HSLDA frequently reminds their members "how effective capitol lobby days are in preventing bad legislation. If legislators from either party meet a good homeschool family face to face, it makes it hard for them to vote to restrict homeschooling. If they never meet a homeschooler, they will often vote against homeschooling when given the opportunity."

But not everyone—even within the homeschooling community—is pleased with HSLDA's political involvement and clout. Critics accuse the organization of habitually framing issues in dire, even apocalyptic terms, and frequently overreacting with adversarial zeal when a more measured, collaborative approach might foster better relations with other relevant stakeholders, whether they be legislators, public school officials, or community leaders.

The most prominent example of this approach occurred during what Farris reputedly calls homeschooling's finest hour, when HSLDA mobilized an avalanche of phone calls and faxes to Capitol Hill in 1994 to protest language in the massive Elementary and Secondary Education Act (ESEA) reappropriation bill. The contested sentence required states to verify that each school district has teachers "certified to teach in the subject area to which he or she is assigned." HSLDA interpreted this as a possible means by which states could require homeschool parents to be certified as well, and their emergency mobilization in response to the reappropriation bill (known as HR 6) forced a quick alteration in the language to specifically exclude homeschoolers from such requirements.

Many other prominent homeschool organizations and leaders criticized HSLDA's hyperkinetic response to HR 6. They felt the bill was not intended to apply to homeschoolers and, since any final vote would be months away, they believed their concerns could be addressed through more measured, nonconfrontational means. Raymond Moore, a pioneer in the homeschool movement, summarized this view when he accused Farris of "losing crucial homeschool friends by pushing state and federal alarm buttons, alienating state and federal legislators and officials by treating them as pressure-vulnerable political hacks instead of befriending them, informing them, and reasoning with them as statesmen, as we have done for years."

But the lesson HSLDA apparently learned from that episode was that their tactics worked. As former congressman Dick Armey observed, "They made a big impact on people's minds that fateful day. They got a taste of the game and found out they could be a major player." Not only does HSLDA employ the same pattern of alarm and mobilization on newly arising issues, but they continue to use the HR 6 controversy itself as political ammunition—such as when they warned members in 2006 that Congressman George Miller (who authored those contested lines about teacher certification) was poised to lead the House Education Committee if the Democrats gained control in that year's elections.

More recently, HSLDA played a significant role in a high-profile controversy in 2008, when a California appellate court ruling implied that parents need a teaching credential in order to homeschool their children. HSLDA joined numerous homeschool organizations—as well as California's governor, attorney general, and superintendent of public instruction—in condemning the decision and urging a rehearing by the court. Michael Farris participated in this rehearing, after which the court ruled that homeschooling qualifies under the private school exception, which doesn't require teachers to be licensed by the state. (Significantly, however, the court let stand its earlier contention that parents do not have a constitutional right to homeschool their children—and closed with the observation that California regulations, with their "near absence of objective criteria and oversight for home schooling," could benefit from "additional clarity.")

Some critics question HSLDA's advocacy regarding issues not directly related to homeschooling, such as strong support for state bans on same-sex marriage. HSLDA counters that since courts have based parental rights on "western civilization concepts of the family," it's essential to preserve that traditional concept of marriage, or "the foundation upon which parental rights are based is completely removed." Western civilization is based on biblical precepts, Farris asserts, and "it is impossible to say that the God of the Bible would sanction rights of homosexual marriage." This conservative Christian worldview of HSLDA—and the political stances that emerge from it—leads many homeschoolers who do not share those beliefs to view HSLDA as indifferent or even antagonistic toward more "inclusive" state and national homeschool organizations.

As Hanna Rosin's book *God's Harvard* describes, the HSLDA kingdom is hardly free from internal turmoil either. Nearly a third of Patrick Henry College faculty resigned in 2006 to protest what they saw as Farris's heavy-handed intrusion on their academic freedom. More recent was the abrupt resignation of Ned Ryun as director of Generation Joshua in the summer of 2007. "Dissent is not allowed in Mike Farris' world," Ryun wrote afterwards. "I hate to disappoint some who think that freedom of thought and conscience are allowed at HSLDA." Ryun's disagreement with Farris over the official endorsement of Mike Huckabee by HSLDA's political action committee appeared to be the breaking point, but after he left, Ryun commented, "I think HSLDA members need to ask, is the defense of homeschooling still the priority for HSLDA, or are there other things that are priority? And really, what are membership dues being used for?"

Despite these various organizational controversies, I'm more interested in spending my brief time with Michael Farris exploring the possibilities of common ground between homeschoolers and policymakers when considering the relative interests of parents, children, and society. Farris— selected by *Education Week* as one of one hundred individuals who shaped American education "in ways big and small, for better or sometimes for worse" in the twentieth century—is an intense personality. He sits across from me at his desk in Founders Hall, the wall behind him filled with framed plaques, certificates, and diplomas.

When I ask Farris if he thinks there are families who don't do a good job with homeschooling, he acknowledges there are some, but then quickly turns to the familiar comparison with public schools: "Public education systematically does a worse job than homeschooling families who do a less-than-great job," he asserts. The families who don't do at least as well as public schools, he contends, are "very, very few."

"Anecdotally we might have a sense that there aren't a lot of home-school families doing a poor job," I say, "but how do we *know* that, because in so many states we don't even know who is homeschooling?"

"No system is going to be perfect," he responds, "and we have to decide if we're going to be a free country or not. And a free country has to allow people to make mistakes. And if the goal is to prohibit *any* child from receiving a substandard education, then not only do we need to license and rigorously regulate homeschoolers, we've got to shut down the public school system." Disdain fills Farris's voice. "I mean just entirely, it should be shut down, because the fact that high school graduates can't rank order common fractions or write a normal paragraph—this is utterly unacceptable."

For Farris, the value of trying to protect all children is far outweighed by the principle of parental freedom to direct their children's education without state involvement. When I suggest that requiring homeschoolers to take a basic skills test wouldn't be tremendously intrusive, Farris responds, "The problem is that all of this is entirely subjective. There is no such thing as an objective standard. A test is fair, according to due process standards, only if it measures the content of what you've been taught." This is what testing experts refer to as *content validity.* No test for homeschoolers can meet the demands of content validity, Farris argues, because their curricula are so frequently customized for individual children. "You'd have to write an individualized, content-valid standardized test for every child that's being homeschooled in America. You just can't do that."

Farris raises one example of how content validity becomes more complicated in the homeschooling context. "I won a case on content validity in the supreme court of South Carolina where they tried to test home-

school teachers. You just simply can't do it." Farris describes with satisfaction how James Popham, a prominent expert in educational testing
and measurement, "got his comeuppance in that case, because he thought
he could get a bunch of professional educators together and judge the
content and validity of a math and reading exam for homeschool teachers.
I was able to demonstrate to the satisfaction of the supreme court of South
Carolina that public school educators didn't know what they were talking
about when it comes to homeschooling."

What Farris refers to here is an attempt by South Carolina in the
early 1990s to require homeschool parents to pass an examination intended for college students applying to teacher licensure programs. The
state supreme court overturned a lower court decision on the grounds
that the test makers were not sufficiently familiar with homeschooling to
determine whether test questions were appropriate measures of what is
required to effectively homeschool one's child.

I agree that the challenges of homeschooling and public school teaching are distinct enough that requiring homeschool parents to obtain state
licensure doesn't make much sense. But imposing such a requirement—
or something akin to the South Carolina teacher assessment—is a far cry
from the idea of basic skills assessments for homeschool students themselves. *All* children, homeschooled or not, have a fundamental interest in
gaining basic skills of literacy and numeracy.

When Farris tells me that "unless you have standardized curriculum,
it's impossible to create content validity—you just simply can't do it," he
is vastly overstating his case. "When do you learn fractions?" he asks. "Is
that the third-grade test or is that the fourth-grade test? When do you
learn the word 'undoubtedly'? The sequence of learning will vary from
curriculum to curriculum. All those things, I think, make the pragmatics
of it incredibly difficult—it would take *multimillions* of dollars to even
approach a curriculum-based examination that would be broad enough.
Maybe it's not impossible, but it's highly improbable and extraordinarily
expensive, and not worth it."

Farris's concerns about curriculum sequence are not without merit,
and any test would need to focus on skills basic enough that widespread
agreement would exist that if a student hadn't developed a particular skill
(say, multiplying two-digit numbers or comprehending a short passage
from *Charlotte's Web* by eighth grade), then further questions about the

effectiveness of the child's homeschooling ought to be asked. Even then, the assumption shouldn't automatically be that homeschooling has failed that child—plenty of other variables deserve consideration as well. But contrary to Farris's assertion, such a basic test need not dictate the broader shape and content of a homeschool curriculum. I'm confident that most of the homeschoolers profiled in this book would pass such tests, and yet their curricula vary widely in method and content.

But Farris disagrees with regulation on a more fundamental level as well. "I don't see why education is different than feeding a kid or clothing a kid or providing them with shelter," he says. "They're all essential. And we don't have a system of prior restraints or testing on those areas of parenting. We have a system of, 'If we the government can demonstrate abuse, then we prosecute you.' That to me is the standard that should be followed in homeschooling."

In response, I point out that a parents' caretaking of their children *is* tested—it becomes clear to outsiders if a child is not fed, clothed, or housed. But Farris believes the same informal community oversight is just as effective when it comes to the basic educational needs of homeschoolers. "*Every* child," Farris asserts, gets examined informally by extended family and people in the community. "They've got grandparents, they've got aunts and uncles, they've got people they interact with at church. They've got all kinds of people that see them on a regular basis." He offers the example of kids reading aloud during Sunday school class. "There are going to be people who hear them read and see them in context and if there is genuine abuse going on, just as concerned citizens should turn people in where they find out that the kids are starving to death, there is a mechanism in every state when kids are being educationally starved. It's a form of neglect. And so we've got the system already built; we've got the legal standards already in existence."

The other problem with regulatory proposals, Farris adds, is that homeschooling is "so dominantly religious." Regulating it, therefore, violates prohibitions again excessive entanglement with government. "You cannot give government officials discretion to license religious activity," he argues. "It's an issue of speech; this is religious speech."

While plenty of homeschoolers would contest Farris's claim that homeschooling is largely religious in nature, this question of religious freedom does complicate the issue. The courts themselves appear conflicted about how much religious conviction should matter in protecting parental interests, not to mention what distinguishes religious conviction from other deeply held beliefs often so central to parenting decisions.

Some states have a "religious freedom" component to their legal code, and some specifically extend this to homeschooling regulations. In Virginia, for example, families who file for a religious exemption avoid all other requirements imposed on the state's homeschoolers, such as submitting a description of their curriculum and having their child's performance evaluated on a yearly basis. Approximately one-quarter of Virginia's homeschoolers are granted religious exemptions, and school districts rarely turn down these requests. As one administrator told a local newspaper, she has no way to judge whether parents have genuine religious beliefs or if they are simply abusing the law to avoid additional requirements. Not surprisingly, HSLDA would like to see religious exemptions available in all states. "It makes no sense for government to regulate how you worship in a church," argues HSLDA attorney Scott Woodruff. "Educating my child is a form of worship."

Perhaps the biggest item on HSLDA's agenda, however, is their effort to champion a Parental Rights Amendment to the United States Constitution. "This is the fight of our generation," Farris claims, pointing to a "growing trend of anti-parent bias in the federal courts." He raises particular concern that Congress may eventually ratify the UN Convention on the Rights of the Child (UNCRC). Currently, state officials can override parental authority only if they can prove in court that parents have abused or neglected their children—but the UNCRC, Farris warns, would give our government "the right to override every parental decision if it deemed the parent's choice contrary to the child's best interest." HSLDA sees a Parental Rights Amendment as the best defense against attempts by "internationalist social workers and child-care 'experts' to substitute their judgment for that of parents."

Some advocates of increased homeschool regulation propose a "multicultural curriculum" requirement, arguing that democratic citizens need to learn to engage respectfully with the diversity of beliefs and perspectives of fellow citizens. Not surprisingly, Farris—along with every homeschooler I've ever met—rejects such a proposal. As a homeschool parent, he says, he would want his children to "learn about a variety of other views, but I wouldn't want the government to coerce me to teach *my own view*, much less anybody else's view. I just don't think the government can dictate the content *of anything*. They can't dictate the content of tolerance or pluralism." Farris's tone becomes even more passionate: "And if they're going to force you, upon penalty of some criminal sanction, to teach tolerance, I view this as the jack-booted thugs trying to promote tolerance. To me, it's utterly inconsistent. I mean, why would we let tyrants teach tolerance?"

When I suggest to Farris that part of respectful citizenship amidst ethical disagreement is understanding *why* someone believes in a particular way, he agrees, but then contends that the secular Left is more blameworthy in this regard. "The Left has no clue as to what's going on in the minds of the Religious Right," he says, shaking his head. "They just don't understand us at all. They don't understand the differences between various theological viewpoints. There are huge differences in why we think some things. I think that Christian civic education does a better job of understanding alternative viewpoints than the reverse, by a long measure. And so I think that there's value for everybody to get out more and to listen to each other."

As we conclude, Farris offers me a closing statement of sorts on the question of regulating homeschooling. "It's one thing to operate an education system for the willing and say, 'If you want this, come get it; if you don't want it, you don't have to come get it, you can go do your own thing.' But when the government then tries to come over to the unwilling and say, 'Yeah, you're doing your own thing but we're gonna regulate so it's as much like our thing as we can,' we've lost the distinction between the willing and unwilling. We've lost the difference between freedom and socialism. Having a well-educated people to run the machinery of something other than a free republic isn't worth it." He shakes his head dismissively. "I really don't want to play that game. Does my family get to decide what my family does or somebody else's family? Do *you* get to tell me how to raise my kids or do *I* get to tell me how to raise my kids? Do I get to tell *you* how to raise *your* kids? No It's self-determination and there's spheres of authority. And when we lose respect for those spheres of authority, we've lost the essence of what it means to have a free country and a free nation."

I rise to leave, shaking his hand and thanking him for his time. "You're welcome," he says, then adds with obvious sarcasm and no trace of a smile, "I've never thought about these matters before."

After exiting Farris's office, I step across the hall to Smith's office. In contrast with his partner, Mike Smith's demeanor is genial and easygoing. While Smith clearly has firm convictions about homeschooling, his responses to my questions are not self-assured declarations delivered with a tone of ultimate certainty. Contrary to Farris, he seems willing to consider what I have to say before responding. He is certainly the better public face of HSLDA.

"What we try not to do is tell homeschoolers how to teach their kids," Smith explains to me. "We have resources available here, we have high school coordinators, we have special-needs coordinators available that our members can call and they can get help. But we don't tell them what curriculum; we don't tell them how much time they should spend on math, science, and so on. We do not want to get into that, because we believe in parental freedom and parents need to be making those choices themselves."

I wonder how much of this emphasis on homeschooler freedom extends to the students themselves as they get older. "A common view of adolescent development," I say, "is that there needs to be a sort of gradual process of helping kids to become independent, to learn how to think for themselves. I wonder how you conceive of that—I know HSLDA was opposed to an Arizona bill allowing children sixteen years or older to decide whether they wanted to go to public school or not. So clearly that degree of autonomy is not acceptable to you?"

"No," Smith replies quickly. "I just think until a child reaches adulthood, whatever the states determine—eighteen, let's say it is—that the parent should be able to make the important decisions unless it's shown that they're being abusive. Otherwise, I think they should have absolute authority to make those kinds of decisions. I find that you don't have to teach children to be independent," he says, starting to chuckle. "They just seem to naturally progress that way! I trust parents to make those decisions, and I don't see the government being any wiser."

"How important do you think it is for homeschool students to engage with ethical diversity," I ask, "with people who believe differently about deeply held moral—"

Smith interrupts. "I don't think it's important at all, if they're *taught* properly. Ninety-seven, ninety-eight percent of our members say they're born-again Christians. If they're Christians and they read the Bible and they teach them what Jesus said, they're going to love their enemies. That's really hard to do, but one thing is they can't be prejudiced and biased, because the New Testament clearly teaches against it."

Several times during our conversation, Smith mentions the confidence he has in homeschool parents, that they are "trying to do the best for their children" and will make the right decisions. He believes this perspective should form the basis for any approach to homeschool regulation. "As long as we keep the presumption that parents act in the best interests of their kids," he asserts, "then we'll be okay. But if there's a presumption that the *government* has to meet these needs because parents aren't, then we're *not* gonna be okay, because government cannot love a child, cannot raise a child."

I ask Smith if he would agree that, at least in some cases, parents don't live up to that presumption, and the child needs to be in a setting other than homeschooling.

"There's no doubt about that," he acknowledges. "It happens and it's unfortunate. But what we're saying is, just because a few are bad parents, let's not impose all these regulations on *good* parents. Let's continue to presume that parents act in the best interest of their kids. And a lot of times, this is the problem with social workers. When they come to that house, they presume—they've gotten some report, *it could be anonymous*, it could be *fabricated to hurt the family*—'Okay, got a report, the parents are bad, here we go.' *That's* what we try to work against."

As I've mentioned, HSLDA sends out regular "state alerts" to their members, many of them describing harassment of members by social workers or public school officials. While it's impossible to gain any sense of perspective from these reports about how often homeschool parents are investigated on spurious charges, or what percentage of social workers presume homeschool parents' guilt, it's true that some public officials hold unfair stereotypes of homeschoolers and at least occasionally overstep their authority when interacting with families.

Again, however, it seems to me to be a balancing question: not wanting to impose overly burdensome and intrusive regulations on parents who do a good job homeschooling just because of the likely few who don't. "I wonder if there is room for a very low level of regulation that is not highly intrusive that could be agreed upon by the vast majority of homeschool parents," I say. "For instance, that there be an occasional, *very* basic check of basic literacy and numeracy that any kid whose parents are doing a halfway decent job will have no trouble with—but it will help to flag the situations where there just isn't education going on. It would not only help protect the interests of some kids but it would perhaps also be another validation of homeschooling's effectiveness."

Smith pauses for a moment before responding. "I wouldn't be for it," he finally says. "There are a lot of states that regulate and there are very few states where there isn't any kind of notice of intent; there are only five or six states where there isn't some kind of regulation. But I know in those five or six states that it's not going to be any different in terms of whether kids are being educationally neglected than these other states where they have high regulation. I know that innately; I can't prove it statistically."

He then adds that when they compare homeschooler test scores in states that require testing to scores from homeschoolers who do it voluntarily, the results are similar. But here we run into the same problem of self-selection: it's reasonable to assume that in states where testing is not required, parents who do a lousy job with homeschooling probably won't bother to have their kids tested. So it's not surprising that test scores from a low-regulation state will compare favorably with states where testing is mandatory.

Smith continues, "I think we have to keep regulation to nil or minimum, because I know if we start at 'merely literacy'—how do we determine that? Well, we have to have a test. Well, what kind of test is that? Then we're gonna have to get a curriculum to *drive that* and then the next thing you know, and it won't take long, we're gonna be back to where we were forty years ago!" Both Smith and Farris depict any sort of test—no matter how focused on basic skills—as inevitably and unreasonably dictating the entire shape of homeschooler curricula.

"I think the reason homeschooling is so successful," Smith concludes, "is because we put the responsibility on the parent to do the right thing.

And the parents I'm familiar with and who are doing testing and joining HSLDA, they're just doing a great job, and I don't think they should be subjected to proving that to the state."

With Aaron Branson in mind, I present Smith with the anonymous example of a teenager who is still counting on his fingers—and in this family situation, there hasn't been any significant opportunity for outside accountability or intervention.

Smith surprises me by questioning whether basic math skills are an essential form of literacy. "If you're gonna get into that, maybe next critics will say they need computer skills. And that's gonna happen." He says the next three words with slight pauses between each to emphasize his point, albeit with a smile. "*It. Will. Happen!* Every time you get these bureaucrats involved and the politicians and the legislators, they all have different ideas about what literacy and self-sufficiency is. I don't think it's workable."

This refusal to give ground on testing even the most basic of skills leaves us with no reliable way to identify homeschoolers whose fundamental educational interests are being neglected. I mention to Smith that in all the research studies of homeschooling I've read, I have yet to find one where the homeschooler sample is not self-selected or somehow limited in a way that doesn't allow for generalizations to homeschooling in general. Comparing public school and homeschool student performance on tests isn't possible, because it's either optional for homeschoolers or they take a different test, or parents administer the tests or avoid them altogether by not registering. "So what this leads me to," I say, "is that while I think there is ample evidence that a sizeable chunk of homeschoolers are doing a very good job, there aren't any hard data to tell us about the other end of the spectrum."

"I just don't think it's significant," Smith replies. "If I thought it was significant, I wouldn't make the representations that we make. I just don't believe it's significant at all. Because I know moms. The moms who are typically testing kids are the ones who are a little more insecure about how they're doing. They want to make sure. They have to be able to show their in-laws: 'Look.'"

I'm not convinced. "Is it possible, though, that the moms who really aren't doing a good job are the ones who don't even bother to show up at the conventions to talk to you?"

"Possible," Smith concedes. "But again, if it's happening, it's a very insignificant number of homeschool families."

"So would the ultimate goal of HSLDA, regulation-wise, be a place like Illinois," I ask, "where parents don't have to report, register, anything?"

Smith nods. "Ultimately, yes. But we also tend to be realistic. I mean, there are organizations that stand for the proposition of no compulsory attendance. Do I think that would be good? Probably, but it's not gonna happen. I mean, that's unrealistic. So we operate within what's realistic, incrementally making changes, but ultimately to get to the point where we have as few regulations as possible."

I've spent hundreds of hours reading HSLDA materials, considering their arguments, and observing their strategies to promote homeschooling and reduce regulations. I understand why they keep careful track of legislative developments, and I recognize that their role as an advocacy organization is to put homeschooling's best foot forward. While I find their tone overly combative, I realize that some of this is in response to uninformed criticism and even antagonism on the part of some public education officials and other outsiders.

But there's no good excuse for their ongoing distortion of research. I've already mentioned their controversial use of the Rudner study, but plenty of other studies get oversimplified into sound-bite assertions that simply are not supported by the details of the research. While the fine print of studies such as Brian Ray's *Home Educated and Now Adults* advises readers to "keep in mind the limitations of representativeness and generalizability," the glossy HSLDA pamphlet trumpets: "The results confirm what homeschoolers have thought for years: 'No problem here.'" Such "evidence" then becomes widely cited elsewhere, such as in the gubernatorial proclamation of Nebraska Home Education Week, which asserted that "dozens of studies confirm that children who are educated at home score significantly above average on national achievement tests."

In spring 2008 HSLDA announced plans for a major new study of homeschoolers' academic achievement. But like the Rudner study they sponsored a decade ago, it draws from volunteers who have already opted to test their children through mail-order testing services. Any conclusions about homeschoolers' academic achievement drawn from a study of volunteers who administer the test to their own children may serve as potent public relations material but will tell us little about the big picture of homeschooling.

For all its political influence and vast resources, however, HSLDA is hardly the final word on homeschooling, nor the only conservative Christian organization offering programs designed to encourage religiously informed citizenship. There are plenty of groups whose vision of Christian citizenship is at least as adversarial as Generation Joshua, but in the interlude that follows, I learn about one organization, and one student, who follow a different path to civic engagement

CIVIC ENGAGEMENT DONE DIFFERENTLY

Six years of following Generation Joshua gives me confidence in my characterizations of the program, but they remain broad brushstrokes. Quite likely within GenJ—and certainly outside of it—plenty of conservative Christian homeschoolers have a different idea of what constitutes good citizenship and desirable civic engagement.

Consider the example of Noah Grant. I meet Noah while giving a public lecture about homeschooling and civic engagement at a New England university. Now a college freshman, he and his five siblings had been homeschooled their whole lives, and he considers himself a politically active conservative Christian. He's familiar with Generation Joshua (his family holds an HSLDA membership), but he had been more involved with a somewhat similar program called TeenPact instead.

Like many conservative Christian homeschoolers, Noah sees his educational experience as a soul-shaping endeavor much broader than formal academics. While religious beliefs certainly permeated his homeschooling, it went deeper than that: "Everything in our life was focused around the Bible," he emphasizes, "not just the education aspects."

TeenPact was a great experience for Noah. In many ways similar to Generation Joshua, it describes its mission as "training young people to be leaders who will impact the nation and the world for Jesus Christ." Involvement in TeenPact begins with a four-day class at the state capital that includes mock legislature sessions, and then continues with participation in civic and political events as they arise (for instance, TeenPact teams attend the annual "Values Voter Summit" in Washington, D.C.).

Many of Noah's friends were involved with Generation Joshua, but he preferred the TeenPact approach. "I think that government's important, but what I liked about TeenPact was it focused on your whole life as a Christian, which includes your civic participation but so much more than that: how you live your life toward others, serving others, leadership. It involved everything, whereas I felt like Generation Joshua was just too focused on the political. And sometimes I think that parts of our movement get too focused on the battleground for political victory as if that were the most important thing, and it's not."

Echoing this perspective in a *Practical Homeschooling* magazine article, a teenage girl writes about TeenPact: "I know what you're thinking: 'But my son or daughter doesn't want to be a politician! Why should they go to TeenPact?' I don't want to be the first female President of the United States either; I want to get married and be a mother. But I also want to be a good citizen, I want to know how to make a difference, understand legislation, and be aware of current events."

The biggest benefit of being involved with TeenPact, Noah tells me, is learning that "you want to be able to defend your beliefs but you don't want to do it bombastically, you don't want to do it aggressively, because your Christian witness is far more important than winning any political issue. And in every discussion you want to show grace to the other side and be respectful." This is vital, he says, because "both sides often stereotype the other side as the one who has no sincerity and wants to destroy America."

Although many of Noah's friends encouraged him to enroll at Patrick Henry College, he felt it was time to step into a more diverse context than homeschooling or PHC provided. "You have to hit the world at some point and learn to stand up for your beliefs and learn to test what's right and not right," he tells me. "You don't want to just blindly believe what your parents told you—at some point you're going to have to begin figuring out for yourself, 'Do I really believe this is true?' And I felt like I was ready to do that for college." It hasn't been easy, he admits. "Not being surrounded by a ton of Christians has been very different," he says. "And I'm glad for the challenge. It's not good to believe something just because everyone around you believes it." He has learned even more about the importance of genuine, respectful interaction with people whose beliefs differ from his own. "It has been eye opening," he admits, "to get a lot more firsthand interaction with people where I may disagree with them." He uses the abortion controversy as a telling example: "I now see what makes them believe so strongly in a woman's right to choose."

Besides the ethical diversity of his college environment, Noah also sings in a community chorus in which most participants are politically liberal. This has provided "plenty of contact with people who have vastly different belief systems. It has been fun to talk to them; sometimes it's gotten heated but usually it's a pretty good discussion," he says. Noah believes these interactions have been valuable learning opportunities: "It's just as important a skill to be able to analyze things that secular people are saying and learn to determine what you think is true and what you think is not true, and learning to work with that."

If America were full of conservative and liberal Noah Grants, it seems likely that our public square—while still abounding with spirited debate—would be a more hospitable and respectful environment. Religious convictions would obviously still be part of the civic conversation, and they should be, lest we ignore the powerful and legitimate ways in which religion shapes many citizens' beliefs about what matters to them and why. But the conversation would likely create more room for genuine consideration of opposing viewpoints—an elusive state of affairs for the next family I visit.

6

THE CARROLL FAMILY
"Public School Is the Enemy"

Oregon often conjures images of rugged coastline, rain-soaked greenery, and liberal environmentalism. I soon discover this is not the Oregon I'm headed for. Getting to the Carrolls' home involves flying into Portland and renting a four-wheel-drive to traverse the Cascade Mountains, which separate those traditional images of Oregon from the high desert beyond. This first visit is in early April—early enough, in fact, that I'm forced to creep through a snowstorm that hits the mountain pass.

I'm headed for an elk ranch. I'm not sure I even knew before now that elk were raised domestically, but this is a full-scale enterprise about twenty miles outside of Cedar Point, the closest town. As I turn off the empty paved highway and on to a dirt road that meanders toward the ranch, I'm struck by how isolated this place must feel from the rest of the world, and wonder how much this feeling is amplified by schooling at home.

I pull up to the Carroll home at seven-thirty in the morning, just after their breakfast. Cynthia and Roger Carroll have four children: the eldest, Abby, is seventeen years old on my first visit; her sister Leah is fifteen; Joshua is thirteen; and Wayne is seven. They live in a double-wide trailer surrounded by various barns, sheds, and lean-to structures. Several old swing sets, a trampoline, and a concrete slab with a basketball hoop complete the immediate surroundings. Beyond that, however, are nearly a thousand acres of grazing land for the two hundred or so elk currently residing there. As the sole full-time employee, Roger is responsible for the many day-to-day operations of the ranch.

Cynthia greets me at the door, dressed in blue jeans and a flannel shirt, her shoulder-length brown hair pulled into a loose bun. The older kids are already outside doing chores with their dad. Cynthia offers me some coffee, and then returns to her spot on the couch. She starts by giving me a little of their homeschooling history.

"We had our kids in public school until Abby was halfway through sixth grade," Cynthia explains. "Roger had always wanted to homeschool, but he never really pushed it. I mean, the kids were doing great in school, enjoying it, and I was able to be involved there as well. But after Wayne came along, I had one over at the middle school, two in the elementary school, and Wayne at home, and we couldn't keep up anymore with what was"—she raises her hand in a helpless gesture—"you know, we spent hours every evening going through their work. We wanted to know, what are you learning? And going over their homework with them and making sure that they were understanding things. We said to ourselves, 'You know, this is kind of silly; we can just do this at home!'"

And that's what Cynthia initially attempted: replicating the schoolhouse in the living room. She researched all sorts of curricula, pored over homeschool catalogs, and talked to other homeschool parents. "It was a disaster," she admits. "I tried to create that public school at home, basically. This is something I've heard over and over again from homeschoolers. And it just wasn't fun at all, and it wasn't really working. Then I found this." She holds up a thick binder labeled "Sonlight."

Sonlight is a popular curricular option for homeschoolers. Started in 1992, the company and its offerings have steadily expanded to a full preschool through high school menu of choices. Its Web site includes not only product information but links to online Sonlight Forums, where homeschool parents can exchange ideas, ask questions, and offer suggestions both to the company's curriculum developers and one another. Sonlight provides a core curriculum of history, Bible, language arts, and science, and then recommends other curriculum vendors for math and various electives. Cynthia says she spent about $1,500 this year on their materials, and she generally can sell their used copies to others online and make back a decent chunk of their cost.

Wayne, a quiet but friendly seven-year-old with short brown hair and an easy smile, comes in and sits next to his mother on the couch. "You ready to get going?" she asks, nudging him with her shoulder. He nods, and she reaches for a Bible on the coffee table in front of them. She begins reading the day's selection, which tells of the arrest and trial of Jesus in Jerusalem. Near the end of the passage, she stops. "Okay, your turn," she

says, handing him the Bible. Wayne complies, reading slowly and halt-
ingly, but with few errors, for about five minutes.

Just as he concludes, his three older siblings make their way through
the side door from outside, hanging up their jackets and kicking off their
boots. After greeting me with smiles and soft hellos, they head straight
toward their bedrooms in the back. They spend much of the morning
there, coming out occasionally to ask Cynthia questions about their work.
As I've discovered already, homeschooling provides tremendous flexibility in terms of schedule and structure. I wonder how this looks in a household whose rhythms must fit within the myriad needs of a thousand-acre
ranch. "Is there a general sort of timeframe that the schooling day usually
occupies?" I ask.

"I try to get Wayne's stuff done in the morning and then that frees me
up in the afternoon to tackle the other kids' schoolwork or work on bills
or anything else I have to do," Cynthia explains. "But with Wayne, his
stuff is pretty easy to get through. If I really sat down and just did what
they recommended, I'd probably have his stuff done in two-and-a-half
hours. But I spread it out a little bit throughout the day. There are some
days where he'll just go hang out with his dad all day and he'll catch up
the next day."

The older kids, Cynthia tells me, get started around eight in the morning and—if they stay focused—finish around one or so. If not, they work
during the evening as well. The girls in particular have little problem
keeping up the pace, Cynthia says. "Besides me just trying to engage in
some discussion on what they've been reading and working on, I pretty
much leave them alone."

The girls play a variety of instruments—guitar, mandolin, fiddle, and
piano—and give private lessons in homes and at their church. They don't
read music, Cynthia tells me, but they haven't found that to be a real limitation in their teaching or their own performing. Abby is even contemplating a career in music. "The music industry kind of scares me," Cynthia
admits, "but if she could find a good, solid Christian band, that style of
music, I'd love to see her join up with a band and tour for a couple years."

The kids also attend an intensive music camp for a week each summer over in Garrison, about an hour's drive away. "They bring in some
pretty high-quality instructors from around the country," Cynthia says.
"They've gone four years now and we've gotten to know a lot of the kids

who come back each year. It's kind of the highlight-of-their-year type of thing." On the whole, however, these types of group activities are pretty rare for the Carrolls. There are some homeschool co-ops over in Garrison, but the two-hour round trip discourages them from getting involved.

Later in the morning, Joshua emerges from his bedroom, math book in hand, waiting patiently for his mother to finish talking with me so she can review his work. Joshua is a taller image of his younger brother, but with a typical adolescent reserve around unfamiliar adults. He and his mom review several problems together, and then he settles himself at the dining room table to work on his own.

Even with Cynthia's college coursework in math and science, she acknowledges that Joshua's curriculum may eventually exceed her current knowledge base, particularly with physics and calculus. She doesn't see this as a huge problem, however. "That's something kind of unique about homeschooling," she explains. "I hope that kids see me as not afraid to tackle that with them. I'm not pretending like I know it and I'm going to teach it to them. I'm going to learn it alongside of them, support them and encourage them while they're learning."

Cynthia sets Wayne to work on his next assignment while she helps Joshua with his math. Meanwhile, the girls emerge from their bedroom and sit on the floor in front of the woodstove, leaning back-to-back against each other while they read. Abby is an energetic, enthusiastic brunette with a loud, easy laugh. Leah is a bit taller than her elder sister; she has lighter brown hair and speaks in a softer voice, but offers a friendly smile whenever we talk.

The boys finish up their math, and Cynthia heads to the kitchen to get lunch started. The clunking sound of cowboy boots echoes from the kitchen as Roger enters from outside. His tall frame fills the doorway, and he smiles my way and says hello. Roger is an imposing figure, with a dusty black cowboy hat and worn boots, and a full gray beard. He speaks in a low voice, so soft that I occasionally find myself asking him to repeat himself. He settles down in a chair opposite me, and we talk for a while before lunch is ready. I learn that Roger dropped out of high school in the ninth grade. As he explains it, he only attended that first year about two-thirds of the time, and still was managing to pull down a B average. He decided it wasn't worth his time, and got a job instead. Later, at age twenty-one, he passed the GED—without studying or reviewing, Roger points out. "And you know what?" Roger adds as we rise to join the family at the table. "No employer has ever asked for my diploma."

After lunch, the kids clear the dishes and head off to their bedrooms, while Roger, Cynthia, and I sit at the table and talk. Roger remarks that it's outrageous how much public schools spend per student—around ten thousand dollars in Portland, he's heard (a pretty accurate figure). "It burns me up that I have to pay for the education of other people's children," he fumes. "Give me that forty thousand dollars and I won't even have to work. You want to turn our economy around, then get rid of public schools."

I wonder aloud whether there might be at least some circumstances where he thinks the government should play a role in education, such as providing support and resources to families with children who have special needs. Roger responds with great conviction: "The government shouldn't help *anybody*. That should be the job of their church. You tell me which is going to have more of an impact—getting checks from some faceless bureaucracy or getting help from a fellow churchgoer who will look you in the eye when he's helping you out. And it will make sure people really need it if they have to go ask a friend every time they need a dollar."

Cynthia is confident that homeschooling is the best choice for her children, but unlike Roger, she doesn't view her decision as a criticism of public school or its teachers. "I know that I couldn't do what teachers do, teaching all those kids with all those different needs," she says. "But what I *can* do is teach my own children, and learn along with them when necessary."

But then she offers an interesting caveat: "I talk to a lot of homeschool parents who boast that they teach to their kids' learning styles, but what they're really doing is teaching to their *own* learning styles." This can cause conflict, she says, when their children have troubles with that approach.

"That's an interesting point," I say. "It's actually a pretty common mistake among novice classroom teachers as well—they tend to teach the way they themselves prefer to learn. It sometimes takes a while for them to really recognize the need to provide a variety of ways for students to learn and demonstrate their learning."

This dynamic underscores both a potential strength and weakness in homeschooling, one I've alluded to in earlier chapters. When I was teaching high school and did a poor job meeting a particular student's learning needs, she got plenty of other chances with other teachers, both that year and beyond. If her parent, on the other hand, teaches most or all of her subjects, the quality of that one individual's teaching carries much more significance, for better or worse. While many parents undoubtedly do a great job of tailoring instruction to meet their child's learning needs, there are some who don't, as I've seen from firsthand observation.

Roger heads out to repair some fencing, and Cynthia gets ready to help Wayne with his next assignment. As she looks at her older kids sprawled out in various spots around the room reading books, Cynthia comments, "Probably an area that we're kind of weak on—and I really need to pursue, especially with Joshua—would be more current event–type things. I'm probably being a little gender biased, feeling like the girls can get away without it. We don't subscribe to the newspaper and we don't watch TV. We do subscribe to *World* magazine; it's a weekly news magazine. It's good for junior-high- and high-school-aged kids, because the articles are short and there's lots of pictures. Boy, when that comes, they're usually fighting over who gets to read it. And, you know," she adds, laughing, "you can tell their father has some strong political views!"

World magazine, the conservative Christian alternative to *Time* or *Newsweek*, claims the fourth largest weekly news magazine circulation in the United States. Their Web site proclaims, "We stand for factual accuracy and biblical objectivity, trying to see the world as best we can the way the Bible depicts it. Journalistic humility for us means trying to give God's perspective. We distinguish between issues on which the Bible is clear and those on which it isn't." Fairly straightforward news items are mixed with strongly partisan editorials, such as the one that proclaimed, "If Democrats secure a majority in either the House or the Senate, they will cripple the war effort and oblige retreat from the front lines in the war. If that happens, the certainty of another 9/11 cannot be seriously argued; only the date." Public education is a frequent target for *World.* As one editorial proclaimed, "Secularism, naturalism, disdain for much of God's created order (especially in gender considerations), anti-authority inclinations, near reverence for popular culture—all these are part of a worldview systematically and self-consciously taught in our nation's public schools for almost as long as many Americans can remember." Dissenting voices occasionally find their way onto *World*'s pages, however, such as the reader who argued, "We should be working harder to make sure there are Christians in our schools. I don't think Jesus strayed away from the difficult places or people."

Cynthia wants to make current events a bigger part of her kids' learning. "I'm hoping next year, with that civics and government class we're planning to do through Sonlight, we can focus on more world affairs. Boy, I tell you, just living out here like this, it's just so easy to forget what's going on and not think about it."

"So are there no good newspaper choices for you here that you'd want?" I ask.

"Not really. I can tolerate them a little more than Roger," she says. "It just makes him angry; he just sees everything as having a liberal bent, and it's not worth having it around for that. There are some that we *could* do, but I just don't think we'd get to them. Roger subscribes to *The Limbaugh Letter.* That's pretty one-sided," she says, chuckling. "But it's interesting."

I float an idea that might give the kids a range of perspectives to consider next year: having them compare a liberal, conservative, and moderate periodical over time.

Cynthia nods her agreement. "Yeah, you can't go about it just thinking they're wrong, when you don't even know *why* they believe what they believe. You really do need to have an understanding of that. There's still time to tackle that. There's so much—I could keep my kids home for another five years and study all this stuff I'd love to study where all the other countries are politically right now and how they got there and how it's affecting them. I know it's complex. I'd love to make a trip back to Washington, D.C. The East Coast would be like a whole other world to the kids."

We all take a break and head outside for a brief tour of the ranch. The sun shines brightly in the big sky of the desert, but the air is cool. We walk along a dirt path toward the barn, where Cynthia shows me the large, plywood-reinforced pen they use to treat individual animals. It's also one of the kids science classrooms, she explains. "Animal health management: they get to draw up the vaccines, mark off records, and help move the elk in and out. We just worked the cattle two weeks ago: branded, dehorned, vaccinated, and dewormed—and castrated the bull calves." She laughs. "You would have gotten to learn all sorts of things!"

In addition to the built-in opportunities at the ranch, they also use science kits recommended by Sonlight. "Some of them we do together as a family," Cynthia tells me. "They had a little module just on genetics, so we ordered a bunch of blood type kits and we all sat around the table and determined our blood type, and looked at how that fit between Roger's and mine and the kids. They thought that was pretty cool."

"Seems like some neat resources are available," I say.

"Yeah, we do dissections, too. I've got a catalog where you can order just about anything you want besides a human body. They have different veins and arteries injected with color to help you determine where things are. One day when we butchered elk, we collected a whole bunch of eyeballs so they could dissect them." She swings shut the heavy wooden pen door and we head toward the back pasture. "Yeah, the kids have gotten a lot of anatomy just from watching animals being butchered and locating all the different organs and things. That's always pretty different."

I think to myself that "pretty different" is an understatement, as I recall the measly little frog I helped dissect one time in high school biology. No doubt—science is clearly the richest curricular subject for the Carroll kids, and their homeschool experience provides much more hands-on science than is available in most schools.

"I was an animal science major, so that's my thing," Cynthia tells me. "So my poor kids, they get lots of science. My biggest weakness is probably language arts, writing stuff and all that. And that's probably the area where I don't push the kids enough. But I learned to write in college. I had some great writing classes and great teachers. So I guess I'm kind of falling back on that: when it's time to do in-depth research projects sorta things, they can tackle it at the college level. They've got the basic skills of how to put it together."

As a former high school English teacher, I'm concerned by their lack of attention to writing. But I also have to admit that plenty of public school students get relatively little practice in extended analytical writing—long essays, research papers, and the like—so this is hardly a flaw intrinsic to homeschooling. But it strikes me that this could in fact be a great strength in homeschooling, for parents committed to putting in the extra time to read and critique their children's writing. It's hard for a tenth-grade English teacher to assign and evaluate 150 essays a week—but an extra half hour for a homeschool parent to read an analysis of Orwell's *Animal Farm* or a research paper on current events seems both manageable and tremendously valuable.

During a supper of elk steak that evening, our talk turns to Roger's passion for debunking evolution, and his avid support of the Institute for Creation Research, a southern California organization that publishes a range of materials asserting a scientific basis for creationism. "All you have to do is sit down and apply five minutes of logical thought," Roger tells me, his voice full of absolute conviction. "Take, for instance, your eyeball, and everything your eyeball does. Then take a one-celled creature from the sea, and compare one with the other. Evolutionists can say whatever they want—it's not logical. I mean, things don't get better, they break down, in real life. And you can do that with any of their theories. Sit down, and apply logical thought."

For Roger, being a Christian means reading the Bible as a literal scientific textbook. "Everything comes together," he asserts. "There are so many pieces of Scripture, just in our lifetime, that have been shown to be scientifically true. Every instance so far of evolutionary theory has been proved wrong. So I find it a whole lot easier to accept a few things on faith, and then look at everything else to see how it fits, than to go with evolution, to take *it* on faith—which is what *they* do. They tell you it's not religion, but it is. They have a whole lot less facts to go on—it's just a theory."

Cynthia remarks that the curricular materials she uses with the kids try to point out these fallacies as well. "I don't see why kids can't read this stuff in public school," she says. "I just can't see how they can get away with teaching a lot of that stuff as *fact.* Your kids aren't allowed to question it at all. It's just taboo."

She points to a magazine on the table titled *Creation*, still enclosed in shrink-wrap. "You can open that up if you want," she says. "It's kind of interesting—pretty sound stuff about what's happening, different discoveries and things that tend to support creationism." I pull off the plastic and flip through it. It's published by an organization called Answers in Genesis, whose purpose is to "train others to develop a biblical worldview, and seek to expose the bankruptcy of evolutionary ideas." Cynthia mentions that AIG has recently finished construction of the new Creation Museum in Cincinnati, Ohio. "It sounds like it's going to be very well done," she says. "Very good quality, hi-tech, big, and it's got potential to draw a lot of people to see the other side." I learn later that the Creation Museum and Family Discovery Center has opened to huge crowds, as many as four thousand visitors a day and nearly half a million in the first year, well surpassing initial projections.

Later that evening everyone piles into the family trucks and heads down the road to their neighbors, the Millers, where the kids are going to put on a little concert for the Millers' visiting relatives. Even in their spacious home, it ends up being quite a crowd, with eight children, both sets of parents, and a half dozen relatives. As we stand around eating ice cream sundaes, it soon comes out that I'm writing a book about home-schooling. Since the Millers also homeschool their children, their interest is immediate and they are full of questions.

With a wry grin, Brenda Miller asks me if I've heard the story yet about Abby's driver's license test. Abby breaks into a broad and embarrassed smile: "No, and he doesn't need to!" This, of course, just eggs the crowd on, and the tale quickly unfolds from multiple sources with guffaws of laughter and only halfhearted denials from Abby: when she went to take her driver's test, the proctor asked for documentation of her school attendance. "I homeschool," Abby said. "Well, I need some documentation," the official persisted. Standing beside Abby, Cynthia started to get annoyed: "*I'm* her documentation!" The man wouldn't relent, however, and eventually Abby and her mom had to go through the lengthy process of obtaining a card from the state education agency. "So, after going through all of this," Brenda Miller concludes, trying to control her laughter, "Abby proceeds to fail the test—*twice!*" The gathering breaks into fresh hysterics, and someone adds, "You did homeschooling proud, girl!"

The family jamboree that soon follows is a real celebration, full of rowdy bluegrass tunes and foot-stomping melodies. All the kids join in, playing cello, mandolin, keyboard, and an assortment of fiddles, backed up by both sets of parents on guitars and an upright bass in the background. Everyone—perhaps with the exception of Joshua, who strives to retain a certain teen male aloofness—seems caught up in the simple

joys of playing music and being together. I'm quite sure that this scene
of family harmony and wholesome fun is one that many homeschoolers
would be quite proud of, and I can see why.

The next day begins pretty much like the one before. The older kids
are working independently—the girls sprawled out on the living room
floor reading their books, Joshua in his room. Cynthia and Wayne read
together from the Bible, then move to language arts and math. When his
mom offers correction or advice, Wayne sometimes tries to argue about
why his way is better.

"I think he'd be a teacher's nightmare in a classroom," Cynthia says
to me at one point, smiling. "A friend of ours teaches second grade at a
private school and we've threatened to send him over for a couple days of
real school, where you have to sit and be quiet while you do your work."

I turn to Wayne. "Sound good to you?" I ask. He shakes his head in
vigorous dissent.

Cynthia laughs. "Homeschool kids learn to read while hanging upside
down from couches! You know, he's certainly not anywhere near an ADD
kid or anything like that. He's done really well, but he can't sit still! And
I think, how does that affect a lot of little kids that have to sit still all
day long at a desk? Would they learn better if they could do their math
facts on the trampoline instead? You know, let them be active!" I think
of several young boys I know who probably would benefit from a learning
environment in which they could run out and bounce on a trampoline
every few minutes—or, as Cynthia suggests, perhaps even practice their
math in mid-bounce.

As Wayne transitions into his geography lesson, which today involves
using a world globe to locate and learn about Caribbean countries, Roger
enters the room and hands me the "values survey" that I'm asking all the
homeschool parents to complete. "The question about a woman for president," he tells me. "That's a tough one."

"Oh yeah?" I say. "What did you put?" Roger gives me the thumbs-
down sign.

Cynthia weighs in. "I'm not totally against a woman as president—
but my specifications or qualifications would probably be a lot different
than others," she says. "I believe if a woman is married and has children
still at home, absolutely not, no matter how qualified she is. I mean, she

might have some other job and utilize, you know, schools or a nanny or whatever. But running the country, that's a full-time job."

"God made us different," Roger says gruffly. "He laid out how we ought to be in the Scriptures. It's not saying anything bad about women or anything good about men; he just gave us different roles." Roger pauses for a moment, then clarifies his priorities: "But I'd much rather have a woman-conservative than a man-liberal any day."

As we talk, I've been quickly scanning his survey answers. Roger puts on his coat to head out again, but I want to ask him about what appears to be a contradiction, or at least a tension, in his answers. "So you say that you agree that the younger generation should be taught by the elders to do what is right," I point out, "and then here you ranked 'kids should learn to think for themselves' more highly than 'learn to obey.'"

Roger has a ready explanation. "They should be *taught* to do what is right and in that process *learn*, not so much to *obey*, but to do the right thing. To learn the difference between right and wrong and hopefully they'll be able to figure that out for themselves. Not 'obey me or else' kind of thing."

As Roger heads out the door, Cynthia adds her perspective. "I don't think children should be flat out taught to obey their elders always, just because they're your elders. You've got to learn to think for yourself and be able to have conversations and other things. You know, at a certain age, you need to obey, until you can learn to think for yourself. It's all a process."

The question, of course, is about *how* and *when* parents encourage this process of kids learning to think for themselves. If children end up thinking pretty much like their parents do, is that a sign that this hasn't happened, or just that they've recognized the wisdom of their parents? How many other perspectives do kids need to be exposed to before we can say with some assurance that they have made a legitimate choice about their values and beliefs? If parents shelter their kids from other viewpoints throughout most of their adolescence, are they "stacking the deck" in a way that unfairly restricts freedom of thought and choice once they reach adulthood?

For example, when I later ask Abby about her views on women's roles in politics and the family, she expresses views closer to her mother's perspective. "I don't think there is anything totally *wrong* with a woman running the country," she answers at first. "Well, running a country might be a little too extreme, so far as being president. In the Congress, I don't think that's a problem. But in the home, I'd definitely have the guy be head of the home and the gal just stay at home and do what she's supposed to do. You know, take care of the kids and whatnot." Abby tells me she wants to be a nurse, but eventually have thirteen children. Why thirteen? Because, she informs me, that's the most you can fit in the biggest passenger van available these days.

Do these more conservative, traditional conceptions of gender roles suggest that Abby has simply imbibed the ethical water of her parents, rather than stepping back to critically analyze those views? Making such judgments from outside a family circle is a guessing game at best. Even with the Carrolls, there's more diversity of perspective than first meets the eye.

As if to remind me of this, Cynthia elaborates on one section of her survey responses. "The whole abortion issue—I mean, I'm very pro-life but yet I don't believe abortion should be illegal. Because I can't control somebody that doesn't believe the way I do. I'd love the chance to talk to that person and share with them my beliefs. But I don't see any benefit in making it illegal."

Cynthia's fairly moderate position surprises me a bit, but I suppose it fits with a libertarian approach to government. She offers another issue along these lines as well. "The same thing with capital punishment. God gave *me* a second chance, and a sinner is a sinner. There are a lot of people who commit murder, you know, who can be reformed, who can learn and grow and become wonderful people. Those are tough issues."

I discover that Cynthia's perspectives on homeschool regulation are varied as well. She thinks it's hypocritical that public school advocates should be worrying about the educational neglect of homeschoolers, but doesn't have a big problem with current state regulations. "Oregon is a not a bad state for homeschooling, for the most part," she says. "You're supposed to register with the state, but there are tons of ways around that. And you're supposed to test in certain grades, just simple standardized tests. If the kids are passing those, at least you know, okay, they're going to make it. That's good, and boy, it shouldn't be threatening to any homeschool family. I don't feel threatened by that at all. But there are an awful lot of homeschool kids out there who just slip through the cracks."

"Is that right?"

Cynthia nods. "I know some families where they just feel pressured to homeschool and it's really not a good situation for them. You know, the mom gets stuck with the majority of it, just doesn't want to relearn, doesn't want to go through it all again, doesn't enjoy it. I think those tests do point out when you've got kids that are not even learning the basics. But then again, I think a lot of those families don't test either, because they know their kids."

"How do they pull that off?" I ask.

"They don't register in the first place," Cynthia explains. "Like the Millers—I think their kids are doing fine and progressing pretty well, but they had their kids in a private school before, so when they pulled them out of private school, they never had to report that they were home-schooling. I know they're not on the list or anything. So there wouldn't be any way the educational services department could track them.

"We're kind of renegades when it comes to this testing," she continues. "I found a test that qualifies. It's a legitimate standardized test that the state of Oregon accepts and I was able to order it online and administer it to the kids myself, which you're not supposed to do—you're supposed to have an outside source do it. But if I'm going to take the time to do one of these tests, I want to see how they do! Where did they mess up? I don't want to just get a sheet back that said they scored this percentage. What's the use of that, besides the state of Oregon knowing they're doing okay?"

I can definitely relate to Cynthia's desire to see for herself where her kids had problems on the exam. Of all the standardized testing that my students did, I rarely got to examine the results in detail, and almost never in time to implement any changes in the curriculum to address whatever weaknesses students may have had.

At the same time, however, I can't see the point in a state testing system for homeschoolers that includes loopholes enabling parents to test their own children and report the results. That's not to mention the even bigger loophole of homeschool families who've never been to public schools and don't bother to register with the state at all. As Debbie Palmer and many other parents have told me, the families who follow homeschool regulations are generally the ones who do a good job in the first place. It seems to me it would be a far better policy approach to establish minimal regulations that can be enforced for *all* homeschoolers—and then to focus state attention on the few families who are truly neglecting their children's education.

The following year brings a big change of scenery. Roger had grown increasingly unhappy with his salary on the elk ranch, so he quit his job there and they moved up in the mountains to an old church camp, which Roger was hired to restore after a huge wildfire gutted it. My return trip is in early October, before the snow starts to fall. The Carrolls are hoping that funds will be available to winterize the camp so they can stay there and keep working on it through the snow.

Despite the move, they remain within an hour's drive of Cedar Point and their church. They don't have a place for me to stay with them this time around, so I'm up at five in the morning to make the ninety-minute drive from Garrison to their mountaintop camp. The last ten miles or so are off the highway and up unpaved forestry roads. Right before the final turn, the road changes from rutted dirt to soft cinders, and a barren tableau of burnt tree trunks and blackened, leafless branches replace the lush forest landscape. A few small, green saplings appear here and there, as nature slowly recovers from the massive ninety-thousand-acre fire that scorched the area three years ago.

I pull in among stacks of lumber, heavy equipment, and partially constructed cabins. Almost everything at the church camp was burned to the ground, save the main lodge, which nevertheless needs a full restoration inside. The Carrolls moved up here in early summer, and are well into renovations on the main lodge.

After we catch up over breakfast, Cynthia tells me about two intriguing new developments in their educational world. One is that Abby and Leah have started to take classes at the local community college. The other is the Sonlight civics curriculum she's starting with the three older kids—this promises to be the most substantive attention to democratic citizenship of any of the homeschool families I visit. I'm eager to see what the shape and content of that will be, as well as Cynthia's vision for how they will explore it together.

The book list recommended by Sonlight includes a rich variety of titles, many of which you'd find in public school classrooms, such as *The Scarlet Letter*, *Black Like Me*, and *The Jungle*. Sonlight even recommends *Lies My Teacher Told Me*, a liberal antitextbook of sorts that seeks to correct common misinformation about American history, and *The Godless Constitution*, a polemic against the "Religious Right." Sonlight's introductory comments about this latter book catch my eye:

> So why would I choose a book like this for you to study? Why study a book written by "the enemy"? Partially because you're getting older and you're going to have to "take on" people like these college professors and you're going to have to be able to *read* their works, *understand* (accurately) what they are trying to say, *analyze* what is true or false, insightful, helpful, etc., in what they say, and then *figure out how to respond*. Should you defend what you believed before you read their book? Modify your beliefs? Join their forces? You're old enough. It's time for you to take on such a task with two college professors as your sparring partners.

This strikes me as qualitatively different from the "opposition research" of Michael Farris. Sure, the Sonlight commentary is still full of combative images, but there's at least the acknowledgment that understanding the arguments of others might be of more value than just figuring out ways to defeat them.

Nevertheless, this curriculum would undoubtedly raise the eyebrows of many outside of conservative Christianity (and even some within it). It also includes titles such as *The Institutes of Biblical Law* and *Tools of Dominion*, whose authors advocate a perspective called Christian Reconstructionism, which calls for the establishment of a Christian theocratic government operating under Old Testament law. Sonlight offers tepid criticism of Reconstructionism; stoning someone who advocates evolutionary theory, for example, is presented as unacceptably extreme. But the editorial commentary also suggests that the current state of affairs in America, where our government "sponsors and actively promotes the killing of unborn babies," deserves perhaps even greater criticism than Reconstructionism.

This Sonlight civics curriculum is a good example of how difficult implementing a "multicultural curriculum" requirement for homeschoolers would be. Is exposure to a variety of values and beliefs enough, even if we assume those beliefs are presented charitably? How would such regulation prevent some homeschoolers from also reading Christian Reconstructionism and deciding, upon the subtle or not-so-subtle urging of their parents, that those whose beliefs run counter to Old Testament law merit ritual stoning?

In response to these concerns, some proponents of regulation suggest that homeschoolers should be required to participate in state-administered civic education classes, to ensure exposure to alternative viewpoints in an atmosphere that doesn't simultaneously condemn them. Of course, such classes would need to be required for *all* students, public and private, as well. And then suddenly the arm of the state has lengthened considerably, endorsing and enforcing a particular version of civic learning and engagement.

This Sonlight curriculum at least has the potential to get the Carroll kids thinking about their role as citizens in a democratic society where everyone doesn't share their religious convictions. But when Cynthia mentions her desire to get Roger more involved in their discussions, I have to ask her: if part of good citizenship is being able to think and analyze for yourself, are the Carroll kids going to have the intellectual and emotional room to do this when Roger participates?

Cynthia isn't surprised by my question, but she doesn't share my concern. "I think they need to be able to listen to their dad and then they need to be able to say, 'But what about this or what about that?' Or, 'I read this and this sure made sense—why don't you agree with it?'"

"And do you think they'll feel comfortable doing that?" I ask.

"I think they could get to that point," she says. "And I think it would be really good for them. And you know, it's good for Roger, too, to learn to be able to back up what he believes and be able to listen to questions and things. I want the kids to get to the point where they're not afraid to question something. You know, anything."

While I don't think that Roger's presence will utterly stifle discussion, I'm skeptical that his children would feel comfortable floating *any* idea about political, moral, or religious issues. But at least with the girls, civics discussions around the kitchen table will only be part of their education moving forward, particularly if their college courses expand beyond music offerings.

When I ask Cynthia if she expects to see changes in the girls as they explore this new world, she seems both accepting and unconcerned about the possibility: "Yeah, I think this is going to throw them into wanting to be more independent, be out on their own real quick—and that's okay. I'm fine with that."

I'm eager to hear from Abby and Leah about their new community college experience, particularly given the resistance that Roger had to the idea. While hardly the equivalent of shipping off to a New England liberal arts college, the first month of classes appears to have qualified as an exciting and worthwhile adventure, especially to an eighteen- and seventeen-year-old who've been homeschooling most of their lives.

Abby tells me about how they got started. No transcripts were required, but they did have to take a placement test. "We were nervous, you know, because it's been six or seven years since we've gone to public school. But we did fine on that."

"Did you have particular high points and low points, in terms of subjects?" I ask.

"My writing wasn't real good. My writing is—ugh." She makes a face of distaste.

"Are you going to take a course in writing, do you think?"

"No, probably not." She chuckles. "Not unless I have some huge inclination to write something some time. But no, not so far."

"Are most of the students around your age?" I ask.

"Yeah, they are!" Abby's eyes light up. "It's like the first group of kids my age. Ever since I left public school, I haven't had friends my age."

The transition to a secular academic environment has been challenging for them, but far from oppressive. Both Abby and Leah are feeling increasingly comfortable speaking up in class, although they do remark on the occasional swear words they hear, and how it's strange to analyze religious songs in music class with people who don't find any personal significance in them.

Even though the experience as a whole has been positive, Abby says it's complicated to live up here on the mountain and make community college work. "Any classes we take right now need to be Tuesdays and Thursdays, because if we did a Monday-Wednesday-Friday class, it would cause us to be gone all week, and Dad doesn't like that idea. He doesn't like us being gone three days out of the week already."

"Did you have any arguments with your dad about taking the courses?"

"Um—kind of," she says. "Mom looked things up and then asked Dad about it. Dad doesn't really like us going to college, because *he* didn't go to college. Mom did, but he just doesn't really like it all that well. He likes it when we're home."

I ask Abby what would happen if she got interested in a field of study that her dad didn't want her to pursue.

"Well, he usually has a pretty good reason for something if he doesn't want us to do it," Abby says. "If I really wanted to pursue nursing—I mean, he's not that stubborn. I can usually soften him up pretty good." She laughs. "But if he *really* didn't want me to do it and he had some good reason behind it, I would probably accept that and find something else or come to terms with him on it. Because I stick to that 'your parents know what's best for you' thing right now, as far as what I choose to do and stuff like that."

"Do you have a sense as to when that might change for you?" I ask. "At a certain age, do you feel like you'll be responsible for making your own decisions?"

"I don't really know," Abby says. "I have a feeling that once I'm really done with school at home, probably next year, I'll have a little bit more freedom. My dad likes to let us go just a little bit at a time. And gradually, I think—by the time I'm twenty-two, twenty-three, something like that—I think I'll definitely be able to go. I might choose something and Dad will say, 'Well, I don't like it,' but he won't say I can't do it." Abby laughs. "You know, he does that a lot!" Here she mimics her father's stern voice: "'*I don't like it, but you can do it if you want.*'"

For her part, Abby's younger sister Leah wants to take some theater classes and perhaps get involved in an acting troupe, on a short-term basis. But what Leah *really* wants to do, she tells me, is major in Christian missions work, even if that means eventually needing to transfer to a college farther from home. She doesn't see this happening for a couple of years, though, since she needs to finish up her homeschool curriculum this year, and then their youth group is planning a missions trip to Africa the following summer.

When I ask Cynthia about the girls' college experience thus far, she echoes their positive appraisal. "I think it's a great way for them to get their feet wet," she says.

"Is your sense that Roger has come around a little bit?"

"I've been amazed," she says. "I'm totally amazed that they are taking two classes at the community college."

"You didn't think it was going to happen?"

"No," she admits, "especially with Leah. I thought he would make them wait until Leah officially graduated before they could do it. I don't think he'd be against them taking more classes next term. He kind of sees that he's got to let them pursue what they're interested in, that this can be good for them."

One of Roger's regular sources of news and commentary is Rush Limbaugh. Roger is one of at least fourteen million listeners, making Limbaugh the top-rated talk-show host, by far, for nearly two decades—an influence frequently overlooked by his liberal critics. Even more disheartening to the political Left, a 2006 Pew survey reported that Limbaugh's listening audience ranked higher on "news knowledge questions" than that of National Public Radio.

"So when you think about the qualities of a good American citizen," I ask Roger, "what are the primary things that come to mind?"

"Vote, absolutely above all," he says. "But you can't just vote; you must be educated. A noninformed voter would be better off not voting, in my mind. It bothers me that people don't bother to find out about the real details of an issue. Citizenship is a tremendous privilege—but it is also a tremendous responsibility."

While I agree with Roger's sentiment, I get the sense that for him, the "real details" of an issue are the ones he agrees with. Certainly there are plenty of times when thoughtful people examine the same details and come up with different, but still reasonable, conclusions. "Why do you think people might think differently about some of these controversial issues?" I ask.

He grimaces and shakes his head. "Stupid," he says. "Or ignorant."

If we stop here, Roger comes off looking like the walking antithesis of reasonable disagreement. I try again. "But couldn't you see them as reasonable, even if you disagreed with their conclusions—you understood how they logically reached that conclusion, even if at the end of the day you think they are wrong?"

"That's a *really* tough thing," Roger says, "because I see most things in black and white." Part of this absolutism, perhaps, stems from Roger's view of the relationship between his politics and his Christian faith: "People want to say politics is something separate. It's just like people saying, 'my Christian life'—it just doesn't make any sense. I don't have *a* Christian life and *a* regular life. I'm not *not* political outside of my regular life. It's all the same life; it's all the same thing." When holding fast to one's political commitments gets equated with holding fast to one's faith commitments, it's not surprising that room for reasonable disagreement, compromise, and accommodation becomes hard to find.

During my individual conversations with the Carroll kids, it becomes clear they don't share Roger's inflexible approach to civic disagreement. Although I get the least amount of explanation from the boys, Joshua does tell me that he "wants to know what the other side believes, so if you're talking to somebody, you can see it from their point of view, too." Unlike his father, he sees politics as more of a "gray area," without always having obvious right and wrong choices.

Abby expresses a desire to search for common ground with people who believe differently, at least on some issues. "Well, you don't have to agree with everything but you've got to be willing to accept certain terms," she says. "And you can argue, but not so far as losing your temper. Kind of meet in the middle on things, not go way overboard, you know?" But then she adds a caveat—there are some things about which she wouldn't be willing to yield. "Like the whole evolution thing," she says, "I think that's just ludicrous. How they could believe that, it just kind of mind boggles me."

"So your sense is that someone who believes evolution is seriously confused?" I ask. "They couldn't have a reasonable basis for it?"

"Yeah, see, I don't understand it *that* well. If I were to argue a case about it with somebody, I don't know if I'd win!" She laughs. "I have my beliefs about it and I know what I believe and so I could argue it for a *while;* I don't know if I could carry it on completely, though."

Her sister Leah, as usual, offers the fullest reflection on my questions. When I remark that the Sonlight civics reading list offers an interesting mix of political perspectives, she agrees. "I think that's really good for us," she says, "because we can see both sides and it will make us stronger on our side, because we understand it."

"And do you have a sense," I ask, "what will inform where you stand on this wide spectrum between liberal and conservative?"

"Um, I'm not sure," Leah responds. "As far as biblical law, I'm gonna have to go back to the Bible and see what it says. And I'll talk to Mom and Dad and just get all sorts of ideas and then I'll start thinking and kind of come up with my own, I guess."

Like many parents and older children I talk with, Leah makes a distinction between legislating behavior and beliefs. She has no desire to force the latter: "It's a free country," she says. "People moved here because we have freedom of belief. I mean, I can try to persuade them that Christianity is right and you need to follow the one true God. But I'm not going to force them to." Of course, the issue becomes vastly more complicated when the policy positions she advocates (such as outlawing abortion and gay marriage) are directly informed by her religious beliefs.

"And when you read these different civics materials," I ask, "do you already have in your head an idea of what a good citizen *should* be? Do you think about that?"

"I haven't much," Leah admits. "We get *World* magazine, and I read that, and we get *The Limbaugh Letter*, which I only read a couple pages of. But Rush Limbaugh is like totally extreme to the Right."

"Yeah, your dad said that you guys didn't like Rush as much as he does."

"No, I think Rush Limbaugh is obnoxious." She laughs. "I'm sure he has some good ideas, but he doesn't need to be that annoying."

"So would you say that Rush wouldn't meet your idea of a good citizen?" I ask.

"Yeah," she says. "It seems to me that sometimes he totally closes the door to people. Like they'll be trying to say their own ideas—I mean, everyone is entitled to their own opinion—and he'll be like, 'No, that's wrong, you can't even say that!' So he's not very open to listening to people."

"And in terms of giving people their say," I ask, "do you think it's also important, when you're listening, to be open to the possibility that they're right?"

Leah nods. "Yeah. It all just depends on what the subject is, but you need to be open to what they're saying and actually consider it and think, 'Maybe they *are* right.' But then you can look back on your own ideas and tell them, 'I really think you're wrong. Would you look at my opinion?'"

"Now what would be the subjects that wouldn't qualify for that type of openness?"

"Well, for me, the matter of creation and evolution," Leah says. "I *strongly* believe in creation. I can listen to their ideas about evolution, but there is no way I'm going to believe that. Partly because I grew up believing creation, but also we did biology last year. Our book covered evolution, and looked at both sides, and the evidence—it was really good for me to see what some people believe. But still I think creation is true."

Here again we can see how the proposal to require all homeschoolers to present "both sides" of social or political issues would be doomed to failure, at least in the eyes of its proponents. Abby and her siblings *did* explore the arguments between evolution and creationism, and their mom could certainly have submitted curricular materials to the state attesting to that. Even if the state had required them to include an unabashedly "pro-evolution" text, it's easy to imagine how that would have been cast in the worst possible light during actual home instruction.

One of the Carrolls' regular trips to town is Sunday morning to Cedar Point Christian Church, a small independent congregation that sees about sixty people in attendance each week. On my first visit, I'm immediately welcomed by greeters in the vestibule and directed into the sanctuary. Here, a well-equipped worship band leads the congregation in singing, followed by group prayers and then a sermon given by one of the elders.

I receive multiple invitations to stay for lunch after the service, and eventually head down to the basement kitchen, where we scoop corn chowder from a huge soup tureen. As we eat at long cafeteria-style tables, I discover that many of the families in the congregation are homeschoolers. One mother remarks that as the years go by, they're starting to see some of the earlier generation homeschool parents offering enrichment courses for newer homeschoolers. I'm also struck by a father's comment that homeschoolers' independent streak leads many of them into business for themselves, rather than trying to fit into a larger organization or someone else's idea of what they should do or how they should do it.

This is a friendly group of people, and before the morning is through, I've probably spoken to half of the adults in the congregation. While some of them remind me of the Carrolls' conservatism and "go it alone" ethos, others appear more moderate in their views about politics, education, and religion. There seems to be more diversity of opinion—theological and political—than I would have expected at a church where Roger was an elder. Since the kids spend each church service in its entirety with the adults, this is likely an important opportunity for them to experience a wider range of perspectives than their home environment regularly provides.

Homeschooling for many Christian families represents an effort to prevent their children from being *of* the world, indistinct from unbelievers and their values. But the physical separation of one's children—especially in a situation like the Carrolls, where they have so little interaction with other children throughout the week—raises challenging questions about how to be *in* the world. I explore this tension a bit with Roger by reading to him the Randall Balmer criticism of homeschoolers as neglecting their duty to be "salt and light" to the world.

Roger pauses for a moment as he considers his response. "If the public school was a neutral ground," he says, "I could agree with it. But public schools are not a neutral ground; public school is the enemy."

"So the deck is too stacked?"

"The deck is absolutely stacked," he says with conviction. "I mean, me sending *my* kid *there* is like them sending *their* kid to *me*. Do you think they'd be willing to do that? I don't think so. The public education system, in general, is teaching exactly the opposite of what I believe. And they expect me to put *my* kid into *their* hands for the better part of every day? How silly. Now they start sending their kids to me—"

I chuckle at the offer. "Would there be a point at which, with your kids, you would feel comfortable saying, 'Okay, they're old enough, they've got a foundation, they know who they are, they know what they believe. I can let 'em go. They may find it challenging, but they're going to be fine'?"

Roger nods. "The oldest ones are there now. They're seventeen and eighteen, and I have no trouble with them going to college. They're well founded. You know, for each kid it would be different when that age was."

"Do you think Joshua is there yet?"

"Joshua doesn't talk very much about himself," Roger says. "And I wouldn't be comfortable yet. He's fourteen. You know, at the rate he's going, another two years probably. And it's a shame that they can't *be* in school and have more impact on the children out there. But their salvation is worth more than that risk to me. We'd be sending them to public schools for indoctrination—and it just don't make sense. It's too tough of a battle."

Then Roger mentions another challenge of being *in* the world. "I see some parents who are homeschooling their children and their kids are *still* getting indoctrinated, through the radio, the songs they're listening to, through the television. I believe television is Satan's most effective tool in the United States of America. Not only for the garbage it presents, which you can find anywhere, but for the *time* that it eats out of our everyday lives. It's a waste, an *absolute waste.*"

Roger recognizes that homeschooling in and of itself will not shield his children from the cultural influences he despises. And clearly there are parents of all political persuasions who would agree with his desire to minimize exposure to the mindless consumerism that pervades much of our popular media. Of course, one can be uncritically accepting of more than just popular culture; with this in mind, I wonder what kind of room there is for the Carroll kids to diverge from their parents' perspectives. "Are there issues or disagreements that you have with the kids as they're getting older and starting to develop their own views on things?" I ask.

"Not yet," Roger says.

"Do you have any premonitions of what might become issues?"

"No, I really don't, because I'm not gonna be picky about the little things," he says. "You know, I'm easy to get along with. And the big things, they can see. They've all got good heads on their shoulders; the education they get at home does them well."

Roger sees his job as a parent as instilling in them a particular Christian worldview in the hope that they will be able to navigate the world themselves after they leave home. This theme of protection and preparation continues to run through my visits with each homeschooling family—although it's not always clear when the protection should lessen and more room should be made for kids to step out on their own.

I try to push a bit on this concept. "So your sense of the turning point for them is when they're done with school, eighteen or nineteen or whatever—they've been prepared to go out and deal with the outside world?"

Roger nods. "If they've got a solid foundation, they won't have to unlearn stuff after college. So many kids jump out and they get pushed in immoral directions, and by the time *they* have children, they no longer believe in any of that stuff they did." He shakes his head. "There's no sense in going there in the first place."

"So what are the signs to you that they are independent thinkers?" I ask.

"They argue."

"Oh yeah? What do they argue about?"

"Oh, not much," Roger says. "They'll ask questions. I don't want my kids to agree with me 'just because I said so.'"

Roger sees himself as encouraging a family and educational environment that allows for genuine dialogue. My private conversation with Leah, however, suggests a somewhat different perspective. "Sometimes Dad's like"—here she mimics his deep, authoritarian tone—"*'This is what you have to believe, end of story.'* I think I'd just be a little more open to different ideas."

"Do you and your parents ever argue about issues?" I ask her.

"No," she says. "As far as beliefs, we believe the same thing. But in pretty much any argument, if I was to argue, 'Dad, you need to be little more open,' he would probably win, because he's the dad." She chuckles.

"Wait," I say, needing clarification. "He'd win just because at the end of the day he'd say, 'Well, I'm the dad'?"

"No, he would listen to me, because he cares," Leah says. "But he also has a temper and sometimes his temper gets a little out of control, I guess."

"And so you'd rather just not deal with the conflict?" I ask.

She nods. "Yeah, and really it doesn't bother me that much."

My sense from our multiple conversations is that it really *doesn't* bother Leah that much, but it's hard to know how much of that equanimity comes at the cost of simply avoiding dialogue about tough issues. She wants to honor her parents' authority and the wisdom she believes they have to offer, but it should be possible for a teacher (and parent) to foster an environment where honest questioning of received wisdom can be done respectfully and without fear of censure.

Joshua is also trying to navigate the realm between parental authority and his own desires. When we talk privately, he expresses at least some dissatisfaction with his current homeschooling circumstances. "It's boring," he tells me, "because all my friends are down there and Abby and Leah are gone most of the week." He then surprises me by confiding, "Next year I want to—there's a school in Garrison, Redwood Christian School. I'd *like* to go to that; I don't know if I could or not. But just to get back in the swing of things." Joshua will be in tenth grade next year, and he wants to experience institutional schooling for his final few years of high school. He also misses their old neighbors, the Millers; the girl closest to his age attends Redwood this year.

"Have you talked to your folks about it yet?" I ask.

He smiles sheepishly. "Not yet."

I ask Joshua how he thinks his parents will react, and he says he doesn't think they will be against it just on principle—and if he keeps at them, perhaps they'll eventually change their minds.

"So when do you get to see your friends these days?" I ask.

"On Wednesdays, we have a Bible study at church," he says. "Usually they all come to that. And on Sunday."

"But those are pretty much the only chances? You don't go down for other stuff?"

"Not usually."

It's hard to separate Joshua's dissatisfaction with his geographical isolation from any disenchantment he feels with homeschooling in general. From his relatively positive appraisal of homeschooling during last year's visit, I suspect his unhappiness is primarily social in nature, but it may also be that as he gets older, he will grow increasingly weary of his relatively limited educational milieu as well.

To my surprise, I soon get a glimpse of how Joshua's conversation with his parents might go if he eventually works up the courage to broach the idea of stopping homeschooling. Later in my visit, Cynthia remarks to me that "I could see Joshua maybe wanting to go to school in a year or two. I don't know if he would want to be in a public school, but he might want to be in a Christian school."

"And you guys would consider it?" I ask.

She nods. "Yeah, it would depend on his reasoning and kind of where we were at, if it was really possible. I wouldn't be against that. But I look at him and think, 'Yeah, right. You spend eight hours in school and then come home and do homework for two or three hours, and you'll change your mind!' But that may be a good step for him before he enters college. I'd totally be open to it."

I ask Cynthia how she thinks she might react if one of her kids openly rebelled against their authority and guidance.

"I don't know," she admits. "I would think you can only butt heads so much with your child. I would like to think that I could handle it in a way of saying, 'I'm concerned about this direction you're headed, and this is why.'"

"Would it be different, in terms of how you'd deal with it, if it were a rejection of your religious foundations, as compared to a political shift, like becoming a hard-core Democrat?"

She nods. "Yeah, I'm sure it would be. Because I'm of the belief that politics are interesting, but that's not where our salvation is. You know, I think there are an awful lot of good Christians that are bleeding-heart liberals who are just a little misled. They certainly mean well and they're real compassionate, they care about people. I think most of those people, the older they get, the more they'll realize that certain kinds of compassion work and others don't. But I think it's very normal for kids who are very curious about our world and how things work, and very curious about God and spirituality and all that, to have a more liberal swing before they really come back to their foundation. And I see that as *way* more common than kids who just stay on the straight and narrow on the Right all the time, and never even choose to consider or think about the other side and what other people are thinking and feeling."

"So you feel like you could ride that out pretty well?"

"Oh yeah, I think so. But it's easy to say, with our kids on the direction they're heading. It hasn't been a real challenge."

A few weeks after my final visit to the Carrolls, I e-mail Cynthia to say that I'd love to see any "letters to the editor" the kids write in response to their civics curriculum, as suggested in the Sonlight curriculum guide. I don't hear back from Cynthia, however, until I write her again at the end of the year with some final summative questions. In her eventual e-mail response, Cynthia admits that they didn't finish the civics curriculum. Furthermore, she writes, "I am realizing my lack of ability (or is it just desire?) to follow up with challenging writing assignments. So we are going to tackle the 'Excellence in Writing' program this next fall and hopefully have more time to analyze what Joshua learned this year."

Cynthia also tells me that Joshua did ask about attending Redwood Christian School next year. "We talked about it and he decided he could meet his goals better at home and through the community college. At home, he will be taking chemistry and writing (one last shot!) and continuing with the civics program. He'll take two courses each term at community college to begin an Associates of Science degree." One of those classes in the spring will be a writing course—"gives me some firm goals to work on his writing skills before then!"

Cynthia reports that the girls continue to love their college experience. "They are the top two students in their math class this term," she writes. "Leah plans to complete a two-year transfer degree and then hopes to go to a private Christian college for a missions major. All three older kids will spend six weeks in Botswana next February on a missions trip."

When considering the Carrolls' educational experience as a whole, several central tensions in homeschooling rise into sharp relief. For Roger and Cynthia, homeschooling is an effort to foster a particular mindset in their children, one that respects the wisdom of parents and will stand against the brainwashing of the outside world. The tension between preparing children for a hostile world while still giving them room to stretch their wings involves an ongoing negotiation with an autocratic father whose criteria for useful education are narrow indeed. In terms of civic preparation, their Sonlight curriculum offers a potentially rich exposure to the complicated questions surrounding Christian citizenship, but it inevitably gets filtered through the instruction and influence of parents. The ultimate impact of these tensions on the lives of their children, of course, remains to be seen.

Race, Homeschooling, and the Common School Vision

Until recently, the stereotypical image of a homeschooler has been a white, conservative Christian. As I noted in the introduction, estimates vary widely in terms of homeschooler religiosity; the same uncertainty holds true for race and ethnicity. The 2003 NCES data suggest that about 77 percent of U.S. homeschoolers are "white, non-Hispanic," compared with 62 percent of the rest of the K–12 population, but many observers contend that racial diversity has been increasing steadily since then. Some homeschool leaders assert that African Americans are the fastest growing subset of homeschoolers, but this—along with all national homeschool statistics—can only be educated guessing at best (others, for instance, claim that Muslim Americans merit this distinction instead).

This apparent diversification is somewhat ironic, in light of the history of the modern homeschool movement. In the three decades following the Supreme Court's 1954 order to desegregate public schools in *Brown v. Board of Education*, thousands of private schools were formed, many by conservative Christians. While some of the public school exodus can be traced to dismay over other legal decisions such as bans on school-sponsored prayer and Bible reading, racism clearly played a significant role as well. Some commentators suggest that homeschooling shares some of these racial motivations, seeing as though homeschooling began to gain traction among white conservative Christians when these small Christian schools began to close down in the 1980s.

It seems likely that of the 88 percent of homeschoolers in the 2007 NCES survey who pointed to "concern about the environment of other schools," some see racially diverse public schools as part of the reason to keep their children away. But this hardly qualifies as a broad generalization about homeschoolers' motivations. There are also many homeschoolers such as the Carrolls (and the families in the two chapters to follow) whose public schools have very little racial diversity to avoid. Their "concern about the environment" clearly focuses on issues other than race.

To the extent that homeschooling is an increasingly popular choice among African Americans, anecdotal evidence points to a growing disillusionment with the promise of public schools and the persistent "achievement gap" between black and white students as primary motivations for the shift. Nevertheless, African Americans who switch to homeschooling sometimes face a backlash within the African American community itself; abandoning public schools, their critics say gives up on the promise of integration that previous generations fought so hard to try to achieve.

As I mentioned earlier, the ideal of the "common school" was based in part on the idea that democracy is strengthened when all its members learn with each other and from each other. Public schools were seen as a means of self-advancement, but also as preparation for democratic life together. When faith in those public institutions wanes, however, the logic of privatization becomes increasingly appealing. As the line between public and private education continues to blur—as the next chapter illustrates—the questions of what counts as public education, and what that means for our preparation to be a public, become even more complicated.

7

THE WALLIS FAMILY

"God Gave Her to Me"

As the preceding chapters illustrate, homeschooling several children simultaneously requires enormous commitment and the ability to balance a wide range of needs. But even homeschooling a single child—and a relatively self-sufficient one at that—poses similar questions about how to prepare her to live in a world full of so many different visions of what is good, right, and true. This chapter will continue to explore these challenges, while also analyzing some emerging trends in homeschooling's use of technology and its increasingly blurred boundaries with public schools.

Twelve-year-old Linda is the only child of Mark and Cindy Wallis. Mark serves as youth pastor of Creighton Evangelical Church, a rural Pentecostal congregation, and Cindy works part time as church secretary. The Wallises live in central Vermont, a place where people give directions by way of landmarks rather than street names. Vermont combines a strong streak of political independence with socially progressive policies—universal health insurance for children, civil unions for gay couples, and significant restrictions on commercial development, to name a few. Conservative Christians, I discover, often see themselves as in the minority here when it comes to social and political issues.

Spring doesn't really arrive in Vermont until May approaches, so my first visit in March finds snow on the ground and temperatures in the 20s—"brisk," the natives call it. The Wallises live in a double-wide trailer that sits on a small hill overlooking farmland and a wooded valley beyond. I pull up the driveway and Cindy meets me at the door.

"Did you find us okay?" she asks. In her mid-thirties, Cindy has shoulder-length auburn hair, a broad smile, and a toned physique, which I learn is a result of her dedicated fitness regimen of weight lifting and cardio work. As I walk into the kitchen, Mark rises from the table to greet me. Like many church pastors, he has Mondays off. Mark is about six feet tall, with long sideburns and a regular five o'clock shadow. Well muscled from his own routine workouts, he has an easy smile and a relaxed manner, but—as I discover during our conversations over the next year—an underlying intensity that emerges when talk turns serious.

The Wallis home is comfortably furnished, with a small galley kitchen opening out to a living room area whose large windows overlook the picturesque valley. A television set sits in the corner, surrounded by videotapes, and a dark leather couch wraps around a coffee table. Linda is at work here, sitting on the floor with her back against the sofa, legs stretched out beneath the low table. She has short brown hair and glasses, and is dressed in casual clothes befitting a day at home. I notice a throw blanket draped across one end of the couch; on it is stitched the same biblical passage that the Palmers display in their living room: AS FOR ME AND MY HOUSE, WE WILL SERVE THE LORD.

As a twelve-year-old, Linda is using an eighth-grade curriculum— about a year ahead of what is typical. Homeschool advocates often point out that individualized, self-paced homeschooling can be far more efficient than institutional schooling in terms of progressing through a curriculum. When Linda needs help, she generally has immediate access to her mother, and her studies advance at the pace that fits her. This flexibility became clear when Cindy told me on the phone that I shouldn't wait too long before making my first visit in the spring, as Linda was quickly wrapping up several of her core academic subjects. "Linda and I always finish early," she explained. "I think we're both sort of overachievers, so we push everything pretty hard. And we like the extra time off—it feels like a relief."

On this late March visit, I discover that they have already completed grammar and composition, math, and science for this academic year. The only remaining subjects are geography, history, spelling, health, and Bible Quiz. The latter is obviously an elective, but it receives a great deal of attention from Linda and her mom. It's actually a competitive activity of sorts, focusing on memorization of Bible passages and textual details, and Linda and Cindy have traveled all over New England for competitions. In fact, Linda just recently won a national award by memorizing, verbatim, twelve chapters from the book of Romans, as well as the entire book of

James (in total, more than ten thousand words—longer than this chapter). This requires intensive daily practice, of course, but Cindy believes it's well worth the time, both spiritually and intellectually.

Not surprisingly, the homeschool routine differs markedly from the larger households I visit. Linda spends much of her time working independently, checking back with her mom when she is finished with a particular subject or assignment. "That's what's so much nicer when they get older," Cindy says. They do spelling and math together each morning, then Linda works on her own while Cindy exercises or does housework. Mark is somewhat more involved with the day-to-day homeschooling endeavor than most fathers I observe, but he is quite willing to let Cindy take the lead in shaping Linda's experience, in terms of both curriculum and pedagogy.

Cindy uses one primary curriculum called A Beka, a popular choice among homeschoolers. Founded in the 1970s to serve the private Christian school market, A Beka now provides materials for homeschoolers as well. In the latter case, parents can follow a comprehensive, accredited K–12 program complete with A Beka report cards and transcripts, or—as Cindy does—purchase pieces of the curriculum package for their own use and recordkeeping. (Interestingly, the University of California has refused to recognize some Christian high school courses that use A Beka textbooks—such as a biology course that apparently gave short shrift to evolution. After a Christian schools association filed suit, the UC decision was upheld in U.S. District Court in 2008.)

Based in Florida, A Beka describes itself as "unashamedly Christian and traditional" in its approach to education. "Our skilled researchers and writers do not paraphrase progressive education textbooks and add biblical principles," their Web site claims. "They do primary research in every subject and look at the subject from God's point of view. Of course, the most original source is always the Word of God, the only foundation for true scholarship in any area of human endeavor." The Bible as the primary authority for learning remains a central emphasis in all the families I visit.

And like many homeschool parents, Cindy forgoes teachers' editions and supplemental materials. As she describes her curriculum to me, I'm flipping through one of the A Beka guides. "I notice toward the end, this has them write essays," I say. "So how do you evaluate whether or not she's doing what she's supposed to?"

Cindy pauses as she considers my question. "Well, I'm not a licensed teacher, but I've done a lot of writing and I used to edit for a magazine, if you're talking about grammatical errors and things like that. Plus there are lists of rules that I can look up, too, if I'm questioning something. And I'm not really very concerned with that with her, because she reads so much and she writes stories for fun and her grammar is good."

The only joint activity Linda and Cindy do that morning is a spelling and vocabulary review, about a dozen words for each. They spend about ten minutes reviewing the words, discussing particularly tricky spellings, and then Linda provides definitions from memory for her vocab words. Her mother hands back the spelling list. "Okay, time for the next section of history," she announces. "If you want, you can go see what your dad is doing, if you'd like to read it to him. I know sometimes it's more interesting when you do it together."

As Linda heads off to the kitchen, Cindy confides, "She hates history. I know where she gets it—I don't like history either. We'll read it together sometimes, and I try to have a little dialogue about it just to make it more interesting, but the majority of the time she does it by herself. When her dad is home, I'll suggest she work with him, because he enjoys history and I feel she'll benefit more from it."

Here we see another tension in the homeschool teaching and learning dynamic: while a parent skilled and enthusiastic about a particular subject can inspire great learning, her dislike of (or lack of ability in) a particular subject may result in its neglect, or at least the implicit message that it is somehow less worthy of attention or devotion. This need not be the case, of course, particularly if the parent finds other means of providing a positive experience in that subject—through co-ops, community classes, and so on. Perhaps Linda wouldn't have liked history anyway, but it seems likely that her mom has influenced her significantly in that regard. While it's true that students in conventional schools may sometimes have teachers who lack passion for a particular subject, it's generally only a yearlong arrangement. Linda, on the other hand, has had a decade of what her mom admits is unenthusiastic history instruction.

So when he's available, Linda does history with her dad. This generally involves them taking turns reading to one another, and then Mark asking Linda the questions at the end of each chapter. If she gets any wrong, she has to review the chapter to find the answers. These questions focus primarily on factual recall—names, dates, and so on—or summarizing the historical interpretations provided by the text. The book they're using is called *America: Land I Love*, and it describes its purpose this way: "Through the story of America's rise to greatness, students will learn to recognize the hand of God in history and to appreciate the influence of Christianity in government, economics, and society." Again, God and Christianity serve as the reference point from which academic exploration and understanding occurs.

Cindy firmly believes that Linda is receiving better academic preparation at home than conventional schooling could possibly provide. "For me, one of the biggest benefits of homeschooling is you can provide an education that they're never going to get in a public school," she says, "because in public school, the teacher can be an awesome teacher but they're shooting kind of in the middle. You've got your kids who are really struggling to catch on and then you've got the really bright kids. You just kind of shoot in the middle and try to hope for the best for the class. But there is nothing that compares with that one-on-one, going at their pace in different subjects, because you're looking at the individual needs of the child and learning how they best learn and working with them that way."

There's no doubt that a one-to-one student-teacher ratio has tremendous benefits, and it's true that classroom teachers who just "shoot in the middle" will likely frustrate students who need additional assistance or challenge. But such an approach is not inevitable. An "awesome teacher" can be responsive to the ways that different students learn as well, and can make the experience of learning alongside others more of a strength than a liability. Public school critics will argue that such teachers are in short supply, and I wouldn't dispute that we need more of them. My point is simply that the quality of the learning experience depends more on the skills and commitment of the teacher than whether it occurs in a traditional classroom or around the kitchen table—and these homeschool visits around the country confirm as much, for better and worse.

———

A half hour later, Linda returns from reading history with her father. When I ask her opinion of other subjects, she tells me she doesn't like science much, either—the curriculum follows a similar format of reading the chapters and answering factual recall questions at the end. She doesn't do any experiments, although her mother notes that they did more of that when Linda was younger and the science was simpler.

On the other hand, Linda loves doing creative writing—"I have three books started on the computer," she tells me—and reading fiction. Her reading list from the previous year, fifty books long, points to a range of authors. Many of the books would likely be categorized as "Christian fiction," by authors such as Beverly Lewis and Frank Peretti, but interestingly, one of Linda's favorites from the list is Philip Pullman's His Dark Materials trilogy, a supernatural fantasy strongly critical of organized religion.

The Wallis homeschool curriculum, while providing the core subjects for Linda, is only part of her overall schooling experience. In what is often termed "dual enrollment," Linda takes several classes at the local public school, and also participates in extracurricular activities. So far, this arrangement has worked well. "What's really cool is that Vermont schools allow you to take whatever," Cindy says enthusiastically. "I do all the basics here at home with her, but this year she took Introduction to Foreign Language—which I certainly couldn't do with her—and then she did art, and she's done band. She plays the clarinet in band and she plays the trumpet in jazz band."

The question of whether states or districts should allow homeschoolers to take individual classes or participate in extracurricular activities at public schools has become increasingly prominent in recent years, with many homeschoolers pushing for greater access, either by urging lawmakers to champion their cause with new legislation or even taking the issue to court themselves. Currently, fourteen states have laws mandating that homeschoolers be allowed to enroll as part-time students, and seven states explicitly prohibit it; the rest leave it up to district discretion (the numbers are similar for policies about extracurricular participation).

Some districts resist the idea of part-time participation by homeschoolers. While the logistical challenges of accommodating unpredictable enrollment can be significant, it seems the underlying objection of some public school officials rests on the belief that students should either commit fully to school or stay away—no ordering a la carte, as one administrator put it. Participation in extracurriculars adds another layer of complexity. In many activities—sports especially—rosters are often limited, and some people object to the idea of a homeschooler with no other involvement at the school coming in and taking a spot on the team, or a lead in the school play, away from a full-time public school student. Homeschoolers often respond that they pay just as many taxes to support those programs as anyone else.

Another sticking point for extracurricular participation is accountability, and the concern that homeschoolers can't be held to the same eligibility standards (such as maintaining a C average or better in their classes) if they're being taught and assessed by their parents. During my days coaching basketball, for example, a star player in the league who had trouble with his grades switched to homeschooling and was never ruled ineligible again. Granted, homeschooling may have been the environment that improved his performance—a possibility that would have been easier to accept if he hadn't been scoring all those points against my team.

Nevertheless, I support the idea of public school districts trying to accommodate homeschoolers' desire for involvement in classes and extracurriculars. I certainly appreciate the desire of public school administrators to foster a cohesive community, and I understand how students dropping in for a couple of classes or band practice may complicate that goal. At the same time, however, many public schools—particularly high schools—are recognizing the need to broaden their vision of education beyond the school walls anyway. As students engage in service-learning projects, pursue local internships, and access community college and online courses, the boundaries between school and the wider community become increasingly permeable. To the extent that schools can provide opportunities for members of that community to interact and learn from one another, the richer the learning experiences can be, both for homeschoolers and the learning community they join.

An increasing number of districts offer a hybrid option for homeschoolers. These programs provide a kind of auxiliary support for parents, including consultations with licensed teachers, access to school resources and facilities, and the opportunity to take classes that might be more difficult for parents to provide themselves, such as foreign language, music, driver's education, lab sciences, or physical education. Many of them still allow parents to make all curricular choices and specify what kind of support they would like to receive. Because they are publicly funded, however, these programs bring external accountability with them, and homeschoolers are often required to take state assessments or have their progress reviewed by district personnel.

While some homeschool families see access to public school resources as the best of both worlds, other homeschoolers and their organizations reject the idea of dual enrollment, extracurricular participation, or public school support programs of any kind. Deeply suspicious of public schools, these skeptics interpret such overtures as a strategy to gain additional state funding, or even a sinister plot to gain access to homeschool children's hearts and minds. "Baltimore County Public Schools wants to give you some freebies," warns HSLDA in a state alert to Maryland members. "All you have to give them is your freedom." The district will receive thousands of dollars for each child who enrolls in their hybrid program, HSLDA asserts, "because each child will become a public school student. For the same reason, parental control of subjects and lesson content will vanish. Parents will remain involved as an appendage, but the real control will be in the hands of the public schools."

The Wallises don't participate in any such comprehensive homeschool support program, however. The local public school oversees Linda's public school classes, of course, but beyond that, Cindy still directs her daughter's educational process. Linda tells me that next year she wants to take several new classes: world drumming, word processing, piano, and Spanish. She also just talked with the athletic director, who told her that she could try out for basketball.

Given Cindy's enthusiasm for the opportunities that Linda has at the local public school, I'm curious if she thinks it provides her daughter with important experiences that Linda simply would not have otherwise. Cindy says no. "Not with me, because I would find a way. Before I realized that I could do this at school, we would do Creighton Community Center for art—I would just pay for it. And my husband and I are both musical, and he's the worship team leader for the youth. She sings on the worship team. I teach drama at the church, and she does that. And we're very fitness oriented. Three times a week we go to the gym. So I think that anything the school can provide, I could. Even foreign language—I could buy a CD for the computer and she could learn it that way. But it's convenient and I'm paying the taxes anyway, so I might as well benefit from it. The one thing that she would miss is a couple little girlfriends that she's made at the school who she wouldn't have. But we're so active in church activities, and we already know so many people."

Mark appreciates the balance that Vermont's flexibility with dual enrollment provides for Linda. "What you're talking about is your child being acclimated to society and operating in it. At what point do you say to her, it's time for you to make some choices? We feel like we've been able to keep her under the protection that we desire her to have and also raising her in the values and morals that we believe are important. And she also goes to school and sees how it is, and I think there's a value in that as well. Kids who never experience that, at some point, they're going to come to the reality—"

Cindy cuts in here, apparently to head off the impression that public schools provide an essential slice of reality: "People do ask about protecting your child and all that, and worry that the child won't know what it's like to live in the real world—it's so silly. When again in your lifetime will you sit in just a classroom with only people your age, that peer group? You'll never be under that peer pressure again. You'll go to work and you'll work with people twelve years younger than you, thirteen years older than you, and everything in between." Her voice grows passionate with conviction. "*That's* the real world, *that's* what you're really around. So school isn't the real world; that's one little piece of our life that prepares us academically for the real world."

I return to visit the Wallises the following September, just three weeks into their new school year. In a few short months, Linda is looking more like a teenager; her glasses are gone and she's sporting a stylish haircut with blonde highlights. She's taking four classes now at the local high school—band, piano, typing, and Spanish—and both Linda and her mom are struggling to balance her homeschool work with a significantly more robust public school experience. Cindy admits to me, "I don't know if we've bit off more than we should have for this year or not."

Part of the challenge for Cindy is the growing sophistication of Linda's academic material—not that it's too complicated to understand, but it does take additional time. "It was a lot easier when she was little," she observes, "because the concepts were so simple. As it's gotten more diffi-cult, I wish I had more time to look ahead, because I like to think of ideas to make it more creative. Right now, I feel like I'm just frazzled, catching up, asking, 'Okay, now what are you doing with this?'"

Even self-directed students sometimes need guidance and modeling on how to approach their learning, what questions to ask and which areas to probe more deeply. This type of inquiry isn't likely to happen when Linda is pretty much just moving from chapter to chapter on her own, an-swering recall-oriented questions. But when I wonder aloud if such guid-ance might be available in their local school, Cindy doesn't buy it. There are a few teachers who make their subjects come alive, she concedes, but most don't—Linda and her peers tell her that most of their classes are downright boring.

Linda finds that some subjects lend themselves well to homeschool-ing, such as math: "I'm good at math, so I don't really like the idea of having to sit in a big class, hearing them explain the same thing over and over." Science, on the other hand, seems to her like it would be much better in school. "They do more experiments and stuff like that," she says. "With science, I just read it and don't enjoy it." Linda's disenchant-ment with science, I suspect, has more to do with her read-the-book-and-answer-the-questions approach than with any inherent limitation of homeschooling. Although some advanced work would require access to a formal science lab, plenty of experiments are possible in the home (or out-door) setting, and co-ops can provide access to capable instructors with strong science backgrounds.

After beginning the morning with their typical spelling and vocab review, Linda and Cindy turn to Bible Quiz. The text this year is the New Testament book of Acts, but due to Linda's busier schedule, she's not planning on memorizing everything this time around. Cindy begins by having Linda practice reciting about fifteen verses from memory, and then they transition into the quiz format. "For ten points, who was from Antioch?" Cindy asks.

"Nicolas." Linda's answers are generally quick and decisive.

"Okay," Cindy says. "For twenty points, give a complete answer: it would not be right for the Twelve to what?"

"Neglect the ministry of the Word of God to wait on tables," Linda finishes.

The next forty minutes are spent in this back-and-forth quiz format, with questions based entirely on information recall from the text. Linda gets almost every answer correct—it's a pretty impressive display of memorization.

Next up this morning is math, and the Wallises have switched curriculum providers this year. The new one includes a computer program to assist with instruction. Cindy found their old curriculum, Saxon Math, to be less than user-friendly. "Unless you're a teacher, it was more difficult because they didn't break it down for you, *why* you're doing things," she says. "It gave you the answer, but you're trying to figure out *how* they got it."

The use of technology in homeschooling—as with education more generally—continues to expand, from Linda's simple math program all the way to complete "virtual schools." In some cases, "real-time" interaction is provided with a teacher and other classmates who are simultaneously logged in; other formats have students work independently and then submit their work for evaluation and credit. Everyone from private, for-profit companies to local school districts themselves are offering distance learning courses, many of them intended to serve as a complete curriculum. Both public charter schools and local public schools are increasingly turning to distance education as a way to draw more students and thus increase their funding from the state, without having to expand costly physical facilities. Other charters are dispensing with the "bricks and mortar" approach altogether, and providing all classes online for children throughout the state and even beyond.

Estimates vary widely on how many students use online learning in their education—anywhere from half a million to more than twice that, and increasing as much as 30 percent a year. Nearly one hundred thousand students attend full-time, public charter K–12 cyberschools, and some scholars even predict that by 2019, half of all high school courses will be offered online. Many parents and students express great enthusiasm for the rapid rise of online learning, but cyberschooling has its critics as well. Even programs funded by the state generally have little accountability or oversight, and concerns exist about their academic quality. Other critics worry about the prospect of students sitting isolated in front of a computer screen all day.

The popularity of homeschooling is also playing a role in the debate over whether states should be funding these virtual forms of education, as critics contend that many enrollees will be homeschooled children. It's unclear how many cyberstudents were homeschoolers who decided to "virtually" rejoin the public school system, but in some states that keep track, homeschool numbers have dropped as cyberschool enrollment increases.

In a case of rare agreement with public school advocates, many homeschoolers and their organizations are wary of public school distance learning as well. As with dual enrollment in public school classes and participation in extracurriculars, the prospects of governmental oversight gaining traction—however ancillary—in the homeschooling world sparks alarm and resistance. As one HSLDA e-mail alert warned, "Public school at home programs are an educational flop," and curriculum will inevitably "be sanitized to remove truth about God" and "injected with the most pernicious fads the government school system believes your children should be exposed to."

Nevertheless, homeschool curriculum companies themselves are starting to ride the cyberwave. Some now provide the option of online classes to supplement their traditional curricular packages. Other homeschool providers exist entirely online, in some cases effectively supplanting the parent as instructor entirely. As one cyberschool advocate boasted, it "takes most of the homeschooling burden off parents' backs."

But some homeschoolers see this as part of the problem, even with nonpublic cyberschools. Homeschooling, they argue, is fundamentally about parental control and oversight of their children's education. Even if parents select the curriculum provider, they don't organize and direct the instruction. In fact, HSLDA has a specific membership policy: parents must direct at least 51 percent of their child's education. As a result, if parents enroll their child in a comprehensive cyberschool, they are no longer considered homeschoolers in the eyes of HSLDA and are ineligible for membership.

Interestingly enough, however—in what may be a case of "if you can't beat 'em, join 'em"—HSLDA recently developed its own distance-learning program in conjunction with Patrick Henry College. Designed and taught by PHC faculty members, "these courses will provide the student with a classical liberal arts foundation rooted in a biblical world view." Whether these courses will count against HSLDA's 49 percent limit remains to be seen.

As the popularity of distance learning and virtual schooling continues to grow, the complexities of regulation and quality assurance extend well beyond traditional homeschooling. State oversight aimed at protecting the triad of interests—parents, children, and broader society—must now contend with a limitless and fluid virtual world of materials and delivery systems, making the prospect of substantive curricular oversight even more daunting.

The opportunity to visit with the Wallis family over these two years offers a few unusual "homeschooler demographics": an only child, pastor's kid, part-time public school student. But another distinctive is the high level of homeschool regulation in Vermont as compared with most other states. The central requirement is a year-end assessment, either through standardized achievement tests, a portfolio of student work, or a written evaluation from a Vermont-licensed teacher.

Cindy uses this latter option. "That's really nice," she says, "because we have a teacher who goes to our church. He's supposed to type a letter saying what Linda did in the last year and if she was successful or not." Cindy digs through her teaching folders and finds the forms she submitted last year for Linda's evaluation. "And it's so easy, because for me he says, 'I don't want to mess with it; type the letter saying what she did and put my name on it. I'll read through it, maybe ask her a couple questions, I'll sign the letter, and we're done.' So that's the way we do it," Cindy says, handing them to me. The cover letter reads:

To Whom It May Concern:

Linda Wallis has successfully accomplished the 8th grade by successfully completing the following courses: 8th grade Saxon math, A Beka Books' 8th grade Language Arts, Vocabulary, Spelling, Poetry, History & Geography, Science and Health. Linda read a booklet from the public school explaining the purpose and procedures for Howell County's town meetings as part of her Vermont study. In addition to this, she took a field trip to the State House in Montpelier and met Howell County's Senator Jim Stone.

Linda also read many books (see attached list) and took art, band (clari-net), jazz band (trumpet), and combined chorus at Creighton High School. She was actively involved in several programs at her church such as teaching children, and weekly practices and all performances with the youth worship band and drama team.

Linda participated again this year in Bible Quiz, competing against other junior high/high school students from Vermont, New Hampshire, and Maine. She did exceptionally well, taking first place over all. She also earned a national honor for memorizing (word for word) 12 chapters of Romans and the entire book of James out of the Bible.

Linda stayed physically active this year by attending Vermont Bodyworks three times per week. Her training included cardio machines, weight lifting, rock climbing, swimming, kick boxing and swim classes.

The school year was more than satisfactory. Linda received a well-rounded education and is ready to advance to the 5th grade. Thank you for your co-operation.

The letter was signed by the Wallises' friend from church, a licensed Vermont teacher. In states requiring a licensed teacher's evaluation, it's not uncommon for homeschoolers to ask a family friend to do it. On one hand, this makes sense—what parent wants to impose on some random, overworked public school teacher who may be biased against homeschooling in the first place? On the other hand, this arrangement obviously has great potential for abuse. Even though I'm confident Linda did everything listed in this letter, it would be easy enough for parents to misrepresent their child's educational experience.

I ask Cindy whether she resents the higher level of homeschooling regulation in Vermont, as compared with the Midwest, where they used to live. "In some ways it's really good because they stay on top of it," Cindy admits. "You know, the majority of homeschoolers I've met are very smart, and I think their parents take it seriously. But you have some where their parents are just keeping the kids home, and you're thinking, 'These poor dumb children are never going to be able to do anything in life.' It's really sad. But Vermont stays on top of it, and even though it's a pain in the butt—because I do it well and I don't like to have to go through all the red tape all the time—I can see why they do it."

Mark echoes his agreement here, mentioning a specific family he knows whose kids are being "robbed of an education" because of their poor homeschooling experience. At the same time, however, both are quick to point out that they see—both in their church youth work and in the substitute teaching they do in the local public schools—many kids with dreadful academic skills who are routinely promoted to the next grade level each June. It's an unfair double standard, they say, when homeschool critics imply that the public schools are any more successful in meeting the learning needs of all their students.

Despite relatively high levels of regulation, the relationship between homeschoolers and education officials here in Vermont seems relatively constructive. In an interview with the state's largest newspaper, Commissioner of Education Richard Cate expressed confidence in Vermont homeschoolers: "I think that the vast, vast majority are getting an excellent education. It's just different than what students might be getting inside the classroom. There's some really good things going on in some of these situations."

Many public school teachers and administrators do not share Cate's positive appraisal. The National Education Association, whose 3.2 million members make it the largest union in the country, is generally critical of homeschooling. They call for greater regulation, asserting that homeschoolers should be required to meet all state curricular and testing requirements, and that instruction should be provided only by those with a state teaching license. They also argue against homeschooler participation in public school extracurricular activities. Likewise, the National Association of Elementary School Principals expresses concern with the growth of homeschooling, and urges that "those who exercise these options are held strictly accountable for the academic achievement and social/emotional growth of children."

I suspect that at least part of this relatively hard line toward homeschooling emerges from administrators' frame of reference involving homeschooling issues. In a survey of Indiana superintendents I conducted a few years ago, for example, every respondent expressed concern about inadequate homeschool environments. A frequent complaint was that parents often begin homeschooling to skirt disciplinary or attendance problems their children are facing—which suggests that administrators' perception of homeschooling may be skewed because they're primarily interacting with parents who misuse the option. Public school officials would have little opportunity for ongoing engagement with families who are deeply committed to quality homeschooling, particularly if their children had homeschooled all their lives.

Linda's involvement with public school life creates some additional questions for the Wallises as they strive to be in the world but not of the world. One simple but telling example is that most curious of traditions, the high school prom. "Mark has always said she's not allowed to go to school dances," Cindy tells me, "because we don't care for the type of music, and some of the dancing is inappropriate. I support him completely and I understand where he is coming from and tend to think like he does. But I understand Linda's desires, too." Cindy's tone grows wistful and it's clear she's torn about this. "I am a girl and I've been to prom and I know every girl wants to be the princess. When Mark and I discuss this alone, I say that I can understand where she's coming from—and what's *one* dance? She knows what's appropriate and what's inappropriate, but she just wants to be the princess. Her heart's right." Cindy shrugs and smiles. "But he has a desire to protect her and it's set in his mind."

"So what's going to happen?" I ask.

"I don't know," she says. "Some youth groups do prom alternatives to keep their kids from going to the prom, but it still gives them the opportunity to dress up and be beautiful and have their pictures taken and go out to eat real fancy. But we keep so busy, and it's a brainchild that takes a lot of work." She hesitates, then adds, "But it's also my daughter. So I may just take it under my wing and try to do something big like that."

Proms and other formal dances for homeschoolers have become increasingly common across the country in recent years, often organized by local co-ops for the reasons Cindy mentions. Homeschoolers have recreated many other features of school life as well, including sports teams, yearbooks, class rings, and formal graduation ceremonies complete with embossed diplomas, caps and gowns, and commencement speakers. Companies seem quite happy to market their wares directly to homeschoolers and their organizations.

While Linda is hardly a social hermit or awkward misfit, she mentions on several occasions her desire for more time with friends. "I don't really get to be around my friends very much," Linda tells me when we talk privately. "I love my parents to death but, you know, being around them *all day*—sometimes I just have to tell them, 'I want to be around someone my own age!'" Linda laughs as she says this, and it becomes clear during our conversation that their relationship is generally marked by comfortable, open communication.

"What types of interactions do you have in your life where you come into contact with people or situations that conflict with your beliefs?" I ask.

"There is always public school," Linda says. "I'm not afraid to stand up for what I believe in." She mentions an assignment her class received to write and film a movie, and her classmates wanted it to be about a wizard. For many conservative Christians, wizardry is seen as part of the occult (think Harry Potter protests). Linda did not feel comfortable participating, so she asked the teacher if she could do something else. "She was fine with that," Linda says. "And she actually told my mother that she thought it was neat that I could stand up for what I believed in."

Linda mentions another opportunity she has to engage with differing beliefs, a program called The Way of the Master, which trains Christians to proselytize strangers. Although she finds it easy to answer Bible study questions from a peer, Linda acknowledges that sharing her faith with an adult can be more challenging. They sometimes "get on the defensive side and they start asking *you* questions. So that requires a lot of thinking—you know, this is what I believe, this is *why* I believe it." She echoes something I hear her mom say on several occasions: "If someone challenges my intellect, I know where my beliefs stand. Everything has to be in check with God's Word."

Mark continues to be pleased with Linda's part-time enrollment at the local high school. "It gives her an opportunity to do some of those things that Cindy and I really are not qualified to do," he says, while still letting them remain the primary influences in subjects such as science (evolution) and health (sex education). But Mark doesn't think that the increased course load at the public school indicates any desire by Linda to stop homeschooling; she regularly mentions to him that she's glad she doesn't have to be a full-time conventional student. Regardless, Mark also makes it clear to me—and no doubt he has to Linda as well—that attending public school full time is "not an option."

I ask Mark if he has a sense, now that Linda has entered her teen years, what challenges he and Cindy might be likely to face in terms of parenting, and especially Linda wanting to go her own way or speak her own mind. This prompts a rueful smile. "Well, I think that boys are going to be a problem," he says. "And beyond that, we try to have open communication around the house." He doesn't want Linda to follow their lead simply because they say so, but because she recognizes it's the right thing to do. "There's going to be that separation where she is gonna have to be able to spread her wings a little bit or she won't ever fly. And so as parents, whether public school or homeschool, you have to learn the art of release. How do you release that child into the world in such a way that you're giving them enough freedom to learn but not get hurt?"

The art of release strikes me as a fitting image, as is the need to strike a balance between freedom and safety. Mark has been around adolescents enough to know he won't do it perfectly, and he also acknowledges that Linda will "fall down some" as well. Chuckling, he adds, "And I'm sure we'll have our times of saying, 'Oh my gosh, why don't we send her over to Grandma's house or something!'"

Mark seeks to provide Linda with the social freedom she needs to make decisions about the kind of person she wants to be. But I also wonder about Linda's intellectual freedom, and what opportunities she will have to explore and consider a range of perspectives and beliefs. "So besides the social challenges that adolescents face in terms of how they want to conduct themselves," I ask, "do you think the same thing will go on academically? Will Linda have the opportunity in her homeschooling to read and explore different philosophies about life, or is your feeling that your job as parents is to just infuse what you see as the right way of thinking?"

Mark's response echoes the idea of protection and preparation that I've heard from the other homeschool parents during my journeys. "My personal style would be more to equip her now with biblical standards and truths and principles that would take root in her," he says, "not just by education but also by experiencing God's power and his life-transforming love and provision. I don't believe I need to make part of her curriculum books that are going to cause confusion that she's going to have to work through at an age that she is basically not prepared for *spiritually*."

This is why Mark doesn't want Linda taking a full slate of classes at the public school. The ones she takes now aren't as likely to delve into issues that might challenge her core values and beliefs. It's not that Mark doesn't want Linda to consider these questions eventually, but he wants her to be secure in her own convictions first—and he's particularly leery of an educational environment where authority figures might apply pressure, even unintentionally, for her to reject what she has been taught at home and at church.

Later, I explore this same issue of intellectual freedom with Cindy. "One of the reservations that some people have about homeschooling," I say, "is if the vast majority of kids' educational experience is guided by their parents, they don't have sufficient opportunity to develop their own way of thinking and looking at the world, to become their own person."

Cindy nods, obviously familiar with this concern. "I do try to teach her my values, but at the same time I can say that she's a very strong personality and she doesn't always see things eye-to-eye with me. But she does take after her father and me in a lot of ways. We have strongly influenced her," she says unapologetically, "but that's the way I want it."

Homeschool parents probably influence their kids more than other parents, Cindy acknowledges, but "unless a parent is controlling and doesn't allow them to experience anything," they'll still become their own people. And even with parents who try to control everything, Cindy adds, "those children are probably going to buck that system somewhere along the line—they're gonna get out there, they're gonna see, and they're gonna form their own opinions." Ultimately, Cindy concludes, her daughter's faith must become her own if it is to mean anything—a sentiment echoed by Mark as well.

Conservative Christian homeschoolers see broader culture, its messages and morals frequently at odds with their own, as the eight-hundred-pound gorilla. They themselves are the underdog, merely trying to hold their ground. (I suspect most parents, religious or not, have felt this way, particularly as their children enter adolescence.) Again, the desire to protect and preserve emerges most strongly in educating their children. "In the formative years when they're so young," Cindy says, "why would you want to send your child away for the majority of the day and let someone else's ideas and personality be placed in your child every day? *I'm* her parent; God gave her to *me* to form and to raise, so I feel that's my responsibility. And the things we learn, we're able to learn from a Christian perspective."

The right of parents to raise and educate their children—and the complete lack of government authority in that regard—is perhaps *the* foundational conviction in homeschooling. For conservative Christian homeschoolers, this clearly has theological underpinnings. As Cindy expressed on multiple occasions, "God gave her to *me*."

Creighton Evangelical Church is a modest, white clapboard building with a tall spire at one end. A large wooden cross stands out front, and an American flag flies from a pole in the courtyard. CEC draws around 250 parishioners each week to its narrow, low-ceilinged sanctuary. During one of my visits, the sermon focuses on living in but not of the world. "We should be living a lifestyle that stands apart from this polluted world," the preacher advises. "Holiness is evaluating everything we do in light of God's Word." But holiness is not just about keeping oneself holy, he continues: "We advance the gospel of Jesus Christ through extending mercy to others and telling them who Jesus is."

One way that the Wallises seek to do this is through missions work with an organization called Convoy of Hope, which travels to low-income urban areas and provides a variety of services, such as food distribution, job fairs, medical attention, and children's activities. A Christian ministry, it also presents a brief sermon message for attendees. So far, the Wallises have participated in projects in Indianapolis, Boston, Philadelphia, and Washington, D.C.

In all my visits to Creighton Evangelical, I hear few explicit references to politics or the civic role of Christians. Serving others—in one's congregation but also beyond—is presented as a Christian's obligation rather than a citizen's. The only place I see sociopolitical issues addressed is in the denominational magazine that is handed out with the church bulletin. Although the main articles generally focus on applying biblical principles to everyday life, regular sidebars include conservative commentary on issues such as abortion, homosexuality, public religious displays, and updates on current legal issues that "can threaten Americans' religious freedoms."

When I ask Mark and Cindy about the relationship between their Christian faith and their role as democratic citizens, they describe a vision of citizenship that some might find internally inconsistent. On the one hand, they don't advocate a theocratic state or imposing their religious beliefs on others. "To make children recite a piece of Scripture or a prayer," Mark explains, "becomes nothing more than just saying words. To impose that everyone pray like I do, or live like I do—I just don't see that biblically." On the other hand, however, they clearly draw on their religious convictions in their support for policies or candidates.

And while they value their democratic citizenship, it is clearly subordinate to their religious commitments. "I'm proud to be an American," Cindy says, "and I still think this is the greatest country, even with all its problems. But I am a citizen of heaven first and foremost: I will follow every law unless it goes against God's Word. And then if I have to break a law in order to stand on *God's* Word, that's who I am, that's who I will always be. But I'm not one who believes in blowing up abortion clinics—none of that. That's not God's way either. We are good law-abiding citizens; we just live like Christ lived."

To illustrate, Cindy draws upon one of the few gospel stories that describes Jesus's view of civil authorities: "You know, when they brought the coin to Christ and asked him about that, he said, 'Well, whose picture do you see on the coin?' 'Caesar's.' He told them, 'Give Caesar what's due to Caesar, give God what's due to God.' Your life, honor, everything that you are, goes to God. But pay your taxes, take care of your financial responsibilities, vote, and try to make the country the best you can make it."

This notion of dual citizenship, with the obligations of faith taking priority, hardly qualifies the Wallises for the fringe of American society. But the certainty they hold on many social and political issues makes the possibility of productive dialogue across disagreements more remote. "If I believe it lines up with God's Word then it's hard for me to bend or yield at all," Cindy acknowledges. "To me the Bible is not full of a whole lot of gray; I think it's pretty black and white."

If Linda continues using A Beka for her social studies curriculum, she will soon be reading texts that offer a similarly dichotomous view of U.S. history, government, and civics. The *United States History* text makes clear the lens through which it peers: "The Christian perspective is the key to a proper understanding of history, for it enables us to see God's purpose and plan in human events." Furthermore, it makes no pretense of political neutrality in its analysis, identifying one of its goals as contrasting "the harmful effects" of liberalism and "the benefits" of conservatism in the American political system. The story it tells "exposes the error and consequences of Marxism, humanism, modernism, and other false philosophies; and it presents the blessings of the Biblical principles and philosophies on which the United States was founded." The textbook's approach to pluralism is particularly striking: "The 'melting pot' concept is important because it encourages our unity as Americans and gives strength to our nation." Multiculturalism, it cautions, is "a dangerous philosophy that promotes division" and will "keep minority groups from being assimilated into mainstream American culture."

The *American Government* textbook shares this strongly conservative message. In claiming that citizens need to feel that laws are backed by divine authority, the text points out, "Even many of the world's most wicked rulers have in times past invoked the blessings of God upon their actions, realizing that people are more likely to follow when God is mentioned." The irony of this danger, however—leaders citing divine authority—seems lost on the textbook authors. Hopefully it will not be lost on Linda a couple of years from now.

At the end of the school year, Cindy sends me a final update. "I'm still working outside of the home," she writes, "so I wasn't quite as active in the 'schooling' as I would've liked to be. However, to my knowledge, most homeschool students Linda's age do a good deal of self-teaching. Linda's work and testing results indicate that she didn't have any trouble with the curriculum." Linda's public school grades were good, Cindy reported: all As except for a B+ in band. Summer plans include Linda spending several weeks at a church youth camp in New Hampshire, and the family hopes to participate in another Convoy of Hope service project in Indianapolis.

Looking back, some parts of Linda's academic experience seem particularly strong, such as her love of reading and her obvious skills in memorization. Others facets, such as history and science, haven't been as successful or rewarding. But the learning dynamic that strikes me as particularly unfortunate here is the pattern of "read the book, answer the questions, take the quizzes, and move on" that seems to characterize much of Linda's independent work.

How significant a criticism of homeschooling is this? I think back to the public high school where I spent most of my teaching years. There were two social studies classrooms near the stairwell I always took. As I passed by the first room, students were invariably hunched over their desks, staring blankly at the endless stack of worksheets they were required to complete. In contrast, I could always hear the other social studies class well before I reached the door—an animated buzz of thoughtful, informed discussion about historical and current events.

My point is that both kinds of education, and everywhere in between, happen in public schools. To argue that Linda is assuredly missing out on a public school education rooted in higher-order critical thinking is to overlook the real possibility that she ends up in the first classroom. On the other hand, it seems likely that she'd get a chance to be in the second class a few times as well over the course of her schooling. Many homeschoolers believe they'd be giving up too much in return for that possibility.

Indiana Homeschool Convention

I'm driving up Route 37, headed to the home of Carrie and Tom Shaw and their four children, who live in a university town in northwest Indiana. On the way up, I plan to stop in Indianapolis at the annual convention for the Indiana Association of Home Educators (IAHE) Many of the cars surrounding me on this rural highway have the new Indiana license plates bearing the words IN GOD WE TRUST in front of a waving American flag. While not the standard Indiana plate, it's the only specialty option available without an extra fee (an exception the ACLU has seen fit to challenge in court), and provides an apt symbol of the cultural backdrop here in the heartland.

Upwards of five thousand Hoosiers attend the state homeschool convention each year, and as I meander through the Indiana Convention Center, the feel is fairly similar to the one I attended in California. Although the crowd here seems less racially and culturally diverse, I do spot a number of Amish families, the men dressed all in black and the women in long dresses and white bonnets. Overall, I see plenty of large families walking around together, although there also appear to be a fair number of women with neither husbands nor children in tow.

The cavernous General Assembly room has thousands of chairs lined in rows leading to a raised dais in the front; a massive set of bleachers, at least forty rows high, fills the back portion of the room. While nothing in IAHE's title suggests a religious bent, this event is unabashedly Christian in nature. The first speaker opens the proceedings in prayer, and then asks everyone to rise for the singing of the hymn, "To God Be the Glory." Following this, a handful of special convention guests are introduced, including several state legislators who offer brief statements of support for keeping Indiana homeschoolers free of government regulation.

The keynote address by John Stonestreet of Summit Ministries is titled "The Biblical View of Education: Why Students Must Have a Biblical World-view." If our kids have the wrong worldview, he tells us, they will get lost amidst a culture of materialism and secular humanism. If the church is silent, other voices will fill the gap. "Evangelicals suffer from a case of Alzheimer's," he asserts, and stresses the need to recover a sense of Christian history that recognizes how their message differs dramatically from that of our present age.

After Stonestreet's talk, I make my way to the exhibit hall where, similar to the California convention, thousands of homeschoolers mill around hundreds of vendor booths containing shelves upon shelves of curriculum materials for kindergarten through high school, computer software, lab supplies, arts and crafts—an overwhelming array of options. I can't help but think that the abundance of smartly marketed products might give some homeschool parents—especially those just starting out—the impression that everything they need for successful homeschooling is here at their fingertips. This is the same mistaken assumption I have seen some public school administrators make as well: the curriculum product has all the answers—is the answer. Quality teaching becomes, at best, an afterthought.

I return to the General Assembly hall later in the day to hear Ken Ham, one of the world's foremost proponents of "young earth creationism" (the earth was created by God in six literal days) and founder of Answers in Genesis, whose publications are favorites in the Carroll household. But before Ham takes the stage, the moderator introduces Eric Miller, founder of Advance America, whose promotional literature describes itself as "Indiana's leading pro-family, pro-life, pro-church, pro-homeschooling organization." Miller bounds up to the podium and delivers a dramatic plea for support for Advance America and its mission.

"People have got to know the truth about the issues," he proclaims. "I've been involved in defending homeschooling since the beginning, about 1983. We face some of the most serious, ominous, immediate, and dangerous threats to families and churches and homeschooling that we have faced the past twenty-three-plus years!" Miller highlights four of these: same-sex marriage, high taxes (supported by the same folks who want same-sex marriage, he charges), abortion, and homeschool regulation. On the latter point, Miller warns, "We can lose our freedom to homeschool in one legislative session! There are powerful interests working against you in the Indiana General Assembly."

Miller then highlights some recent state legislation aimed at improving screening and assessment procedures for children's social, emotional, and behavioral health. Miller predicts that 15 percent of Indiana children will end up being assigned to mental health counselors and prescribed "strong psychotropic drugs." If your child is tested, Miller warns, "your children can be taken away from you and placed in foster homes with homosexuals. This is real—this is dangerous." (In the two years since this legislation was enacted, by the way, we have yet to see such dramatic consequences.) "Don't sit on the sidelines any longer," Miller concludes. "We are going to reclaim lost ground for our families, our churches, and our freedoms. Working together we can make this happen. God bless you all."

Not all convention presentations are as inflammatory or adversarial. For instance, I attend a thoughtful session by David Hazell, creator of a K–12 curriculum called My Father's World, who gives a talk titled "Expanding Your Child's Understanding of the World and Its Cultures." A former missionary to Russia, he advocates practical ways to enlarge homeschoolers' appreciation of cultural diversity and teach them to serve others, rather than expecting to simply be served by others. "I don't own my children," he asserts; instead, he sees himself as a steward of God's children, and it's his responsibility to give them a range of experiences and opportunities to develop their own gifts and calling in life.

As I depart the convention and continue my drive northward toward the Shaws, I reflect on the prediction that conventions such as these will become increasingly less important as technology allows homeschoolers to network and shop online. In his excellent book *Homeschool: An American History*, Milton Gaither suggests the Internet's impact extends even farther, ultimately diffusing the power of movement leaders to control the shape and agenda of homeschooling moving forward. Given the broad—and apparently growing—diversity of homeschoolers themselves, such a shift might ultimately present a broader and more accurate image of who homeschoolers are and what they're about.

8

THE SHAW FAMILY
"Nobody Can Teach My Kids Better Than I Can"

The Shaws live in a quiet, tree-lined neighborhood, within easy walking distance of a newly opened elementary school up the road. Tom is an electrical engineer at a small company in town, and Carrie worked as a nurse practitioner for five years before turning her full-time focus to homeschooling. I sit in their bright, airy kitchen with Carrie and her four tow-headed girls: seven-year-old Sarah, five-year-old Elise, two-year-old Ruth, and infant Samantha. "We usually start the day with praying, saying the Pledge, and singing," Carrie explains to me. Sensing that the girls are feeling a little self-conscious in my presence, she offers the prayer this morning by herself, thanking God for the day, and asking for wisdom, cheerfulness, and diligence as they study. Next they stand and recite the Pledge of Allegiance, which Ruth finishes off with a rousing yell, eliciting a burst of laughter from Sarah, Elise, and their mom.

"You know what we haven't sung for a while?" Carrie says to the girls. "How about 'The Name of the Lord'? Now, this is *not* a 'Mom solo.'" The girls sheepishly agree, and they begin to sing in beautiful voices: *"The name of the Lord is a strong tower, the righteous run into it and are safe—"* Carrie breaks in with a smile: "You guys want to dance?"

"No!" the girls shout, with the most energy I've seen so far.

"We usually dance with this one," Carrie informs me, chuckling, "but I can tell that they're not going to want to." Carrie picks up the song again, encouraging her daughters to clap along with her as they sing. When they finish, Carrie turns to me with a grin: "The restraint was palpable. Normally we're wild," she says, as the girls laugh embarrassedly.

Carrie then asks Sarah to read the proverb they are focusing on this week—"Apply your heart to instruction and your ears to words of knowledge"—and briefly discusses with the girls its relevance to their homeschooling: "The most important part of the whole thing is, 'How can we use this Bible verse today?'" The girls are still a bit bashful with me sitting there, but then Elise comes up with the example of learning from their music teacher. They discuss how it's important to have a "teachable heart," to pay attention and be willing to learn things.

While Sarah and Elise get started with some handwriting practice, Carrie tells me about their curriculum, My Father's World—which happens to be the one I just heard about at the convention. She explains to me that she's using a first-grade curriculum as the base for both Sarah and Elise, "which is pretty much the only way my brain can handle it." She supplements the material for Sarah—who is working at least a grade level higher—with additional materials suggested by the curriculum. "It tells you what you're going to do every day,' Carrie says, showing me the teacher's manual, "including art, music, science, Bible, reading, and writing—"

Elise, the more ebullient of the two older girls, has been getting a little rambunctious, making silly faces and noises, despite Carrie's repeated warnings. She now turns to her daughter and says in a calm but firm tone, "Okay, now your mouth is in timeout. I've asked you three times not to do that. Look at my eyes. Now you cannot talk, until I tell you that you can." Elise complies, mildly chastened.

Carrie returns to her explanation of their curriculum. "In first grade, they're jazzed about getting you reading and writing. And starting in second grade, they really integrate the Bible and history aspects. So here it tells you—Year One, Year Two, Year Three—what period of history you'll do, with timelines and all. And they're very much into making sure you have a good view of the whole world, of what's going on. You read a lot of missionary books and do a lot of geography."

My Father's World doesn't include a math curriculum, but it recommends a program very popular among homeschoolers called Singapore Math, whose approach balances mastery of basic skills with conceptual reasoning. As the name suggests, it's used by Singaporean students, who consistently rank at the top of international math comparisons—often the initial reason homeschoolers give it a try. (Singapore Math is starting to gain traction in U.S. public schools, with more than six hundred schools using it, and California recently adding the curriculum to its list of approved options.) This is the Shaws' first year using the program.

"I'm not a math expert by any stretch," Carrie says, "but I can tell you it's completely different than the one that Sarah started out learning. She's not doing just rote repetition; she's building on concepts earlier, and they use a lot of pictures and manipulatives, so you can actually see and feel what you're learning."

A few minutes have passed since Carrie's rebuke of Elise, and she now turns to her daughter and tells her that her mouth can "come out of time-out." Carrie asks her, "Do you understand why we don't babble when people are trying to do their work?"

"Because it's distracting?" Elise ventures.

"Thank you," Carrie affirms. She turns to Sarah and asks her to show me what she's doing. Sarah hands me a booklet filled with partially filled-in charts, where she records her daily homeschool activities. "Sarah does her own," Carrie explains. "I help Elise with hers."

Homeschool regulation in Indiana is minimal. Like California and many other states, there are technically no statutes specifically for home-schooling—it is treated as nonpublic, nonaccredited schooling, and state permission is not required. Schools in this category must provide a minimum of 180 days of instruction, the same as public schools, and attendance records must be kept. They are required to provide "instruction equivalent to that given in the public schools," but the state does not define what "equivalent" means, and they are exempt from the specific curricular and programmatic requirements of public schools. Parents who remove their children from public schools (in order to homeschool or place in private school) must notify officials, in order to avoid truancy. If parents begin homeschooling from day one, opinions differ on whether formal notification is required; state officials say yes, whereas HSLDA claims such "enrollment" is voluntary. Regardless, the state doesn't enforce any such enrollment requirements, and many Hoosier families never add their names to the department of education list.

Carrie announces that it's "*Little Women* time," and they all head to the living room, where she spends about fifteen minutes reading aloud to the girls, stopping every paragraph or two to make sure the older girls are following the storyline and understanding the vocabulary. For almost fifteen minutes, Ruth and Samantha play quietly on the floor, just enough time for Carrie to finish the chapter. Closing the book, she asks the older girls for a brief summary, which they give with minimal prompting.

As we head back toward the kitchen, Carrie says to me, "You know, as you kind of go along, you add things here and there to the curriculum. I was inspired by our church's missionary fair and the missionary book that they put together of all their missionaries. So we're going to go through and pick a family, once a week, learn about them, a little bit about the country, pray for them, and put them on our map." Today's missionary family is the Sowettas. Carrie provides some basic facts about their country, the Philippines, and the girls locate it on the big map on the back wall. Carrie then describes each of the family members and holds up the page displaying their photos. She reads off the list of the Sowettas' prayer requests, and then they all spend a couple minutes praying for the missionary family.

Following this lesson, Carrie asks seven-year-old Sarah to try to recite "One, Two, Three," a poem she has been memorizing over the past couple weeks. "Now where do you want to stand?" Carrie asks her. "Pick a place."

Sarah eyes me, the outsider. "Upstairs in my room."

Carrie bursts into laughter. "It would be so hard for us to hear you," she says. "It would make me sad. Can you come over real quick, I want to tell you something." She whispers in Sarah's ear, but I can make out most of it: "—you've been doing a good job and working hard, okay, so I want you to be brave and give this a try."

Sarah nods, returns to the other side of the table, and begins reciting her poem. Thirty-two lines later, with only one pause for prompting, she finishes with a sigh of relief, and her sisters and mom clap appreciatively.

"Yessss!" Carrie says. "Nice job! You're on the home stretch. When we do it next time, I think we can go ahead and add the last two stanzas. And the one thing about it, if I didn't have the book, there are some words that I wouldn't have caught, because it was hard to do it slow and loud, but we can keep practicing on that. It was very good, very good!"

The rest of the morning remains a juggling act for Carrie, as she balances the needs of two young, sometimes restless kids with the formal learning agenda of the older two. While she occasionally reminds or reprimands her daughters, the overall tone is positive and playful. This is a woman who knows what she's doing, and she does it well.

Carrie says she and Tom are open to the possibility that God may one day lead them to put their kids in institutional schools, but their plans right now are to homeschool "for the long haul." Carrie and Tom both attended public schools while growing up, and their experiences were generally positive. But after getting married and having kids, Carrie says, "we really wanted to provide as much saturation as possible in the things of God and his Word in our kids' early years. So I guess our first thought was, 'Let's send them to a Christian school—they're going to pray for our kids, they're going to study the Bible.'" But then they got to know some families at church who homeschooled, and in particular one family. "You just looked at them and said, man, they are doing something right. Just the godly children they were raising and the way things were working for them." So Tom and Carrie began investigating the idea, talking with others, and then decided this was the way God was leading their family.

After lunch, Sarah and Elise do some independent reading, until Carrie gets her younger two girls settled down for their naps. Their last activity of the day together is art appreciation, focusing on a painting by Francisco José de Goya y Lucientes. Carrie reads a bit of background about the artist, then opens it up for the girls to make any observations that strike them about the painting, occasionally interjecting with a question to spur more thinking. "See how he used different colors of red?" she says at one point. "It looks very rich and soft, like velvet or something." After about ten minutes, Carrie wraps it up and tells them they're going to visit the university art museum soon to look at some paintings like this one.

My next visit with the Shaws, a couple of months later, begins much like the first one, with prayer, hymn singing, the Pledge of Allegiance, and Bible reading. The Bible verse for today is 1 Corinthians 14:40, which Elise reads aloud from her Bible: "Everything should be done in a proper and orderly way." They also read together a short morality tale from *A Child's Book of Character Building* about a boy who learns the importance of orderliness after misplacing a special watch his father had given him. Carrie asks the girls if they can think of ways that they have learned that lesson as well, and then points out how much better they've become at keeping the basement less cluttered with their toys, and how that makes things easier to find.

As they settle into their language arts curriculum, toddler Ruth is occupied at the kitchen table by mounds of brightly colored Play-Doh, and infant Samantha picks at Cheerios while secured in her high chair. The older girls pull out their language arts workbooks and get busy. After a few minutes, Carrie checks Elise's progress, and notices she has misspelled *table* as *tabble*. She leans over to her and says, "Elise, you're doing a good job. These are very good and very neat. I have one thing that I want you to do—I want you to go down through each word and read them and make sure that you've spelled them the way that you want to spell them. Let's read them."

Elise reads through the list of words, and then Carrie asks, "Are there any words that you think have a spelling that is not what you want?" Elise isn't sure, even after reading them aloud once more at Carrie's request. "See this double consonant here? What does that do to this letter?" Carrie asks, pointing to the *a* in *tabble*.

Elise now recognizes her mistake and explains it to her mother. She erases and rewrites her answer, then continues on with her work. A couple minutes later she stops and looks up, a plaintive look on her face. "Mom, can I have a snack?"

Carrie suppresses a laugh. "No, you may not have a snack!"

"I thought part of school was lunch and recess," Elise argues sweetly.

Carrie dissolves into laughter at this. "You know those kids who always say, 'My favorite class is lunch and recess'?" she says to me. "That's Elise Marie!"

I ask Carrie if she's noticed a big difference since adding baby Samantha to the family, in terms of her impact on the rhythm of the homeschool day.

"It's actually Ruthie," she says, pointing at her two-year-old. "She has different ways of distracting the homeschool environment. We end up doing a lot of our read-aloud time and crafts and painting and stuff when Ruthie's down for a nap because we just can't accomplish that very well." She pauses, then adds ominously, "But Samantha will be a toddler soon! And when she is, we'll be—" Carrie grabs her throat in a choking motion, laughing.

The girls have gotten started with their math, and Sarah sits staring at her book. "How do I do this puzzle?" she asks her mom

"Let's read the instructions out loud," Carrie suggests. They work together for a minute, and then Carrie turns her attention to Elise, who has been working on a coin problem in her math book, trying to figure out the different combinations that will equal a dollar. With the coins spread out on the table before them, she and her mom start to move them around, and Elise jots down her answers as they go.

When I ask Carrie if she has any teacher's guides, she says she hasn't found them necessary yet, with her kids so young. For now, "they're pretty easy concepts. I don't feel like I need someone to tell me how to teach how to add single digits. Maybe I think a little too highly of myself or something," she says, chuckling. "But I can see where they would become extremely useful as the kids get older."

Carrie rewards Sarah and Elise for finishing their work by letting them play a few games of math bingo. Amidst Carrie's job as the "caller," we talk about the role that co-ops play in their homeschooling experience. She estimates that they probably spend about three-quarters of their homeschooling time actually at home, and the rest in co-op activities or other community learning experiences. As the kids get older, she expects their outside involvement will increase. As for now, she says, "there are many things we say 'no' to, because with young kids, it's just too hectic. Part of why I like homeschooling is because we don't have a hectic schedule. For us right now, the general rule is, if it's something that I cannot reproduce here—physical education is a good example. We can do exercise, but not group activities. Like right now, our co-op is doing a soccer unit. So PE and then drama and music time are things I can't reproduce here."

Carrie remarks that the parents leading the music co-op are professional musicians and the woman who runs the drama workshop was previously involved in New York City theater. "And those are things that will be a lot of fun for them. It's got to be fun and it's got to be something that's not reproducible here." At Carrie's invitation, I had originally planned on attending one of these co-op activities this year, but when she checked with her group, some members told Carrie they weren't comfortable with me, an outsider and researcher to boot, being there.

"We're doing a science co-op again this summer, too," Carrie continues. "So I'll have that one day a week for the whole summer. My friend lives out east toward Galston, near woods and streams, and it's just a great outdoor place. Last year we did botany."

"We did trees and plants and flowers and insects," Sarah interjects.

Carrie nods. "Yeah, we learned about germination and pollination. It was really fun and it's about a chance to get the kids together for a couple hours—it's some of the families that we do PE and drama with, maybe six or seven families. This summer we're going to do 'Flying Creatures of the Fifth Day: Zoology,'" she explains, referring to the biblical account of God creating birds on the fifth day.

During our conversation, Ruth has been getting more and more disruptive in the background, with her mother periodically attempting to placate her. The bingo game has ended and Carrie decides everyone needs a short break before lunch. The three older girls head downstairs to their basement playroom while Carrie picks up the kitchen and starts making sandwiches. She points to a large book over on the opposite counter. "We have a homeschool yearbook for the area, too. A mom kind of put that together. You know, it's not a professional production, but it shows kids' individual pictures and their grades, and then snapshots of things they're doing, their activities and stuff." I pick it up and look through it; it has obviously been paged through many times already by the Shaws.

After lunch, with the younger girls finally napping upstairs, Carrie turns her focus to the next activity. "We're going to study birds this summer in our co-op," she tells Sarah and Elise, "so today we're just going to read a little bit in this book about some of the birds we've seen in the neighborhood." She informs me that they have a robin's nest outside their back door, and invites the girls to go check on it. Moments later, they burst in the back door, with the exciting news that the eggs have hatched. They settle into chairs and Carrie reads to them about robins, interspersing her reading with a few comprehension checks. She draws their attention to the length of time between hatching and leaving the nest, and points out, "So in a couple of weeks, we should be paying attention to see those little robins flying out of the nest. We'll have to keep an eye out and see what happens."

Shortly thereafter, we head back to the living room for the final piece of the homeschooling day, and Carrie asks the girls to tell me about the book they've been reading together.

"It's called *Silver Lake*," Sarah volunteers, "and there are four girls, like us." She and Elise take turns giving me a detailed summary of the story thus far.

Carrie opens the book. "Anyway," she says, "here we are: it's Christmas Day in the Dakota Territory, in the middle of the winter." She begins to read aloud, not stopping much this time—it's a pretty straightforward and engaging narrative that benefits from reading without interruption. Twenty minutes later, it's now just past two o'clock, and the formal home-schooling day is finished. As I take my leave of the Shaws, Sarah and Elise are headed outside to play, while Carrie tries to make the most of the hour or so she has left before her younger two girls awake.

When I return the following year, Carrie welcomes me at the door and ushers me inside. "How's homeschooling going so far this year?" I ask, as I take off my coat and grab my notebook and tape recorder from my bag.

"Well, let me tell you," Carrie says with a smile, "there's many times I thought, *What in the world am I doing?* Sometimes in the morning with the two little ones—like after being interrupted in Sarah's spelling lesson for the ninety-sixth time—I just want to say, 'I'm done! I'm outta here! See ya later!'" She laughs. "Because you have Ruth who, in spite of her abilities to entertain herself, chooses not to, and Samantha, who's still a baby, but now she's mobile and curious." She pauses, and shrugs. "I just have to cut myself a bit of slack because I find myself going, 'Think of what we could have done today!'"

We enter the kitchen, where all the girls are finishing up their break-fast. "As far as Sarah and Elise," Carrie continues with her update, "they have more academic things I put on them this year. Sarah started Latin this year, and writing, which she didn't do before. So it takes more time. Last year, we were in the phase where I was still getting done in the morn-ing for the most part, but maybe a little tiny bit after lunch. And now it's kind of evolved into morning, big break, nap, and then finish. It's longer and more spread out than I'd prefer—we usually finish by two thirty or three—but it still gives the girls time enough to play and hang out."

Carrie gets things started, asking the older girls to take turns reading the Bible passage for today. Afterward, Carrie asks, "Sarah, can you tell me in your own words what happened? If I never heard that story before and I wanted to, but we didn't have a Bible with us?" Sarah provides a brief summary, prompted occasionally by Carrie for details.

After some hymn singing, it's time for spelling. While the girls re-view their words, Carrie tells me about a big curricular change in the works for next year—they're switching from My Father's World to a pro-gram called Veritas. Started in 1997, Veritas promotes "classical Christian education," a systematic, chronologically based approach to learning, and one of the fastest-growing curricular approaches in the homeschool marketplace. It was a hard decision, Carrie tells me. Although she likes *My Father's World*, it provides only Bible, science, and history, then recommends a variety of other resources. "I felt like we were a little bit all over the map," she says.

Carrie started investigating Veritas after reading *The Well-Trained Mind*, a book that describes in detail a rigorous program of classical education called the "trivium": a three-stage approach of grammar (emphasizing memorization), logic (developing tools of analysis), and rhetoric (focusing on persuasive communication and self-expression). "If you use a classical approach with younger kids," Carrie explains, "you do more memory work, laying a foundation of facts, facts, facts, while their brains are little sponges, and then later on, when we come back and do the same material, they'll have a reference for this. That jived with me. And then I liked the logical approach to following history in a chronological cycle."

Veritas is not the only classical curriculum available, Carrie tells me, "but they were the one that kind of inspired me; in their catalog they do a lot of explaining the philosophy and the system." A support network called Classical Conversations has grown increasingly popular around the country, aimed at providing resources and guidance for homeschool parents using classical curricula (interestingly, I later learn that Debbie Palmer is looking into joining a CC group in Los Angeles—perhaps a curriculum shift is in store for the younger Palmers as well).

When I get a chance to sit down and talk with Tom Shaw, he offers his take on why they decided Veritas is the best choice for their homeschooling. "When Carrie and I did our education, we kind of stayed in the memorization phase. We went through high school and college memorizing stuff to get through a test, and then we forgot it, essentially. We would do well on a test because we could study and retain facts and then they would go away. So all along we've approached homeschooling as developing kids who can problem solve and can think better than we could ourselves. As we started looking at Veritas, we saw that the kids do a lot of memorization when they're young and their minds are able to do it, but then there's a step out of that. We like the way that goes into that logic phase when they're more in middle school, and then gets into the rhetoric phase toward the middle of high school."

Like most of the homeschool fathers I speak with, Tom describes his homeschool role as primarily one of supporting his wife. He keeps abreast of the "big picture" and discusses broad curricular issues, such as the switch to Veritas, with Carrie. When he has a weekday off from work, he'll sometimes step in and lead a lesson, and occasionally teaches a science unit here or there. Beyond that, however, Carrie is the central homeschooling influence.

Later that morning, Carrie asks the older girls to get some coins from the counter and look at what's written in Latin on them.

I ask Sarah if she knows what *e pluribus unum* means.

"One out of many," she tells me confidently.

"So why do you think *e pluribus unum* is written on American coins?" Carrie asks her older daughters. "It means one out of many, but what does that mean, in terms of the United States money? You put important things on money, like 'In God We Trust,' pictures of presidents, the date it's printed."

Distractions from Ruth and Samantha derail the conversation for almost five minutes, but then Carrie doggedly returns to her question. "Let's think about what we've been studying about states and the Civil War and people coming from all over the world to live here," she tells Sarah and Elise. "What could it mean?"

"I'm not sure," says Sarah.

"One out of many," Carrie reminds them. "What if you took many, many people from different countries and put them all together into one country—could it mean that?"

Sarah nods. "Yeah."

"One United States of America," Carrie continues. "One country made up of many different people, different states, et cetera. Does that make sense?"

"Yeah," Sarah replies. Then, turning to her little sister, she says, "Ruth, that's my seat. Would you mind getting out of it? Please."

Ruth shakes her head defiantly. "No."

Carrie gestures toward this scene. "This is what I call intentional sabotage. It began about five minutes ago. It's different than random interruption—because I have given multiple, excellent options for Ruth to choose from." She walks over to the table and calmly but firmly redirects Ruth into an activity that doesn't involve antagonizing her older sisters, and they eventually finish up the coin activity.

This little episode reminds me of a follow-up question I have for Carrie, as Elise goes off to the living room to read library books and Sarah heads upstairs to get her Latin book. "I wanted to ask you about the survey you filled out for me," I say. "One question asked whether you agreed that 'it is sometimes necessary to discipline a child with a good, hard spanking.' And you crossed out 'good, hard'—and then agreed. Can you tell me about your approach to discipline?"

"With these older two," she says, gesturing toward the seats formerly occupied by Elise and Sarah, "we don't spank anymore. With them, they know their expectations and they know when they've veered off. So with them, it's usually withholding of a freedom or making restitution. We really try to have them take time to work through it, think about why what they did was wrong, what should happen next time, how their actions affect their relationships with other people and their relationships with God."

"So the spanking is based on the idea that at the younger age they don't really have the capacity to do that type of reflection and recognition?" I ask.

Carrie nods. "Right. I don't have one ounce of belief in spanking anywhere outside of a loving parental-child relationship, done in a way that is helpful to the child. In other words, not getting mad and swatting, but more of a 'Did Mom ask you to do this? Did you obey what Mom said?' And reserved only for willful defiance. I think that's the crucial point, where kids learn to obey and respect authority, and always followed by restoration and forgiveness."

"So even if you have open defiance from Elise and Sarah at their age, you would use other means?"

"Yeah, Tom and I are both pretty much on the same page; it's counterproductive at this point, I think." Carrie mentions a situation in her old neighborhood where local parents were circulating petitions to ban corporal punishment in the school system. "Yeah, I'm totally opposed to spanking in schools. It has no context; it seems violent to me for no purpose. It's because you don't have that beautiful parent-child forgiveness. I think it's *very* counterproductive."

Sarah returns with her Latin book and gets started. Her text comes with a CD to help with pronunciation, but Carrie has already decided to switch next year to a different program, one she "test drove" at the state homeschool convention, called Latin for Children. It has DVDs with it, and uses songs and jingles with the material, so "it's fun—you're learning something and you're singing it and they're singing it back and it's very interactive with music."

Many homeschoolers view teaching foreign languages as particularly daunting, and thus seem to avoid it. Carrie acknowledges the extra challenges but says, "We're planning definitely to do it, we're just not sure when. We're thinking late elementary, early middle school age." They will probably use Rosetta Stone, another popular curriculum choice for homeschoolers, unless something better comes along in the meantime.

"You think, oh, when kids are little they should learn a foreign language, because your brain is receptive to it, and I agree," Carrie says. "But if you really want to learn it, you need to speak it, you need to be immersed in it, either by friends or if your family is bilingual. Ideally, you could learn it as a kid and then have someone to speak it with you. Because neither Tom nor I are fluent, we can't really speak it with them. So I think probably what we'll do is start when they're a bit older and we can create opportunities for them to speak, whether they want to learn Spanish or whatever language they choose. But the good thing about doing the Latin is that we're doing a lot of the groundwork for all the Romance languages and plus we're learning English vocabulary, which is very helpful."

A few minutes later, Sarah returns with her Latin work finished, which turns out to be the text of the Lord's Prayer. They practice reciting it together several times, after which Carrie tells Sarah she can go play for a while with Elise while she gets lunch ready.

After a half-hour break for lunch, the girls head back to the living room for independent reading, clearly one of their favorite parts of the homeschool day. A short while later, Carrie returns from putting Samantha and Ruth down for their naps. The girls want to keep reading on their own longer, but Carrie holds firm. "No, the clock is ticking," she says, referring to the limited amount of tranquil nap time she has to work solely with her older girls.

"How long do they usually nap?" I ask.

"Usually about three hours. I usually try to do it so Sarah and Elise have some free time at the end, just to go play dolls or whatever they want to do. But we usually spend nearly two hours working together." They're learning today about the First Transcontinental Railroad, and after providing them with some historical background, Carrie has them trace with their fingers on a map the path the Central Pacific and the Union Pacific took to meet in Promontory Summit, Utah. "So now we're going to find out how you build a railroad, okay?" Carrie says. "Elise, can you read in box one: what's the first thing they do?"

After a few minutes of reading and discussion, Carrie wraps things up and asks the girls to go get their notebooks and timelines, to show me what they've been learning. They return and begin to flip through their binders, which are filled with evidence of a busy year: pages on the Declaration of Independence, "The Star Spangled Banner," maps of the thirteen colonies and westward expansion, how to write with a quill, Morse code and the telegraph, Abraham Lincoln, lists of state capitals, and so on. Another binder has science experiments, memory verses, and other "non-history" materials. When I ask the girls a few random recall questions about the contents of their binders, they supply an impressive amount of detail.

Sarah is an extremely shy, quiet kid, although she perks up dramatically when she's interacting with her family at home. During my interview with her that week, however, she is content to outwait my questions with long silences, my considerable charm notwithstanding. A few basic pieces of information I gather: she enjoys homeschooling, isn't interested in going to public school, and most of their friends are either from church or homeschooling groups. She enjoys Barbie and princess movies, and recently saw *Charlotte's Web* in the theater.

Elise, on the other hand, offers me some real gems.

"Does your dad help out with homeschooling at all?" I ask.

Elise smiles. "Well, Mom says he's the president of school board and Ruth is his helper."

"Well, what about Samantha," I say, chuckling, "doesn't she get to be in charge sometimes?"

Elise gives a look of distaste. "Mostly all she does is scream and hold onto Mommy's legs."

"So if you could," I ask, "is there anything you would change about homeschooling?"

"Yes," Elise says firmly.

I'm intrigued, as most homeschool kids I talk with say they are satisfied with the status quo. "What would you change?" I ask.

Elise smiles again. "Instead of learning anything, we would just sit around and eat ice cream sundaes."

Now I'm laughing. "Do you ever wish you could go to public school?"

"No."

"How come?" I ask.

"You waste your time learning things you already know," she says.

"How do you know that?"

"Well, because I would be in kindergarten if I went to regular school and I do first-grade work," she reasons. "And if I went to kindergarten, all I would do is eat snacks, take naps, and listen to stories. That's what Sarah said."

Elise concludes our talk by telling me, with enthusiasm and detail, about what she's studying—naming several U.S. presidents, defining gravity for me, and summarizing *Gold Rush Days*, a book she recently read.

My individual interviews with Tom and Carrie provide the opportunity to explore their thoughts on several of my central questions: the inherent tension between fostering obedience and encouraging children to think for themselves; the vision of democratic citizenship they want to foster in their kids; and their views on homeschool regulation, oversight, and accountability.

As I've mentioned before, the surveys I gave to all the homeschool parents asked them to rank what they think are the most important things for a child to prepare him or her for life, and both Carrie and Tom rank "to obey" as first, and "to think for himself or herself" as fourth. (In between were helping others and working hard.)

When I ask Carrie about this, she explains what she had in mind. "When kids are very little, they learn about obedience to God by his commands for them to obey *us*," she says. "There's lots of obedience and very little freedom. By freedom I'm talking about the ability to exercise your own decision making. But as they get older, then they're having more freedoms and less direct parental input: 'Let's think this through. What are our responsibilities tomorrow, will you be prepared to be able to function to do those things? Then you can make a decision and then we'll have the consequences for it.'"

I wonder if this approach applies to freedom to explore other world-views beyond their parents' Christian commitments. "So do you think that there's a point during their growing up and their education," I ask, "where you will want to actively expose them to differing, alternative perspectives and beliefs in ways that they can really grapple with them and figure out where they stand in relation to them?"

Carrie nods. "Oh, definitely—and we do. I like the idea of keeping their minds and hearts pure when they're little children, but even now there are things we're going to encounter, even as we're studying world history, world religions. We're going to be opening up our *Kingfisher History Encyclopedia* and read about how people evolved thirty million years ago from a speck of dust or whatever; those are not things from which I'll shelter them."

The complicated issue here, to me, seems to be how much parents should try to present conflicting perspectives—that they themselves reject—in their strongest possible light, to allow their children the opportunity to genuinely consider them as potentially reasonable alternatives. "Would you want them to engage with those different viewpoints in ways that emphasize why you believe those alternate worldviews are wrong?" I ask. "Or would you try to provide the best case for them, showing that they may have points worth considering, even though at the end of the day you think they're incomplete or even wrong?"

"We want our kids to be able to give a reason for the hope that is in them," Carrie says. "It's hard to picture having children high school age because I've never had them before. But I'm hoping as they mature in their walk with God, they would be able to articulate their beliefs and to be able to sort through things themselves."

Carrie pauses, then adds with conviction, "What I don't like is the idea of a young teenager being in a hostile environment. I think Christians in some schools are put in positions of hostility or ridicule, whether it's from their teacher, whether it's from their classmates: 'How could you think such a stupid thing, nobody thinks like that, don't you know that science says this?'"

"Is there a time in one's growing up and education where that would be a potentially good thing?" I ask.

"I would think so," Carrie answers. "Like I said, I don't have any teenagers at my house. I don't believe it would have gone well for *me*. I don't believe I would have handled that very well at all."

"You didn't find yourself in that situation at all before leaving home?"

"Not really. I was from what you would call a pretty conservative religious type of environment. But I think some kids could do well, maybe even thrive. For some kids, that could be crushing. Obviously, when they're very young, it's your job to protect them and to preserve an innocence about them and a safety. Not so much when they're older, but at the same time, I believe that as their parents, under your house, it's still your responsibility to preserve that."

When I ask Tom about his ranking of obedience well ahead of helping kids learn to think for themselves, he explains that he wasn't thinking as much about obeying him and Carrie, but obedience to God. "If you can get that obedience to God and to his Word down, then that's going to affect how you eventually think on your own, for yourself," Tom says. "You're processing things through that biblical worldview. I don't mean to sound as though we're telling them what they need to believe, but we *are* saying, 'We think the Bible's true and we want you to obey God and his Word. Things are going to come at you from life; let's filter them through there.' I don't know that we can separate it and put it into an obey phase and a thinking phase. The goal would be, you go off to college and you've got the ability to completely think for yourself, whether you're hearing something that seems heretical from a biblical standpoint or something that seems very humanistic, whatever, that's coming at you from the world."

"Do you want your kids to grapple with those things during their homeschooling years?" I ask.

"I don't know that there is any way they're *not* going to," Tom says. "I mean certainly, there could be something like a protective cocoon set up, but that's not what we're trying to do. Our kids are going out and being with friends, in sports, even in church in different groups. So whether it's next-door neighbors who are Catholic, or people across the street who are Buddhists, or our neighbors in a lesbian relationship who have a daughter, it's going to come through extracurricular activities and neighborhood-type things, and even doing service I mean, if you're going over to Meadowbrook"—a low-income housing development where their family delivers meals once a month—"you're going to run across some different stuff. Their exposure is gradual now, but as their awareness grows and there's more exposure, then that should open up the opportunity for learning."

"So if you could imagine that one of the kids during adolescence really starts to develop perspectives or beliefs that are at pretty significant odds from your and Carrie's, maybe even to the point of questioning her faith, how would you be inclined to deal with that?" I ask.

"I think the goal of starting this young is to develop a core that you hope they are not going to go away from," Tom says. Parenting, he explains, is about working yourself out of a job on purpose. "If we're talking about a sixteen-, seventeen-, eighteen-year-old, there's no way at that point we can hammer them over the head. I can remember being an adolescent and thinking that my parents didn't know anything," he says, smiling, "but you still have to have the ability to have a discussion, a framework to reason through that so we can talk about it. Hopefully that's the kind of thinking that we're developing along the way."

With this in mind, Tom mentions that he's looked through the "rhetoric" phase of the Veritas curriculum, to see what kinds of things they'd be exploring. "They're reading competing stuff, stuff that would make you think. Okay, what's Marxism? Different worldviews, different themes. They are going to look at that as they get older. So I don't think there's going to be an insulation from other worldviews and I don't think we would want that necessarily. In fact, I don't know how you teach someone 'this is what we believe' without telling them what other people believe, to some degree." He pauses and smiles. "The more kids there are, the odds are greater one of them is going to, you know, develop some kind of thinking that is not in line with Mom and Dad. I mean it could even be a theological difference, regardless of a major worldly difference. Even still, I think that discussion has to be had."

Tom then adds a thoughtful point about the need for parents to retain their credibility as their children get older and encounter diverse perspectives. "If we're trying to pigeonhole them completely, then when they hear something different elsewhere, does that start planting the seed of 'What are you teaching me?' As opposed to us saying, 'This, this, and this are ideas that are out there about this topic, and let's run them through God's Word and let's talk about them."

When I ask Tom what he wants his kids to learn about the rights and responsibilities of citizenship, he answers first in terms of Christian service. "I don't view Christianity as 'out of the world' but rather us being 'in the world' to reflect Christ's image," he says, alluding to the same Bible verse I've encountered time and again in my journeys. "So how are we going to be in our local community, serving? What does service look like in a larger world community? It's a little hard at their age, but simple stuff like, you know, we have new neighbors: we took them a meal, we went over and introduced ourselves. You know, we go to Meadowbrook: why do we go there and take them food? I'm big on what we can do as a local church to help our community, not just be a little building where everyone comes in and sits and goes home. So hopefully we're approaching it from that standpoint, being someone who's a follower of Christ: how did he live and how did he interact with the people around him? And how can we do things like that?"

Tom pauses, then mentions some more conventional notions of civic responsibility as well. "We haven't been what I would call political activists, as far as joining groups, but we do emphasize the rights that we have as Americans that others don't have in the world, and how to realize those. We can vote; not everyone can vote. We need to go vote. We need to know who we're voting for, why we're voting, all the different issues, you know."

Carrie begins her description of good citizenship where Tom leaves off. "Voting is huge in our family, and I always take the kids with me to vote and we get donuts afterward. And I really like teaching my kids about the foundations of our country, about our forefathers, about the importance of voting and how we became a nation because we had no rights in that respect."

I ask Carrie whether she thinks that a Christian should advocate public policies that directly mirror one's moral-religious convictions, or whether citizenship in a diverse democracy entails moderating one's positions when deciding how we should all live together.

"I find it difficult separating strong personal, moral convictions from how I would *like* for everything to be," Carrie says. "Now, going through with a wrecking ball and steamrolling into the public arena is not going to be beneficial either. But that doesn't mean that I won't vote a certain way; that does not mean I will not stand for certain things in a public way, such as volunteering with certain organizations. But it also doesn't mean pointing and being hateful about it. I think you can stand for what you believe to be right." Carrie mentions her opposition to gay marriage and abortion as examples. "If we're talking about matters of law," she says, "why wouldn't I do something about it if I could?"

Another view, I suggest, might be that in a democracy populated by fallible people with a diversity of beliefs and perspectives—and often no airtight case to be made for any of them—striving for compromise and accommodation might be a civic good in and of itself.

"Yeah, I think there are issues that would apply to," Carrie says. "It just so much depends on whether you're talking about matters of life and death, such as abortion. In that case, I see a difference between compromise and incrementalism. I see incrementalism as a pragmatic means to get rid of abortion, which I believe is a stain on this country. What I see in American society is less of a coming together, as a rule, and more of a, 'Well, my convictions are very strong; I'm going to stand for them here, and your convictions are strong and you're going to stand for them there.' That's a balance, but not a compromise."

Carrie's vision of American politics is an adversarial one, but not necessarily an angry or vicious one. It's certainly a more accurate picture of how laws and policies are actually made, as compared with my hopes for a society in which recognizing reasonable disagreement leads to compromise and accommodation. But Carrie's model also assumes a level playing field, and a certain degree of balanced power; if one side gains overwhelming power, there's no reason to exercise restraint for the sake of a sincere but embattled minority.

Carrie sums up her perspective: "In my role as a citizen, I have a responsibility to God first and foremost, and I believe that his Word is infallible. I don't believe that there's error in it. And I believe that as a citizen, so blessed with the freedom to participate in our form of government, I have a right to act as his citizen on Earth. And I believe that the way that I vote, the way that I do things, should reflect absolutely his law, because his law is written on my heart. And so I feel like to compromise would be a sin against God, between me and God.

"Now my responsibility to God also is very much to love my neighbor," she adds. "So if I were to do that in a hateful, irresponsible, violent way, I would be likewise sinning against God. So I have a dual responsibility. I just feel like God's purposes are served when our country reflects his will, even though everybody doesn't choose to be a Christian—I respect that, I see that's the way it is. But I feel like the better we are, the more good we can do for God's Kingdom. 'A nation will cease to be great when a nation ceases to be good.' Is that Alexis de Tocqueville? Anyway, I believe that, and so whatever little part I can play in making this a good country—as defined by God—then I'm going to do it."

I spend quite a bit of time with Carrie discussing homeschool regulation as well, and start with some of the broader philosophical questions that those issues raise. "So I'd assume you'd say the parents bear the primary responsibility for raising their kids?"

Carrie smiles. "Good assumption."

"Do you believe they have the *sole* responsibility?" I ask.

"Yes. And I believe that you can rationally and correctly delegate," she adds. "I don't believe that every person must homeschool their child."

"But it's the parents' choice as to what should happen?"

"Absolutely."

"Do you see any circumstances beyond physical abuse where it would be appropriate for the state to step in and intervene somehow?" I ask. "I'm thinking here in particular of educational neglect, such as parents saying they're homeschooling but they're just not."

"That's a tricky question," Carrie admits. "It really is. You hear about these isolated cases that have happened where public officials have overstepped their authority. It makes you think I'm a hair's breadth away from that—one person gets honked off at me. Do you know what I'm saying?"

I press here a bit more, trying to see whether Carrie's reluctance is a matter of basic principle about state intervention or more a concern about misuse of state authority. "I guess the question, at its core," I say, "is *does the child have any basic interests apart from the parents?* For instance, two fundamental skills of self-sufficiency: literacy and numeracy. Is there ever a point where the child's basic interests in that regard, if they have those, trumps the parents' interest in deciding everything about their kids' education or lack thereof?"

Carrie pauses before answering. "It's very hard, because I don't want a kid out there being uneducated and unable to become a self-sufficient individual. That's a very, very negative thing. But there are all kinds of ways families aren't working well—whether it be that kids come home and they're not properly supervised after school because their parents are working and they don't want to pay for them to stay at after-care. Or whether it be that they watch TV from the moment they walk in until midnight. Or whether it be that they eat donuts and potato chips for every meal. There are so many things that could be harmful to a child that keep them from being self-sufficient and productive that I don't think that the educational neglect would rise above other kinds of dysfunctional family things."

While I appreciate Carrie's point, it seems to me that some interests of children—such as gaining basic skills of literacy and numeracy—could be more effectively accounted for by outside authorities than these other parenting examples she offers. Sure, it would be great if all parents encouraged good eating habits, but even if we wanted the state to try to enforce that, it would be much more cumbersome and intrusive than requiring kids to take a basic skills test periodically to make sure they're learning to read and write.

"What I don't like is the concept of someone *saying* you're not homeschooling just because it doesn't look like a classroom," Carrie continues. "I'm not a big proponent of unschooling, just letting the kids drift around and learn as they will. But you know what, that's education. I'm afraid that you'll get families who are well intentioned and educating according to the convictions that they have, and to the outsider, it could look like educational neglect."

"But I wonder if there's some point at which people would agree that a child is being ill served educationally," I suggest. "For instance, if your thirteen-year-old is functionally illiterate, then maybe your unschooling stinks. I agree that there's legitimate concern from homeschoolers whenever requirements are proposed, that it could be a slippery slope to further regulation. But at least on a level of principle, wouldn't any reasonable person be concerned about the educational environment of a teenager who didn't have those basic skills?"

"But there are public schools all over America where thirteen-year-olds cannot read, cannot add, cannot subtract," Carrie says. "I wouldn't want to single out homeschooling for standards that are not met by people who are in school and get by with it, year after year, graduating illiterate, completely unfunctioning members of society. I don't understand why—if you're in school and not learning things—why *that's* okay, but if you're at home and you're not learning things, you're not testing well, then it's *not* okay.

"And what about the nonsense from academics that says I can't educate my children?" she continues. "That is *extremely* offensive to me. Because there is no chance that I could go in the classroom right now—I could not walk up the hill to the elementary school right now and teach. I couldn't teach somebody else's twenty-five children to save my life. I'm not a teacher in the sense of being prepared to teach large groups of strangers. But if I didn't think I was the best teacher for my own children, I wouldn't do it. There is *nobody* who can teach my kids better than I can."

Carrie's passionate conviction in this regard underscores a point often overlooked by those who argue that homeschool parents should earn a teaching license just like public school teachers. Homeschool parents are not asking to do the job of public school teachers, nor are they necessarily claiming they could. As a teacher educator who prepares candidates for the public school classroom and signs off on their application for an Indiana state teaching license, I can say with some authority that, while overlapping in some respects, the job of a public school teacher is markedly different than that of a homeschool teacher. This doesn't mean I think that anyone, without preparation and support, can homeschool their children—just that public school licensure isn't the most sensible measuring stick.

While Carrie is obviously convinced that homeschooling is the right choice for *her* kids, she surprises me with her frank admission that this isn't always the case: "Here's the thing about this: *I* am getting my eyes opened. Until the last couple years, I didn't even realize—honestly, Rob, I know that's really naïve—but I did not even realize that there were people homeschooling their kids who weren't as excited and diligent about it as me. This opened my eyes to the fact that there are people out there who are educationally neglecting their children, under the name of homeschooling. I honestly did not know that."

Carrie seems genuinely torn here, concerned for children whose educational needs are being neglected, but also resistant to state oversight. "I don't want people checking up on me," she acknowledges. "I want to be accountable, but I have my accountability to God. I answer to *God*. I have no higher authority there. However," she adds, "if I look now with my new knowledge that there are people out there totally hosing their children, I'm more open to it."

"For a lot of homeschoolers," I remark, "it seems to come down to how to deal with the outliers, the arguably small percentage of kids who are blatantly ill served by homeschool freedom. Most homeschool parents that I talk to say that's really tragic and unfortunate, but trying to fix that is not worth imposing additional regulations on the rest of them."

Carrie nods her agreement, and points out that the ones who ignore the regulations will likely just go farther underground.

But might there not be, I ask, a significant swath of homeschoolers —if they knew their kids were going to be tested for basic literacy and numeracy—who would be impelled to improve their efforts?

Carrie seems willing to concede that possibility, then adds, "Now, if we had a new testing law in Indiana, I'd be like, 'okay, let's just go prove it. Let's just go and do the darn thing.' I would do it, but I wouldn't like it. I'm going to do standardized testing with them by choice, because I think it might be instructive."

When considering changes to homeschooling regulation, it's worth keeping in mind that this can be more complicated than might first appear. As I noted earlier, Indiana is one of a dozen states that don't recognize homeschooling as a separate educational category with its own specific regulatory statutes. Any efforts to establish testing or add other requirements, therefore, would need to apply to the broader realm of nonpublic, nonaccredited schools of which homeschooling is a part—raising the degree of complexity and expense significantly.

Carrie concludes by underscoring what she considers nonnegotiables for homeschooling freedom. "Where I would start to get really agitated is if they started trying to tell you what you *had* to teach, and how you had to teach it. That would get me entirely agitated and I would get behind the opposition in a heartbeat. *Because that's the point.* A lot of homeschool parents would say that the whole reason we're homeschooling is so that we don't have children immersed with the idea that everything is equal. Because if you are a committed follower of Christ, everything is *not* equal in *many* aspects."

Carrie takes perhaps strongest issue with homeschool critics who question her desire to instill a particular belief system in her children. "I completely disagree with the concept of 'your children should be exposed to *x, y, z, p, d, q*' and that 'oh, no, heaven forbid, they turn out and believe just like you!'" She shakes her head in mock horror. "To me, that's biblical parenting. 'Write these laws on your children, put them on your doorframes, carry them with you as you walk along the road,'" she says, paraphrasing Deuteronomy 6. "I want my kids to think like me, not because I'm perfect, but because I love God and I want to follow him. I don't want them to be bound up in sin as much as I am, but I want them to look and say, 'Mom and Dad showed us how to know God; they're not perfect, they screw up, but they showed us'—and I want those beliefs to become *theirs*, obviously. The notion that they can learn and know God is of utmost importance in this house."

I'm sympathetic to Carrie's position here, not because I don't think it matters whether kids get exposed to diverse beliefs and perspectives, but because reasonable disagreement exists about what that exposure should consist of, much less how it needs to happen in a schooling context. It's one thing to endorse the value, in principle, of civic virtues such as tolerance and respect, and another to have enough certainty about how to police the teaching of those virtues in a homeschool setting.

Carrie Shaw has a clear sense, at least with her children at this young age, of what a good and godly education should be. "We're not going to live in some kind of evangelical, Christian, American red-state bubble," Carrie says, "but at the same time, there are things that may be presumed to be virtuous by others that I may not want them exposed to at a certain age." In addition to providing a rigorous education that would pass muster with any homeschool testing I can envision, she is committed to writing God's law on the hearts of her children—and will resist mightily any attempts by the state to impose a curriculum that sends any other message.

9

BECOMING A PUBLIC

A mother describes her initial discouragement when starting to home-school her six-year-old: the challenges of choosing and planning curriculum, transitioning from caregiver to formal instructor, and continuing to manage the rest of family life felt daunting, even overwhelming. "Then God gave me light," she writes. "Homeschooling was not just about fulfilling the education laws of our state or equipping our daughter to read, write, and compute. Homeschooling was a spiritual battle for the soul of our little kindergartner."

Not every homeschool parent views their commitment in these terms, of course, but most share a determination to provide a qualitatively different (and better) educational experience than institutional schooling can offer. And while not even all conservative Christians see their decision to homeschool as saving the souls of their children, their vision includes not only intellectual preparation but also a desire to shape the lives of their children in profound and lasting ways.

Homeschooling is clearly a significant educational trend, one that shows no signs of fading away. But the rise of homeschooling also holds implications that extend far beyond the phenomenon itself, raising fundamental questions about the purposes of education and the relationship between families, the state, and the society we share. Before turning to these broader issues, however, I offer some concluding reflections on the four central questions that framed my homeschooling journeys: What do homeschoolers do, and why do they do it? Do children learn to think for themselves? What do they learn about the relationship between faith and citizenship? And how, if at all, should homeschooling be regulated?

The variety of homeschool teaching and learning I encountered resists easy summary or sweeping conclusions. As I noted earlier, all four of my central questions contain potential tensions between legitimate but conflicting priorities, and this certainly held true when considering the wide latitude homeschool parents have to design their children's education, for better or worse. I saw how many of the unique features of homeschooling—flexibility of structure and content, close personal relationships, and so on—could be used as a strength or become a weakness. On one end of the spectrum, I observed learning contexts that rivaled or even surpassed the best of institutional schooling; on the other end, I watched in dismay as children floundered in environments marked by poor teaching, questionable curricula, or frustrating interpersonal dynamics. Some parents make the most of homeschooling's unique opportunities and deftly navigate its distinctive challenges, while others unfortunately do the opposite.

My second central question focused on the tension between parents' desire to impart deeply held values and their children's interest in learning to think for themselves. Conservative Christian parents don't apologize for their intent to "write these laws on their children"—they believe this is their God-given right and responsibility. At the same time, I've yet to meet a homeschool parent who says she doesn't want her children to learn to think for themselves and make their beliefs their own. These parents recognize—and are continually challenged by—the tension of encouraging such growth while also instilling an underlying foundation of Christian beliefs and commitments.

It's worth keeping in mind that critical reflection about the belief system in which one is raised—whether religious or not—doesn't necessarily entail rejecting those commitments, nor does it require some sort of massive existential trauma of doubt. The vicissitudes of life and the mix of ethical messages from our wider culture that inevitably permeates all but the most isolated upbringings seem likely to spur periodic reflection on what one believes and why. It's also worth recognizing that at least some of the important work of learning to think for oneself can be done from *within* a given ethical framework. Many religions, Christianity included, have rich traditions of theological disputation—critically evaluating various doctrinal interpretations and their implications, even while accepting core beliefs of their tradition as givens.

Outsiders often perceive conservative Christian homeschooling as a straightjacket of conformity, where kids have to toe an ideological line without the opportunity to consider other ways of being in the world. But I've also encountered plenty of public school students who rarely, if ever, bring a critical eye to their own way of life, their understanding of the world. Perhaps for some kids, whether homeschoolers or conventional schoolers, the capacity to step back and critically examine the culture and belief system in which they were raised won't really develop until adulthood. The open question, of course, is what types of educational experiences beforehand will make that eventual self-awareness more or less likely.

The third question framing my exploration of homeschooling considered the idea of Christian citizenship. I began this book with an image of homeschoolers shaping culture at the highest echelons of power. It turns out that most of the people I talk with outside of Purcellville, however, seem less focused on political engagement or transforming the broader culture than Mike Farris's Academy Awards dream envisions. Certainly many of the Generation Joshua participants strive for such power, but it's worth keeping in mind that both GenJ and HSLDA represent only a slice of conservative Christian homeschoolers, and an even smaller percentage of homeschoolers in general. As one mother told me, "I may be a conservative Christian, but I don't take marching orders from HSLDA." It's true that homeschoolers can come together quickly and powerfully when their homeschool freedoms appear at risk, but the fierce independence that leads many of them to homeschool in the first place also suggests more diversity within their ranks than might otherwise be assumed.

That being said, politics is clearly a realm that many conservative Christians have sought to influence, with significant success in recent decades. Some commentators suggest this political run is at an end. In a portrait of a conservative Christian homeschooling family in 2000, Margaret Talbot asserted that "it cannot be denied that as a political force, the religious right is flagging." Coming eight months before the election of George W. Bush, such confidence now seems more than a bit misplaced. Seven years later, the same *New York Times Magazine* alerted us on its cover to "The Evangelical Crackup," and a *Times* op-ed the same day predicted that "Inauguration Day 2009 is at the very least Armageddon for the reigning ayatollahs of the American right." Perhaps. But even if the political power of conservative Christians wanes over the short term, the tension between private faith and public politics—and the conviction among many conservative Christians that the two are inextricably linked—will remain.

However important these questions may be, they aren't the most vital ones for homeschoolers, conservative Christians or otherwise. At the core are the fundamental philosophical questions about who is responsible for the education of children, and the forms that such education can and should take. This is the ground where homeschoolers will plant their flag and not back down.

Some social commentators scoff when conservative Christians portray themselves as an oppressed minority, struggling to preserve their values amidst a hostile secular society. While *oppressed* may be the wrong word, it shouldn't stretch the imagination to recognize the ways in which conservative Christians see themselves struggling to navigate a culture marked by increasing ethical diversity and a seductive consumerist-materialistic value system that threatens to weaken their communities and commitments. For those who choose to homeschool, public schools often symbolize much of what is to be avoided or resisted in contemporary culture.

Although the courts have made clear that parents have the right to opt out of the public school system, recent judicial decisions have also underscored the near-total control public schools have if parents choose to send their children there. While such authority has been granted in legal terms, the moral authority that public schools have in this regard, to be trusted with the education of our children, must be continually earned. As I mentioned earlier, some homeschoolers use the term *government schools* to emphasize their perception that these institutions are imposed and operated by an outside force, rather than the public that represents and is made up of all of us. As a former high school administrator, I know from firsthand experience that it is no small task striving to satisfy the wide array of parental expectations about their children's schooling, both in terms of intellectual content and social values. But if parents don't feel any sense of partnership, if they feel that public schools are unwilling to

22

listen to what matters to them and why, it should not be surprising when they opt out.

A telling example of this difference between schools' legal and moral authority occurred in 1992, when parents sued a Massachusetts public high school for holding a mandatory "AIDS Awareness" assembly that allegedly included the outside presenter having students simulate group sex on stage accompanied by her graphic commentary. The First Circuit Court of Appeals—while acknowledging that the assembly "may have displayed a certain callousness towards the sensibilities" of the students—affirmed that the school did not violate students' legal rights (*Brown v. Hot, Sexy and Safer Productions*). The court's reasoning was that "if all parents had a fundamental constitutional right to dictate individually what the schools teach their children, the schools would be forced to cater to a curriculum for each student whose parents had genuine moral disagreement with the school's choice of subject matter." While this makes sense from a logistical standpoint, it still does not relieve public schools of the moral obligation to demonstrate sensitivity and caution in how they exercise their legal right to educate the students who walk through their doors. If they neglect or abuse this obligation, parents may decide the "public" in public schools doesn't include them—and the ensuing loss to our civic life together will extend well beyond a school's daily attendance count.

And what, if anything, can we conclude about homeschool regulation? In the midst of my journeys, I finally recognized a key reason why homeschool parents react so negatively to calls for regulation. Most parents—whether homeschoolers or not—see education, broadly construed, as part of their job description: raising a child involves constant teaching, and the most important lessons in life generally occur outside of school walls. But what I didn't fully appreciate at first is that homeschoolers take this a step further. They don't see any real distinction between this broader notion of education and formal schooling itself—which makes sense, if homeschooling is just woven into the fabric of everyday family life. And if homeschooling is seen as simply part of parenting, then it becomes easier to understand why many homeschool parents view regulations as unjustifiable intrusions into their sacred domain.

This expansive concept of parenting appears to run counter to at least some legal opinions, however. Homeschool advocates are fond of pointing to the language of a 1925 Supreme Court decision (*Pierce v. Society of Sisters*), which, in striking down a law requiring all children to attend public schools, emphasized that "the child is not the mere creature of the State," and parents have the right "to direct the upbringing and education of children under their control."

But this landmark decision also made clear that "no question is raised concerning the power of the State reasonably to regulate all schools, to inspect, supervise, and examine them, their teachers and pupils, to require that all children of proper age attend some school, that teachers shall be of good moral character and patriotic disposition, that certain studies plainly essential to good citizenship must be taught, and that nothing be taught which is manifestly inimical to the public welfare." By contrast, the state is not permitted this degree of latitude in the general upbringing of children, a realm that clearly belongs to parents.

Similarly, a 1972 Supreme Court decision (*Wisconsin v. Yoder*) allowing an Amish community to end formal education for their children earlier than state law permitted also acknowledged that "there is no doubt as to the power of the State, having a high responsibility for education of its citizens, to impose reasonable regulations for the control and duration of basic education." (This decision also served to complicate matters involving religiously motivated homeschooling, by asserting that the regulatory power of the state over education is not absolute when religious beliefs enter the equation. When educational requirements impinge on "the traditional interest of parents with respect to the religious upbringing of their children," then a "balancing process" must ensue. As the idea of *balancing* suggests, however, this doesn't provide parents unlimited discretion, either, even when religious convictions are involved.)

So what role should the state play in the regulation of homeschooling? Even if we don't insist on a clear distinction between schooling and parenting, the state still has an obligation to protect children from educational neglect. Homeschool parents typically insist that they should have sole authority over the education of their children, whereas advocates of regulation frame the issue as a triad of interests, arguing that children themselves and society as a whole have much at stake as well. Ideally, these various interests will align—parents, for instance, generally want to raise self-sufficient children. But while most parents believe their efforts are dedicated to what's best for their children, this isn't always the case.

A complete absence of regulation (the current situation in a few states) obviously provides the most latitude for parents to educate their children as they see fit, but runs the greatest risk of neglecting the interests of children and the state. Extensive regulations (such as a prescribed curriculum or licensure requirements for parents), on the other hand, jeopardize the flexibility that makes homeschooling an effective educational choice for many families, and may offer relatively little added benefit compared to more modest requirements.

With this in mind, I want to propose three necessary conditions for homeschool regulation to be justified. First, vital interests of children or society must be at stake. Second, general consensus should exist on standards for meeting those interests. Third, there needs to be an effective way to measure whether those standards are met.

Basic skills testing for homeschoolers meets those criteria. Few would disagree that children have vital educational interests in basic literacy and numeracy, and it seems likely we could reach agreement on what skills are involved (some people would undoubtedly push for more than others, but even a lowest common denominator of simple reading comprehension and basic computation skills would be worth verifying). Finally, such straightforward skills would be relatively easy to assess objectively, despite Michael Farris's claims to the contrary.

The current mishmash of homeschool regulations aimed at academic accountability, on the other hand, doesn't measure up. The Wallises, for example, work the system in Vermont by having a friend simply sign off on a letter that Cindy composes—but at least they aren't hiding a lousy or nonexistent homeschooling program. In a 2004 series on homeschooling, the *Akron Beacon Journal* related the story of Coloradoan Nick Campbell, who sought an assessment of satisfactory progress for his six-year-old, Missy. He mailed a progress report and twenty-five dollars to the assessor, and received in return a satisfactory evaluation for Missy—who turned out to be his dog.

The states I visited—California, Vermont, Tennessee, Oregon, and Indiana—represent nearly the full spectrum of regulatory approaches to homeschooling, ranging from essentially nothing (Indiana) to required testing (Oregon) to curriculum approval and/or review (Vermont). What each has in common, however, is the easy opportunity for poor homeschooling situations to slip through the cracks. I can't help but wonder how this might change if consensus could be reached among homeschool-ers and policymakers that focused limited regulatory resources on the likely few situations where children are clearly being educationally ne-glected. Would it cost any more in time or resources for a state to admin-ister a basic skills test every two or three years to a child than it would to try to make informed evaluations from a vast array of curriculum records and work samples? Wouldn't homeschoolers prefer a simple, straightfor-ward assessment that most students would (I suspect) easily pass so they can get on with their studies?

What about regulations aimed at protecting other vital interests, such as children learning to think for themselves and society needing citizens capable of democratic self-rule? In both cases, even if most people recog-nize them as important goals, there is plenty of reasonable disagreement on what the threshold standards would be or how the state could reliably measure if students meet them. Therefore, I do not advocate regulations intended to foster or assess either of those interests.

Nevertheless, I heartily endorse an education in which students are provided the opportunity to engage thoughtfully with a variety of ways of understanding the world (and I'd argue that society should give our public schools more space and encouragement to do so as well). I strongly support an education that encourages students to think for themselves and contemplate leading lives beyond the contours of their present com-munities. In fact, I believe these emphases are just as important as skills of literacy and numeracy, and make for richer lives and better citizens.

But I also believe that a liberal democratic society needs to tread lightly when it comes to defining the boundaries of possible good lives, and even in specifying the virtues of good citizenship. In a real sense, our liberal democracy must risk its own well-being as it strives to persuade rather than compel its citizens to be generous listeners, tolerant neigh-bors, and willing to compromise in the face of reasonable disagreement. The challenge before us is how to foster an identification and commit-ment to a broader public that connects all of us while also recognizing that it is our narrower communities and private identities that sustain us in ways at least as powerful and important.

Regardless of whether homeschooling continues its rapid growth, the on-going shift toward school-choice policies more broadly compels all of us to confront fundamental questions about the purposes of education: What knowledge and skills are essential? What virtues and commitments can and should we instill? What kind of people do we want our children to become? How do we learn to live together amidst disagreement about social and political issues? What role should religion play in our public square? And who decides the answers—each community, each family, or all of us together as a larger public?

In this book's opening pages, I observed that these questions are especially pertinent and personal for homeschoolers, beginning with their choice to step away from institutional schooling and extending to their selection of curricula and deciding how they will spend their days. I would also suggest that homeschoolers' answers to these questions of educational purpose and priority offer important reminders for those of us who work in or for public schools: In quality homeschooling, relationships are central—parents know their children as people and students, and they understand that education is more than formal academics within the classroom walls. Elaborate facilities and cutting-edge technology, while potentially useful, are no substitute for good teaching. Standardized testing may provide a helpful snapshot of a student's progress, but it is at best a partial glimpse of important learning. And perhaps most fundamentally, homeschooling should remind us that, in the words of historian David Tyack, there is no "one best system," no single ideal model for schooling.

Running through these chapters are several vital concerns: the relationship between parents and children, the rights and responsibilities of religious believers as citizens, and the purposes of education in a democracy. Each issue, I believe, prompts reasonable disagreement. But recognizing reasonable disagreement requires a certain degree of humility, an acknowledgement that we are fallible creatures, that none of us have direct, unmediated access to truth. Even for conservative Christians who believe firmly in the reality of absolute Truth, the apostle Paul observes that "for now, we see through a glass, darkly; but then, face to face: now I know in part; but then shall I know even as also I am known." So the question before all of us remains: how much room will we make for reasonable disagreement, for holding firm to our beliefs while also acknowledging our civic obligation to find ways to live together in mutual understanding and respect?

The implications extend far beyond concerns about homeschooling, or even religiously based schooling more generally. The range of ethical sources, values, and commitments held by students, families, and society at large presents both challenges and opportunities for our public square and the realities of democratic citizenship. Although the shape of both public and private schooling—and the relationship between them—may shift over time and context, the need for us to learn to *be* a public, to engage with fellow citizens in mutual respect, will remain as present and vital as always.

Acknowledgments

This book has been more than five years in the making, and many people and organizations have helped make it possible. At the heart of this book are the stories of the families I visited, and I am grateful for their gracious hospitality and willingness to open their homes to an outsider. My hope is that they see a fair and respectful portrayal of themselves in these pages, even if our views on homeschooling or citizenship don't always align. My sincere thanks as well to the individuals (who must also remain anonymous) who provided initial introductions to these families.

The National Academy of Education provided generous financial support through their Spencer Foundation Postdoctoral Fellowship, enabling a year's leave from my teaching at Indiana University. The Center for Evaluation and Education Policy at IU graciously provided a quiet office and clerical support during that time.

Indiana University provided many other sources of support as well: the School of Education Proffitt Endowment Grant supplied initial project funding, and the Poynter Center for the Study of Ethics and American Institutions offered a wonderful opportunity to learn from many wise colleagues through a yearlong Interdisciplinary Faculty Fellowship. Many other individuals at IU have encouraged and supported me along the way. In particular, Gabrièle Abowd and Nicole Bigg meticulously reviewed transcripts, raising important questions and insights that generated new lines of inquiry over the course of my family visits. Sara White and Sara Sturgeon provided valuable clerical support.

Beyond a variety of informal settings in which I shared my ongoing research, I had the opportunity to present portions of my work at Brandeis University through the Mandel Center for Studies in Jewish Ed-

223

ucation, and at annual meetings of the American Educational Research Association and the Association for Moral Education.

Many thanks to Amy Caldwell and everyone else at Beacon Press for their wise guidance and support. Several other individuals read all or parts of the manuscript, and their advice and encouragement were deeply appreciated: Lucy Kunzman, Sam Intrator, Bill White, Ira Lit, and David Tyack. More friends than I can name spent time talking over the ideas herein, and assured me I had something worth writing.

My many trips around the country and many more hours spent at the keyboard have required great support and patience from my family. My daughters, Hannah, Kira, and Zoe, enforce a joyful balance of work and play, and keep me smiling in gratitude. My deepest thanks go to my wife, Audra. Beyond her careful reading and unfailing support for this work, she teaches me daily about kindness, sacrifice, and being present for the many joys that fill our life together.

BIBLIOGRAPHIC NOTE

For an extensive—and growing—compendium of citations on homeschooling research, I invite readers to my Web site: http://www.indiana.edu/~homeeduc.

Several research studies were referred to by name and/or authorship:

Gaither, Milton. *Homeschool: An American History.* New York: Palgrave Macmillan, 2008.

Medlin, Richard G. "Home Schooling and the Question of Socialization." *Peabody Journal of Education* 75, nos. 1–2 (2000): 107–23.

National Center for Education Statistics. *1.1 Million Homeschooled Students in the United States in 2003.* Washington, DC: National Center for Education Statistics, 2004.

National Center for Education Statistics. *1.5 Million Homeschooled Students in the United States in 2007.* Washington, DC: National Center for Education Statistics, 2008.

Ray, Brian D. *Home Educated and Now Adults: Their Community and Civic Involvement, Views about Homeschooling, and Other Traits.* Salem, OR: National Home Education Research Institute, 2003.

Rudner, Lawrence M. "Scholastic Achievement and Demographic Characteristics of Home School Students in 1998." *Education Policy Archives* 7, no. 8 (1999). http://epaa.asu.edu/epaa/v7n8/.

Smith, Christian, and David Sikkink. "Is Private Schooling Privatizing?" *First Things* 92 (April 1999): 16–20.

Stevens, Mitchell L. *Kingdom of Children: Culture and Controversy in the Homeschooling Movement.* Princeton, NJ: Princeton University Press, 2001.

Welner, Kariane M., and Kevin G. Welner. "Contextualizing Homeschooling Data: A Response to Rudner." *Education Policy Analysis Archives* 7, no. 13 (1999): http://epaa.asu.edu/epaa/v7n13/.

The quote that opens the concluding chapter is taken from an editorial written by Ronna Brown in the *IAHE (Indiana Association of Home Educators) Informer.*

INDEX

A Beka curriculum, 90, 164–65, 182–83
academic achievement research, 97–98, 124, 126–27
Advance America, 186–87
Akron Beacon Journal, 219
Armey, Dick, 115

Balmer, Randall, 32, 154
Bible Quiz, 163–64, 171–72
Blue Back Spellers, 46, 90
Bob Jones University Press, 48, 97
Bridgeway Academy: requirements and regulations, 18–19, 47, 49, 54, 61, 65, 66–70; resources, 19–22, 50–51, 53, 58–59
Brown v. Hot, Sexy, and Safer Productions, 217

child abuse/neglect, 68, 77–80, 119, 120; and state investigation, 47, 76–77, 120, 123. *See also* corporal punishment; discipline methods; social workers
Christian Home Educators Association (CHEA), 38, 49
Christian Reconstructionism, 146–47
Classical Conversations, 197. *See also* Veritas curriculum
Coburn, Tom, 105
college, 15, 97, 113, 138, 146, 159,

168; experiences at, 27–28, 80–81, 129–30, 148–50
conservative Christian, 2
considering homeschooling, 76
content validity, 117–18, 124
Convoy of Hope, 181, 183
cooperatives, homeschool learning, 19, 28, 50–51, 134, 153, 165, 171, 177, 194–95
corporal punishment, 77–80, 84–85, 199
cyberschooling, 40, 100, 172–74

discipline methods, 77–80, 84–85, 199
distance education. *See* cyberschooling
Dobson, James, 4, 42
dual enrollment, public school, 167–69, 170, 178. *See also* extracurricular participation, public school

Eclectic Reader, 45, 46
Elementary and Secondary Education Act (ESEA), 114–15
evolution, 17, 139, 146, 151, 153, 164, 173; and Answers in Genesis, 135–40, 186; and *Creation* (magazine), 139–40; and Creation Museum, 139–40. *See also* Institute for Creation Research
Excellence in Writing curriculum, 159